Media Law in Denmark

Media Law in Denmark

Second Edition

Søren Sandfeld Jakobsen
Sten Schaumburg-Müller

This book was originally published as a monograph in the International Encyclopaedia of Laws/Media Law.

Founding Editor: Roger Blanpain
General Editor: Frank Hendrickx
Volume Editors: Peggy Valcke & Eva Lievens

Wolters Kluwer

Published by:
Kluwer Law International B.V.
PO Box 316
2400 AH Alphen aan den Rijn
The Netherlands
E-mail: international-sales@wolterskluwer.com
Website: lrus.wolterskluwer.com

Sold and distributed in North, Central and South America by:
Wolters Kluwer Legal & Regulatory U.S.
7201 McKinney Circle
Frederick, MD 21704
United States of America
Email: customer.service@wolterskluwer.com

Sold and distributed in all other countries by:
Air Business Subscriptions
Rockwood House
Haywards Heath
West Sussex
RH16 3DH
United Kingdom
Email: international-customerservice@wolterskluwer.com

ISBN 978-94-035-1742-1

e-Book: ISBN 978-94-035-1785-8
web-PDF: ISBN 978-94-035-1833-6

The Authors

Søren Sandfeld Jakobsen, PhD, is Professor in the Law Department of Copenhagen Business School, and attorney at the law firm Gorrissen Federspiel, Copenhagen. His primary research areas cover Media, IT and Communications Law, on which subjects he has published a number of books, articles, reports, etc. He has previously worked as a lawyer and manager in the central government.

Sten Schaumburg-Müller, dr jur. & PhD, is Professor in the Department of Law at the University of Southern Denmark. His main research areas cover Media Law, Human Rights (Law) and Legal Philosophy, in which areas he has published extensively, although mainly in Danish. He was an attorney-at-law for eleven years, Women's Human Rights Advisor in Zambia for two years until he joined academia in 2000.

The Authors

Table of Contents

Table of Contents

List of Abbreviations

AJA	Administration of Justice Act
AVMS	Audiovisual Media Services
API	Application Programming Interface
B	(after a judgment or decision published in journal) Byret, i.e., District Court
BGB	Bürgerliches Gesetzbuch
CC	The Danish Criminal Code
CEN	European Committee for Standardization
CERD	Committee on the Elimination of Racial Discrimination
CJEU	Court of Justice of the European Union
DAB	Digital Audio Broadcasting
DPA	Data Protection Act
DPP	Director of Public Prosecution (Rigsadvokaten).
DR	Danmarks Radio
DT	Datatilsynet, the Data Inspection Board. Put before a figure indicates a decision by the Board.
ECHR	European Convention on Human Rights
ECtHR	European Court of Human Rights
ETSI	European Standardization Institute for Telecommunication
EU	European Union
EPG	Electronic Program Guide
FED	Forsikrings- og Erstatningsretligt Tidsskrift, i.e., Journal for Insurance and Compensation Law.
GDPR	General Data Protection Regulation
H	(after a judgment or decision published in journal) Højesteret, i.e., the Supreme Court
IEC	International Electrotechnical Commission
ITU	International Telecommunication Union
MDBA	The Media Data Bases Act
MLA	The Media Liability Act

and there seems to be a deep-rooted tradition for closed administration, in contradiction to Sweden who has a similar legal system, but a much stronger legal protection of access to information and freedom of speech. The Supreme Court was set up in 1661, in principle with the King as the chair, but in reality the King did not participate in the hearings and did not overturn decisions by the court. Presently, the Supreme Court judges still stand up when giving their vote as a courtesy to the king, who has not been present for more than three hundred years. The unprincipled approach is recognizable: in principle, the king has the upper hand, but in practice, the king respects decisions made by the judiciary.

5. In 1849, a Constitution was enacted. One year before the newly installed King was petitioned to let go of absolutism, and he agreed and allowed for a constitutional assembly. The Constitution, as a kind of payback, contains no provision declaring the people as the source of power, contrary to what is common in many constitutions, and according to section 3 the executive power is vested in the King, and the legislative power jointly in the King and the Parliament. In the late nineteenth century this created a political and constitutional crisis, as the King appointed cabinets with increasingly little backing in Parliament as well as among the population. The crisis was resolved in 1901 when the King as a matter of policy decided only to appoint a Prime Minister who would not face a vote of no confidence in Parliament. This 'negative cabinet responsibility' (parliamentarism) was not codified in the Constitution until 1953, after more than fifty years of political practice. Thus, the Danish experience is to a large extent that political compromises work, and there is a tendency to prefer politically worked out agreements rather than more formal solutions made by courts according to legal principles. Denmark has no constitutional court, and there is generally little sympathy towards undemocratically selected judges making politically sensitive decisions. As an example, freedom of speech has not had any strong protection by the Constitution, but rather from the political goodwill in Parliament (*see* Part I).

6. In 1915 women and servants got voting rights, and in 1933 during the economic crisis social rights were introduced, although not with constitutional backing. It is very difficult to make amendments or alterations to the Constitution. According to section 88, changes require two subsequent decisions by the Parliament with general elections in between plus a referendum requiring at least 40% of the voters to be positively in favour of the proposed changes. In 1920, an amendment necessary for the returning of North Schleswig to Denmark was passed, and the 40% was only just reached. The latest change of the Constitution took place in 1953, dealing with succession – the popular issue as the King had only daughters and the then prevailing succession rules only allowed for sons to become heads of state – and with other issues such as abolishing the Upper House. Some social rights were added to the not very comprehensive bill of rights; however, they are hardly operational.

7. Thus, Denmark still has a Constitution stating that the executive power is vested in the King even though there is no King (1972 – a Queen), and had there been a King, he would hold no political power. The formal fact that the Constitution is hard to change adds to the pragmatic approach: we do not pay too much attention to the formal principles, but the legal system works quite efficiently anyway.

8. According to section 4 of the Constitution, the Evangelical Lutheran Church is the established Church of Denmark and is supported by the state. Yet, Denmark is a very secularized society, and the Church does not play any political role. Priests may play a role in their personal capacity, and there are usually priests who are Members of Parliament. However, the Church as such does not have any political opinion. Denmark was one of the first countries to decriminalize pornography in 1967 and in 1973 abortion was made legal, and in 2017 the blasphemy clause was repealed.

9. Even though Protestantism does not play any direct part in the legal and political sphere, protestant ethics is recognizable: belief is a private matter, there is an anti-elitist conception, people are generally conceived of as equal, and hard work rather than luxury consumption is the honorary distinction. The social democratic workers' movement, rather strong especially in the first half of the twentieth century, had as its slogan: do your duty, claim your right – which to the present authors seems more Protestant than Marxist.

10. A scholar[2] has characterized the Danish approach as 'conflictual consensus'. Conflicts are not suppressed, but compromises are sought – with a preference for workable unprincipled solutions.

11. Some will claim that the past ten years have shown a more principled, even dogmatic approach,[3] but it remains to be seen whether the trend is a mere ripple or rather a tidal wave.

§2. The Media Landscape

I. Overview of Media Markets and Main Actors

12. This chapter provides an overview of the Danish media landscape.[4] Over the past years, as in many countries, considerable changes are taking place due to the rapid growth of the Internet and other digital media. Growing consumption of new media has been leading to a decline in the consumption of newspapers and other

2. Carsten Strøby Jensen, *Arbejdsmarkedsrelationer i Danmark. Fra konfliktbaseret konsensus til konsensusbaseret konflikt* [*Labour Relations in Denmark. From Conflict Based Consensus to Consensus Based Conflict*] (Jurist- og Økonomforbundets Forlag, 2007).
3. Lena Sundström, *Världens lyckligaste folk* [*The Happiest People in the World*] (Leopard Förlag, 2009).
4. The Chapter is based on public available reports etc. regarding the Danish media sector and data and statistics from, e.g., the Ministry for Culture and Statistics Denmark.

print media, and to some extent also of traditional radio and television. This represents both a threat and a challenge for the media sector, depending on the eyes of the beholder, but will, in any event, result in dramatic changes compared to the media sector we have seen and got used to over the past decades.

13. The chapter first describes the print media and then moves on to provide an outline of the broadcasting and Internet media.

II. Print Media

A. Newspapers

14. The Danish newspaper market has generally experienced troubled times in the past fifty years, and the crisis has increased considerably recently. At the end of World War II, there were more than 150 daily newspapers. Today, there are less than forty left, most of which are local newspapers dealing mainly with local news. Only about ten are nationwide, daily newspapers covering a broad spectrum of subjects (news, sports, art/culture, business, etc.).

15. The decrease of the traditional printed newspaper has accelerated in the past twenty years with the advent and proliferation of the Internet, where news and most other kinds of media content are accessible for free or by subscription from a variety of sources. Other factors, such as changed media habits among younger people (not only due to the Internet), also play a part. Fewer people seem to be inclined to purchase a print newspaper subscription. The result is a decrease of more than 50% of the total number of newspapers sold annually, compared to 1995.

16. As newspapers in Denmark most often are financed partly from subscription fees, partly from the sale of advertisements, the decrease in sale has in itself hit the business hard. But in addition hereto the financial crisis and competition from Internet-based media and services such as Google and other search engines, Facebook, etc. have also resulted in a remarkable decrease in advertisement revenues in the past couple of years. Hence, the newspapers are hit on both their fundamental income sources.

17. Like in many other countries, several[5] daily newspapers which are handed out for free at traffic junctions and other public places entered the Danish newspaper market more than a decade ago. As they are provided for free, they are only financed by sale of advertisements. The free newspapers have significantly less editorial content than 'normal' newspapers but have nevertheless obtained great popularity, especially among young people who regard the free newspapers as a valid substitution for – at least some of – the subscription-based newspapers. Hence, the

5. At the moment there are three nationwide, free newspapers.

advent of free newspapers has contributed to the vast decrease in the sale of newspaper subscriptions. In order not to cannibalize their regular newspaper business, most newspapers have now closed their free edition, leaving only one nationwide free newspaper on the market.

18. The daily newspapers are subsidized by the Danish state primarily in two ways: they receive direct support for production costs and indirect support due to an exemption from paying Value Added Tax (VAT). Altogether, in 2017, the business received 0.8 billion (approximately Euro (EUR) 105,000) Danish Krone (DKK) on that account.

B. Magazines

19. Printed magazines are sold in subscriptions or in single copies and are published weekly, monthly or quarterly. They normally cover a more narrow scope than newspapers and are thus targeted at a more limited segment of people.

20. Due to digital media development, the number of magazines has declined in recent years. There are less than a hundred different magazines in Denmark today. The Danish market is dominated by magazines published by the Danish media undertakings Aller and Egmont, together with the Swedish Bonnier.

21. The total revenue from the sale of magazines has decreased in recent years, however, with fluctuations among the various kinds of magazines.

22. Magazines do not qualify for the state subsidy measures (neither the distribution support nor the VAT exemption).

III. Radio and Television

A. Television

23. In line with many other western countries, the tendency in Denmark is that the consumption of traditional linear television is decreasing and being replaced by on-demand and streaming television, provided by the traditional broadcasters and new VOD providers such as Netflix and HBO. This marks a fundamental change in the way television is transmitted and viewed in Denmark. Until the launch of TV2 in 1988, Danmarks Radio (DR) had a monopoly to broadcast nationwide television on the Danish territory.[6] A few channels from the neighbouring countries Sweden and Germany could also be viewed locally in nearby places in Denmark due to the surplus of signals which crossed the Danish border from the transmitters placed close to the Danish border.

6. *See* in detail the historical outline in Part III, Ch. 1, §1.

24. Both DR and TV2 were – and still are – state-owned public service enterprises. As opposed to DR, which is financed by public service licences[7] (and is not permitted to sell television advertisements), TV2 is solely financed by sale of television advertisements and other commercial funds.

25. Today, DR also runs the channels DR2, DR3, two children's channels and a cultural channel. TV2 runs the channels TV2 News, TV2 Charlie, TV2 Zulu, TV2 Free and TV2 Sport. Only the 'mother' channel, TV2, has public service obligations.

26. With the technological improvements in cross-border cable and satellite transmission in the 1980s and 1990s, the Danish Broadcasting Act was liberalized in the early 1990s in order to allow foreign television enterprises to transmit channels to Denmark. Subsequently, the advent of the Internet has provided opportunity for IP, on-demand and streaming television. Hence, today a broad variety of foreign channels are available to Danish viewers via cable networks, satellite or the Internet. Furthermore, many people are becoming 'cable shavers' or 'cable cutters', turning partly or entirely away from traditional television subscriptions and instead are forming a personalized package consisting of a VOD streaming subscription, such as Netflix, together with a few subscription channels or simply the channels from DR that are provided for free, also on the Internet.

27. There are two competing cable network operators who cover large parts of the country, YouSee (a subsidiary of the telecom provider TDC) and Stofa (a subsidiary of the large Danish energy provider SE). YouSee and Stofa are not themselves programme service providers, but only distribute programmes provided by other enterprises. However, YouSee has recently announced that they will launch their own television channel in 2019.

28. Programmes distributed by cable are either transmitted directly to the individual households or to communal aerial installations, which are local, relatively small cable networks established as legal entities by, e.g., a housing association or group of parcel owners in a residential neighbourhood. From the communal aerial installation the signal is then distributed to the individual households. There are several hundred communal aerial installations in Denmark.

29. There are two dominant distributors of satellite television to Danish viewers, Viasat (an MTG company) and Canal Digital (owned by the Norwegian telecom provider Telenor). Besides distributing other providers' channels, Viasat and Canal Digital also distribute their own channels. As with cable distribution, the channels are either transmitted directly to the households or to communal aerial installations.

---

7. DR receives about EUR 400 million annually in public service licence fees.

30. Besides, cable or satellite distribution television is also distributed via the digital terrestrial network which from 1 November 2009 replaced the analogue terrestrial network. In contrast to the analogue network, which due to capacity restraints could only carry the public service channels, the digital terrestrial network has a larger capacity and is thus able to carry a large number of channels.

31. Subject to a public tender, the Swedish company Boxer has obtained the right to administer the distribution of channels on the digital terrestrial platform, apart from a number of frequencies which by statute are allotted directly to the Danish public service broadcasters. Thus, the programme service providers must enter into a commercial distribution agreement with Boxer in order to have their channels distributed via the new distribution platform.

32. Finally, a growing number of households receive television via the Internet or other IP-based platforms such as fibre networks.

33. Despite the availability of many foreign television channels, the Danes still prefer the public service channels from DR and TV2, which have a market share of more than two-thirds of the total television viewing. The remaining one-third is divided between a number of foreign enterprises, with channels from the United Kingdom (UK)-established Viasat (TV3 and TV3+) and Discovery Networks Danmark (who in 2012 purchased SBS Media (including the channels Kanal 4 and Kanal 5, 6 and 9) as the dominating ones.

34. There are also a large number of local or regional stations in Denmark, either commercial or non-commercial, which are distributed on cable networks or in 'windows' on the digital terrestrial network. None of these hold a market share of any significance.

B. Radio

35. As with television, a large number of radio channels, Danish as well as foreign, are available to Danish listeners via terrestrial networks, cable, satellite or the Internet. However, the Danes almost exclusively listen to Danish-produced radio.

36. DR's public service obligations also cover radio broadcasting, and DR is currently providing eight radio channels available on the FM network, Digital Audio Broadcasting (DAB) network or the Internet. All DR's radio channels are financed mainly via the public service licence means.

37. Besides DR's nationwide public service radio channels, there are three nationwide FM radio channels, which subject to public tender are allotted to other broadcasters than DR. The public service financed channel Radio24/7 is required to provide news, documentaries, cultural and discussion programmes. Besides Radio24/7 there are two commercial stations, Nova Radio and Pop FM, of which the former is required to send a certain amount of news programmes each year.

38. In addition to the nationwide channels, there are more than four hundred local radio stations, commercial or non-commercial. The non-commercial stations can apply for state funding based on the amount of air-time.

39. DR dominates the Danish radio market with a market share of almost 70%. Most of the remaining 30% market share is held by the various commercial stations.

IV. Internet and Mobile Content Services

40. All significant Danish media providers have established a website on the Internet as a supplement to their main distribution platforms. The most popular newspapers' websites as well as the public service broadcasters DR's and TV2's websites are among the most visited by Danish Internet users. Besides the web services most media also provide one or more apps for tablets, mobile phones or other digital devices.

41. Formerly, the media enterprises' web and mobile services usually consisted simply of parts of the original content transferred to the website, e.g., in the form of newspaper articles or radio/television programmes transmitted either as broadcast (i.e., simultaneously with the transmission on the primary broadcasting platform) or on demand.

42. Concurrently with the rapid growth in Internet consumption, which partly has taken place at the expense of the consumption of the 'traditional' media, the media are developing and improving their digital services, including on the web and apps for mobile, for example by offering new media services which are not offered on the main platform or by offering services which are not typically offered by media enterprises, such as games, chat, purchase of goods and services, etc.

43. The substantial decline in the sale of newspapers, and the fact that revenues from the sale of advertisements are increasingly moving from print and traditional broadcasting media services to various Internet services such as social media and search services, has caused a severe economic situation for many newspapers. The foregoing, again, has led the providers concerned to focus much more on developing their digital services. This change in strategy and scope appears to have slowed down the recent years' substantial decline in revenues.

44. The current transition of Danish media from traditional media platforms to digital platforms is urged by the fact that the Danes increasingly spend time on social media services from abroad, especially services provided by Facebook, YouTube, Google and Microsoft. This illustrates that Danish media enterprises are not only competing with each other but also with the global tech giants that are not media enterprises in a traditional sense but have their origin in the IT and technology sector.

45. The rapid developments in mobile technology, mobile broadband, apps and other technologies specially developed for mobile devices imply that a broad variety of media services, text-based as well as audiovisual media services (AVMS), is available to most mobile subscribers today.

§3. Sources of Media Law

I. Rules and Regulations

46. The Constitution[8,9] does not figure prominently in media law. The freedom of speech clause has never been cited in case law and is not at the centre of legal deliberations on freedom of speech. On the other hand, the Constitution is not without bearing.

47. Section 3 prescribes the division of power, vesting the legislative power with the King and the Parliament conjointly (in real constitutional life, the Parliament passes the bills and the monarch signs), the executive power with the King (meaning the government) and the judicial power with the courts of justice. Section 3 has provided the only case in which the Supreme Court set aside an enacted bill for being unconstitutional.[10] This indicates a certain reticence on part of the courts to mingle in political, legislative affairs, but also a willingness to protect the role of the courts and, arguably, to protect the rights of the citizens if necessary.

48. Section 31(2) requires the Electorate to 'secure equal representation of the various opinions of the Electorate', thus presupposing a free exchange of opinions, and section 57 lays down that the Members of Parliament cannot be held liable for their utterance in the Parliament save by the consent of the Parliament.

49. Chapter VIII provides certain rights such as protection of liberty, of dwelling, property, etc. Erstwhile doctrine questioned whether these sections were constitutional at all, taking their general and vague formulations into consideration. Presently, no one doubts that the provisions constitute a bill of rights, dependent on the wording of the respective sections. Section 77 deals with freedom of speech: 'Any person shall be entitled to publish his thoughts in printing, in writing, and in speech, provided that he may be held answerable in a court of justice. Censorship and other preventive measures shall never again be introduced.' Like the protection of association in section 78, section 77 rejects any requirement of prior approval. Any expression can be put forward and any association can be formed without prior authorization by an authority. The possibility for subsequent intervention is, however, quite different. Whereas associations can only be declared illegal if they are

8. Peter Blume, *Retssystemet og juridisk metodelære* [*The Legal System Legal Methodology*], 3rd edn. (Jurist- og Økonomforbundets Forlag, 2016); Ruth Nielsen & Christina D. Tvarnø, *Retskilder og retsteorier*, 5th edn. [*Legal Sources and Legal Theories*] (Jurist- og Økonomforbundets Forlag, 2017).
9. Act No. 169/1953.
10. *UfR* 1999.841H.

violent or aim to pursue their goals by violent means, an expression can be sanctioned 'in a court of justice', i.e., apparently no restriction on sanctions as long as they are ordered by a court, thus leaving the legislature a rather broad, if not unlimited, discretion as to which expressions can be criminalized.[11]

50. As for publicity, the Constitution provides that the deliberations in Parliament are public (with some possible exceptions). As for the public administration of justice, section 65 merely provides that: 'all proceedings shall be public and oral to the widest possible extent', and there is no constitutional guarantee for public access to activities of the executive. Neither does the Constitution provide for any regulation of the media, including the electronic media. The most recent alteration of the Constitution took place in 1953, and the monopoly then in force of the Danish Broadcasting was not doubted or held to be a violation of the ban on censorship. Legal scholars have now argued that there is an inherent obligation for pluralism in section 77 for broadcasting with restricted access to wave lengths etc.[12]

51. Summing up, the Constitution does not play a prominent part in Danish mass media law, but provides a general framework. This is somehow reflected in the role of the courts: they do not play a prominent role – legislation is the most important legal source in the field, and Danish law is not a common law type – but on the other hand, the courts do play a part and are not merely 'mouth piece of law'.

52. *Statutes* passed by the Parliament (and signed by the King)[13] are generally considered to be the most important legal source. All statutes must be published in *Lovtidende* (the Public Gazette) and are available in Danish on www.retsinformati on.dk. The *travaux préparatoires* are relevant, probably to an increasing degree. It may not be clear whether they are, in fact, independent legal sources or whether they merely serve as an important interpretative factor. At any rate, they are important when implementing the statutes, when the administration generates the executive orders based on a statutory provision and when the courts decide cases.

53. The *Criminal Code*[14] (Chapter 27, sections 263–275) deals with 'crimes against peace and honour', the protection of private life, protection against threats and group defamation, and libel and slander. Even though such issues are often of private character and some of the acts do not involve public prosecution, they are traditionally dealt with by criminal law. Section 23 offers a broadly formulated option for the inclusion of accomplices, by providing that anyone who has contributed to a criminal act by 'instigation, act or advice' can be punished. Taken literally, this would imply that newspaper vendors could be prosecuted for any criminal content in the written or broadcasted material.

11. Whether s. 77 provides any protection of freedom of speech as regards subsequent sanction is contested. *See* Part I.
12. Henrik Zahle, *Dansk forfatningsret 3. Menneskerettigheder* [*Danish Constitution Law. Human Rights*] (Christian Ejlers' Forlag, 2002), 103.
13. *See* General Introduction, §1.
14. Consolidated Act No. 1156/2018.

54. However, this possibility has been circumvented by the *Media Liability Act* (MLA)[15] which generally limits the scope of liable persons to the author and the editor, and only in extraordinary cases, the publisher. Besides, this Act requires the media to act in accordance with ethics of journalism (section 34) and authorizes the Press Council to decide complaints in relation to media ethics.

55. The rather comprehensive *Administration of Justice Act* (AJA)[16] contains several sections relevant for the media: access to court sessions, including special rights for the media to appeal against decisions to hold chamber sessions; access to court documents; protection of the sources of the media, including protection against search and seizure; the requirement to give a loyal account of court proceedings; the ban on revealing the identity of certain actors in the court proceedings such as victims of sexual crimes; and the provision prohibiting media from influencing the court – even though it is questionable whether that provision is in fact part of Danish prevailing law.

56. The *Public Access to Documents in Administrative Files Act*[17] is relevant for journalists' and others' access to documents in the administration. In 2013 a new act was passed after more than eight years of Commission work and several years of political turmoil.

57. The *Broadcasting Act*[18] deals with the right to broadcast as well as the organization and the content of broadcasting. Historically, broadcasting has been regulated much more detailed and tightly than the printed media, and the public institution 'DR' still plays a central role among the broadcasting media even though the monopoly was abandoned in the late 1980s. Following the implementation of the AVMS Directive (2007/65/EC) in late 2009, the Act also contains regulation of on-demand services.

58. Several other acts contain provisions that are relevant to the media. Section 26 of the *Compensation for Damages Act*[19] provides for tort compensation in cases of unlawful violation of other persons' liberty, peace, honour (implying that questions in relation to libel and protection of private life do not necessarily have to be dealt with according to the Criminal Code and the principles of criminal law), the *Copyright Act*[20] protects the media products, and the *Marketing Practices Act* (MPA)[21] contains a general clause in section 3 requiring commercial companies etc. to act in accordance with ethics of marketing, a provision covering a wide range of issues, including the prohibition of unauthorized use of personal pictures or other similar characteristics.

15. Consolidated Act No. 914/2014.
16. Consolidated Act No. 1101/2017 with later amendments.
17. Act No. 606/2013 with later amendments.
18. Consolidated Act No. 444/2018.
19. Consolidated Act No. 1070/2018.
20. Consolidated Act No. 1144/2014 with later amendments.
21. Act No. 426/2017 with later amendments.

59. There is no specific regulation on media ownership. This issue falls within the scope of the general *Competition Act.*[22]

60. In 1992, an Act was passed incorporating the European Convention on Human Rights (ECHR) into Danish domestic law, putting the Convention on par with any other piece of Danish legislation. Whether and how the formal incorporation actually changed the situation is debatable. Even before 1 July 1992, the date of the entry into force of the *Incorporation Act,*[23] Danish courts had made use of the Convention and the decisions from the European Court of Human Rights (ECtHR). Maybe the decisive date is rather 24 May 1989 when the ECtHR for the first time held Denmark to be violating its human rights obligations. (On case law, *see* below)

61. European Union (EU) law is of course also important. The EU Charter of Fundamental Rights Article 11 provides freedom of expression and information, and its significance remains yet to be seen, and the Treaty of the Functioning of the European Union Article 87 on state aid is obviously relevant for broadcasting stations receiving licence.

62. The EU Directive on AVMS (2018/1808 EC) is relevant for the broadcasting and electronic sector, and the EU *General Data Protection Regulation* (GDPR) (5419/16) is partly relevant because the media processes personal data to a very large extent. The Regulation requires Member States to reconcile the right to the protection of personal data with the right to freedom of expression and information, including processing for journalistic purposes (Article 85). The resulting Danish Act, the *Data Protection Act* (DPA),[24] generally exempts journalistic activities from the data protection regime. Also the directives on *Electronic Commerce* (2000/31/EC) and on copyright and related rights in the information society, the *Infosoc* (2001/29/EC), are important.

63. Apart from the supranational EU law and the incorporated European Human Rights Convention, international law does not play a large role. International law is not automatically incorporated into domestic law but requires either a rewriting into domestic statutes or a statutory incorporation, the last of which only happened once. A suggestion to incorporate three human rights conventions, the conventions on Civil and Political Rights, on Torture and on Elimination of Racial Discrimination, has not been politically viable. However, the courts every now and then do refer to international instruments, although this has not happened in cases relating to freedom of speech and mass media.

22. Consolidated Act No. 115/2018.
23. Consolidated Act No. 750/1998 with later amendments.
24. Act No. 502/2018.

64. As a special feature of Danish mass media law, the Guiding Rules for the Ethics of Journalism[25] constitute a mix of a professional code of conduct and state-based rules. The content is generated by the media organizations and the journalists' union – latest update in 2013 – and according to section 34 of the MLA, the media are obliged to act in accordance with the 'ethics of journalism'. The Press Council, set up by the MLA, decides cases according to section 34 of the Act, and in its decisions the Council often refers to the Press Ethical Rules.

65. Lastly, *executive orders* made according to an authorization in a statute are relevant legal sources, which tend to be of a more specialized character. In the broadcasting field there are quite a few, such as the *Executive Order on Radio and Television Commercials and Sponsoring*.[26]

II. Case Law

66. There are twenty-four district courts, two High Courts, one Supreme Court, a special Maritime and Commercial Court and special arrangements for Greenland. There is no constitutional or administrative court, the ordinary courts often deal with administrative cases, whereas constitutional cases are very rare. In principle, the Supreme Court can set aside unconstitutional statutes, but in fact this happened only once.[27] *Judgments from the courts* are perceived as relevant legal sources, and often prevailing law cannot be accounted for without taking judgments into consideration. As an example, for the period 1937–2004 a provision was in force prohibiting the courts in libel cases to take into consideration whether the person in question was a politician. In case law, however, the opposite was the case, the courts giving a certain leeway as regards criticism of politicians.

67. The importance of case law varies. When the rules are vague and general, case law becomes more important, and vice versa. In criminal law, the courts have no power to expand the scope of a provision – there is an absolute ban on expansive interpretation in section 1 of the Criminal Code – but the court can restrict the scope of criminal provisions, e.g., in order to protect freedom of speech.[28] In private law, the courts have more room for being law creating, and also in administrative law, the courts can make law, at any rate when this is done to protect the rights of the citizens.

68. The *judgments and decisions from the ECtHR* are obviously relevant for establishing prevailing Danish law, in particular in cases dealing with freedom of expression issues. Danish courts generally take great care to be in accordance with

25. There is no authorized translation. Previously the webpage of the Press Council used the term 'The National Code of Conduct', now they prefer 'Press Ethical Rules'. Webpage of the council, www.pressenaevnet.dk.
26. Executive Order No. 801/2013.
27. *UfR* 1999.841H with some precedents, in which the Supreme Court defended its authority to set aside statutes, including a partial rejection in *UfR* 1971.299H.
28. Which they have in fact done, *see* Part I, 'Freedom of Speech'.

European human rights and they often explicitly state that the Danish statues must be interpreted 'in the light of the ECHR'.[29]

69. Views from international human rights bodies, such as the Committee on the Elimination of Racial Discrimination, are in principle relevant legal sources of a non-binding character. In practice, however, they are rarely used.

70. Apart from judgments etc. by court, there are a number of organs making decisions pertinent for media law:

71. The *Press Council* is authorized to make decisions in relation to ethics of journalism, and there is a body of case 'law' in relation to important questions, such as consulting procedures when persons are criticized in the media, the use of hidden camera, protection of private life, protection of children, etc. The Press Council cannot make binding decisions except demanding that the media publish its decided view in cases dealing with the particular media.

72. The *Radio and Television Board* has various tasks according to the Broadcasting Act, such as making decisions in cases dealing with programme service authorizations and commercials and sponsored programmes. Besides, the Board generally supervises the public service obligations.

73. The *Data Inspection Board* (Datatilsynet) is the supervising institution in relation to the DPA.

74. The *Ombudsman* is supervising the executive power, and even though his/her views are not binding, they are usually followed by the central administration and perhaps less so by the decentralized administration, the municipalities. In any case, the views from the Ombudsman form a central part of Danish administrative law.

75. Also decisions made by the *Public Prosecutor* may be relevant. Some criminal acts relating to mass media require public prosecution, such as group defamation (section 266b of the Criminal Code). If the prosecutor decides not to prosecute – which was the case in the infamous cartoon case[30] – this will in fact be the decisive outcome. The Committee on the Elimination of Racial Discrimination has in some cases criticized the decision not to prosecute in cases related to group defamation,[31] but the views tend to be perceived as undue political interference rather than relevant legal sources.

---

29. *See*, e.g., *UfR* 2016.151H.
30. Decision by the Public Prosecutor, 15 Mar. 2006, www.rigsadvokaten.dk/media/dokumenter/pressemeddelelse_dansk_endelig.pdf.
31. *Mohammed Gelle v. Denmark*, 34/2004; *Saada Mohamad Adan v. Denmark*, 23/2008.

III. Principles, Doctrine and Custom

76. Legal *principles* are also legal sources even though they are expressed through other sources such as statutes, case law and doctrine.

77. In media law the right to the use of one's image is a non-legislated legal principle. The Supreme Court applied the principle in Ugeskrift for Retsvæsen (*UfR*) 1965.126H in which a producer of TV-sets placed the picture of a famous actor on the screen at TV-sets at display in retail outlets. The lower courts had rejected the actor's claim for tort, but the Supreme Court held that it was against general legal principles to make unauthorized use of another person's images. Subsequently, the principle has been applied a number of times by the courts.[32] When the use is commercial, it falls under the Marketing Act, section 3, and there is a special provision in the Executive Order on Radio and Television Commercials and Sponsoring, section 10, prohibiting unauthorized depicting of and referral to natural persons.

78. *UfR* 1982.179/2H: the organizer of football matches had a right to control the transmission of the match, including the right to prohibit transmission of results while the match was ongoing. Interestingly, the High Court based its decision upon a previous contract, while the Supreme Court employed basic legal principles. In *UfR* 2004.2945H, the dispute was between the organizers of football matches who had given exclusive rights to a broadcasting station, including the right to pass on results of ongoing matches, and a distributor of short messages who picked up the results from the broadcasting station. The Supreme Court acknowledged the right to control transmission as a legal principle but held that it would be an infringement of the news reporting to block information that was already made available.

79. Legal writers have argued in favour of a somewhat broader principle: that once expressions were given free to the general public, they were no longer protected. A grand doctoral dissertation has argued for a range of principles within the broader field of information law, including the right to handle protected information when the particular piece of information has been published with the consent of the rightful holder of the right.[33] The Press Council has decided cases in accordance with this principle.[34]

80. The late media lawyer K.A. Frøbert also argued in favour of a reporting privilege for the media; however, with ambiguous support from the courts.[35] Now,

32. *UfR* 1974.952Ø, *UfR* 1980.945Ø, *UfR* 1983.630Ø, *UfR* 1986.428Ø, *UfR* 1989.1146SH, *UfR* 1991.842H, *UfR* 1995.624H, *UfR* 1998.170Ø, *UfR* 2003.686SH, *UfR* 2008.1974H.
33. Henrik Udsen, *De informationsretlige grundsætninger* [*Basic Principles in Information Law*] (Jurist- og Økonomforbundets Forlag, 2009), 332.
34. PC 4/1999, 2003-6-125, and 2006-6-334.
35. Favourable: *UfR* 1980.1065V; unfavourable, *UfR* 1989.399H (brought before the ECtHR, *see* the following footnote).

this principle has been overtaken by the ‘public watch dog’ principle applied by the ECtHR, entailing that the press has a certain obligation and right to pass on information and ideas to the public.[36]

81. In Danish legal thinking, *scholarly writings* are not conceived of as legal sources in the sense that they are not binding, in contradistinction to legislative acts and court decisions that are binding. Still, legal doctrine may have an influence. In the beginning of the 1970s, Peter Germer published his dissertation *Ytringsfrihedens væsen* (The Essence of Freedom of Speech), arguing that debate on public issues was protected by the Constitution and could not be made unlawful by the legislator. His views were accepted neither by the courts nor by most other writers. However, from the middle of the 1970s, the courts embarked on a more speech protective approach giving weight to the protection of the debate on issues of public interest.[37] And similarly, when Preben Stuer Lauridsen published his book *Pressefrihed og personlighedsret* [Press Freedom and Privacy Protection] in 1988, arguing that freedom of the press as well as protection of privacy were given too little weight by Danish courts, the courts seemingly took his arguments into consideration.[38]

82. *Custom* is generally regarded as a valid legal source, but in practice it occurs rarely, and it does not play any part in media law.[39]

---

36. *Jersild v. Denmark*, 24 Sep. 1994.
37. *UfR* 1980.1037H.
38. *UfR* 1989.726H.
39. In *UfR* 1938.576V, harsh critique of the Minister of Justice was accepted as lawful (except for one count regarding accusation of treason). The Court held that strong political debate was ‘customary’. It could be argued that the case is an example of using custom as legal source. However, it is rather an example of the Court giving some protection to freedom of speech.

Part I. Freedom of Speech

Chapter 1. Freedom of Speech and Section 77 of the Constitution

83. The freedom of speech provision in section 77 of the Constitution runs as follows: 'Any person shall be entitled to publish his thoughts in printing, in writing, and in speech, provided that he may be held accountable in a court of justice. Censorship and other preventive measures shall never again be introduced.' The provision has been in force since the first Constitution of 5 June 1849, except that the word 'in writing, and in speech' was added in 1953 (as a minor part of a larger change).[40]

84. The *second* subsection clearly prohibits censorship. Thus, legislation or other arrangements requiring approval before publication of expressions are unconstitutional. However, the broadcasting monopoly (1926–1988) as well as film censorship (conducted by a now abolished public board deciding whether films were appropriate for children and youngsters), have generally been accepted as constitutional. In the same vein, the ban on 'preventive measures' has not precluded preliminary measures such as interim injunctions or even seizures of pamphlets etc. by the police.[41]

85. The *first* subsection places the clause on par with Article 11 of the French 1789 declaration, the first part declaring the freedom of speech and the second part circumscribing the same right without much guidance as to the limits of the limitations. This is different from the American solution where the First Amendment simply states that: 'Congress shall make no law … abridging the freedom of speech', and the European human rights solution (inspired by the Universal Declaration Article 29(2)), which gives some guidance as to the scope of the limitations, prescribing that the limitations have to pursue a legitimate aim and be necessary for a democratic society. The wording of section 77 leaves open whether there are any limitations on the limitations, or, in other words, whether the constitutional clause in fact entails any protection of freedom speech.

40. Peter Germer, *Statsforfatningsret* [*Constitutional Law*], 4th edn. (Jurist- og Økonomforbundets Forlag, 2007); Henrik Zahle, *Dansk forfatningsret* 1–3 [*Danish Constitutional Law* 1–3] (Christian Ejlers' Forlag, 2001–2007). Jørgen Albæk Jensen, Michael Hansen Jensen & Jens Peter Christensen, *Dansk statsret* [*Danish Constitutional Law*], 2nd edn. (Jurist- og Økonomforbundets Forlag, 2016).
41. *UfR* 1949.922H.

86. The provision does make it clear that any sanction for unlawful expressions must be decided by the courts, i.e., the judiciary, and not by the executive or the legislature for that matter. This meant a farewell to the times when the police could fine offenders. It also meant that a suggestion of providing the Press Council with powers to issue fines was rejected as unconstitutional. Whereas the provision is clear as regards which institution is acting, it is not clear as regards the question of which expression might eventually be sanctioned.

87. Some constitutional history may be interesting in order to examine the substantive content of this provision in Danish media law.

88. At the constitutional assembly, convening 1848 to 1849, there was a focus on avoiding the much-despised censorship (*see* the second subsection of section 77). As for limitations on statutory regulations of the freedom of speech, there was not much debate, the prevailing perception being that the democratically elected legislature, an important part of the coming Constitution, would take care of the general interest and therefore would not circumscribe freedom of speech to a larger extent than reasonable. Seen in hindsight, this has to a large extent proven to be correct, and the legislature has generally not been eager to limit the freedom of speech. At any rate, the provision including the deliberations at the constitutional assembly left very little, if any, guidance neither to the legislature nor to the courts as to the balance of freedom of speech and the various considerations in favour of restrictions.

89. The first account of Danish Constitutional Law did not go much into detail as regards freedom of speech but merely stated that freedom of speech should be perceived as a point of departure, and the cases in which a person could be held answerable to the exceptions.[42]

90. This approach was to be abandoned by two important constitutional scholars, Carl Goos in the late nineteenth century and Alf Ross by the mid-twentieth century. Goos was a conservative member of the Upper House (abolished in the 1953 constitutional revision), and he was active during a politically and constitutionally unstable situation. The King, who had the power to appoint the cabinet, appointed conservative prime ministers (or council presidents, as they were called) with a decreasing backing in Parliament. The Parliament reacted by denying to vote for the financial acts, which in turn resulted in the executive simply making provisional acts, including financial acts and including acts abridging the right to criticize the increasingly unpopular government.

91. Now, Goos presented his theory of unlawfulness (this sounds better in Danish or German: Rechtswidrigkeitslehre): the Constitution does not protect unlawful acts, and consequently any expressed view must be in accordance with law in order to be protected by the Constitution. This was equivalent of stating that the lawmaker, be it the legislature or the executive making provisionary legislation under

42. Carl Georg Holck, *Den danske Statsforfatningsret*, 2. Del [*Danish Constitutional Law*, Second Part] (1869), 345.

the emergency clause of the Constitution, had the unchecked power of making statutes abridging the freedom of speech, only, of course, put more elegantly and couched in legal philosophical terms. After Goos, section 77 was rendered useless to protect freedom of expression.[43]

92. This trend was followed by a sharp and prominent legal scholar, Alf Ross, albeit from a different ideological standpoint. In the middle of the 1940s, he introduced the distinction between 'formal' and 'substantive' freedom of speech, formal freedom relating to formalities, such as prior acceptance, and substantive freedom relating to the content of the expressions. Ross argued that section 77 fully protected the formal aspect, prohibiting prior procedures, but not the substantial aspect, leaving it for the legislature to decide subsequent sanctions for expressions. Thus, he argued famously that the Constitution does not prevent the legislature from passing acts making referral of sport events or criticism of the government sanctionable as long as the sanctions were passed *after* the expressions and by a court of law.[44] Ross argued that it would be very unwise for the legislature to pass such acts, but that it was a political decision, i.e., according to the majority in Parliament, and not a legal decision, involving the courts to judge whether a parliamentary act was in accordance with the Constitution. However, in contradistinction to Goos, Ross was not in favour of restricting freedom of speech; on the contrary, he argued in favour of democracy and freedom of speech. But his main idea was that these kinds of questions ought to be solved exclusively by the Parliament by democratically elected legislators, not by a few judges with no democratic legitimacy.

93. The distinction between formal and substantive freedom of speech was generally accepted for half a century. Ross' rejection of the importance of section 77 in relation to restrictions on the legislative power reinforced the perception that section 77 could not play any part in libel, slander and cases concerning the protection of private life, which were solved with reference to the statutes and their interpretation, not to the constitutional protection of freedom of speech.

94. In 1972, a representative of the next generation of constitutional scholars delivered a direct attack on Ross' view that section 77 is devoid of substantive protection. In his dissertation with the significant title 'The Essence of Freedom of Speech', Peter Germer presented his view that section 77 protects some substantive part, namely the debate of public issues. He argued mainly with reference to American scholars and jurisprudence, even though the American provision has no limitation clause (which he did not mention), and he was heavily criticized for his views, not least by Ross. However, even if Germer's legal analyses were not generally accepted, his views had an impact. From the mid-1970s, the courts (and the

43. Paradoxically, Goos was inspired by J.S. Mill and used his philosophy as a point of departure. However, Goos managed to end up with a very conservative view, arguing that it would bring more happiness to most people if the laws are followed, even laws enacted by the government against the majority of the Parliament.
44. Alf Ross, *Dansk Statsforfatningsret* [*Danish Constitutional Law*], 2 (Nyt Nordisk Forlag Arnold Busck, 1970), 724.

Ombudsman) started to include freedom of expression considerations when dealing with such kind of issues, not merely looking narrowly at the statute in question.

95. In *UfR* 1977.872V the High Court quashed a fine issued by the police.[45] Some demonstrators distributed leaflets against the military close to an army barracks. The police issued a fine according to the then prevailing police regulations forbidding the distribution of leaflets within 100 meters of schools and army barracks. The High Court dismissed the claim that the fine was violating section 77, but found that the police regulation had not sufficient legal backing in a parliamentary enacted statute. The ban on distribution of leaflets close to army barracks had been made in order to avoid disorder, but the High Court held that there was no reason to believe that disorder would be more likely to erupt upon distribution of pamphlets closer than 100 metres than in other situations. The police had the power to intervene if disorder broke out, but this not being the case, the fine was unfounded.

96. In *UfR* 1980.1037H, an artist had made a poster imitating slaughterhouse commercials for pork, however, with another wording: 'Danish pigs are healthy; they are bursting with penicillin.' The slaughterhouses' corporation sued for libel and the bailiff court issued an interim injunction. However, the Supreme Court set aside the injunction and argued that: 'regard to the free exchange of opinions in relation to an important public issue' must carry particular weight.

97. And in *UfR* 1987.726H, a newspaper through several articles made a report on the conditions in a public hospital for mentally disturbed persons, *inter alia*, bringing pictures of persons being strapped. The reports were made through collaboration with the staff and the patients' relatives, but not with the consent of the Regional Council, the public owner of the hospital. The newspaper had announced more reports to come, and the Regional Council was granted an injunction for the reason that the pictures and the story were a breach of privacy.[46] However, the Supreme Court held that the reporting was done in cooperation with staff and relatives of the patients *and* that the professional reporting was of considerable information value, and consequently set aside the injunction.

98. The three cases indicate *first* that section 77 of the Constitution does not play any direct part in such cases, and *second* that the courts take freedom of speech aspects into consideration when interpreting the statutes and deciding concrete cases, this trend being conspicuous from the late 1970s.

99. From around 1990, the courts have started to take judgments from the ECtHR into consideration. This is before the Incorporation Act, but after the first conviction of Denmark[47] and around the time when the government was setting up

45. The formal set up: The police can issue fines, but the sanction can be tried before a court if required by the one having been ordered to pay the fine.
46. According to s. 264a of the Penal Code unwarranted photographing of persons in non-public places is prohibited.
47. *Hauschildt v. Denmark*, 24 May 1989; however, not on a media-related issue.

a Commission deliberating whether the ECHR ought to be incorporated into Danish statutory law. From then on, it was impossible to isolate European human rights from Danish national law, and section 77 of the Constitution still plays no part in the protection of freedom of speech, except for the works written by constitutional scholars.[48]

48. Peter Germer has in subsequent editions of his *Constitutional Law* argued that freedom of speech ought to be protected by the Danish Constitution rather than the European Convention on Human Rights. (*Statsforfatningsret* [*Constitutional Law*], 4th edn., Jurist- og Økonomforbundets Forlag (2007), 351.

Chapter 2. Other Issues

100. There are no provisions in the Constitution relating directly to broadcasting issues or protection of the press. Until the 1980s, the Danish public broadcasting company (presently 'DR' for Denmark's Radio) had a broadcasting monopoly and commercials were prohibited. The monopoly had been in force since the first broadcasting statute and was not disputed when alterations were discussed and a new Constitution was set in force in 1953. In the 1980s, local radio stations were allowed, and they could broadcast commercials, although within limits. TV commercials were only allowed when the second TV channel started in 1988.

101. The Constitution sporadically deals with access to information: section 49 runs as follows: 'The sittings of the Parliament shall be public. Provided that the President [of the Parliament], or such number of members as may be provided for by the Rules of Procedure, or a Minister shall be entitled to demand the removal of all unauthorized persons, whereupon it shall be decided without a debate whether the matter shall be debated at a public or a secret sitting.' Subsection 2 has not been used since the alteration of the Constitution in 1953. Committee meetings do not fall within the scope of section 49.

102. Section 65(1) provides that: 'In the administration of justice all proceedings shall be public and oral to the widest possible extent.' This is not very operational, but the wording may set some limits to closed hearings. A proposal in private cases to exclude publicity for a year was rejected by the Ministry of Justice, stating that this may be an infringement of the Constitution.

103. There are no constitutional provisions relating to access to information from the executive.

Part II. Regulation of Media

Chapter 1. The Journalists' Profession

104. Journalist is not a protected title, and anyone may call himself/herself a journalist. However, most journalists working for the media are graduated either from the Danish School of Media and Journalism or from one of the two universities which presently offer an academic degree in journalism.

105. A certain protection of journalists' reporting privilege can be traced in Danish law. After the ECtHR judgment *Jersild v. Denmark* 24 September 1994, the distinction between quotations and statements emanating from the journalist is clearly seen in Danish case law.[49] Also, there is a rather strong protection of journalists when reporting issues of general interest.[50]

106. An important distinction according to Danish law is whether a journalist works for a media which falls within the scope of the MLA. Journalists covered by this act have special privileges such as a detailed exemption from giving evidence in court and the right to protest against a decision by the court to hold hearings in camera, and these journalists can avoid civil and penal liability if their name does not appear in the media. On the other hand, journalists working for media under the MLA have an obligation to act in accordance with the ethics of journalism. (For further details, *see* below Chapter 2, §3, Chapter 3, §2, II 'The Scope of the MLA', Chapter 2, §3 and Chapter 6 'The Press Council'.)

107. With the advent of the Internet it has become much easier to reach an audience without the interference of professional editors and media. This could be perceived as either a welcomed bypassing of censorship exerted by a professional elite or as a problematic lack of quality checking. Apparently, the easy access even allows for trolls producing all sorts of stories with no respect for the ethics of journalism. Since Danish law does not provide any legal definition of journalism, and since EU law presupposes a broad understanding of journalism,[51] questions arise as

49. *UfR* 2004.1773H (reporting, media acquitted); *UfR* 2003.624H (media's defamatory charge, media convicted).
50. *UfR* 1999.122H (reporting on issues of general interest, *but* forwarding defamatory charges; *UfR* 2010.1859H; *UfR* 2012.2328H.
51. GDPR, preamble No. 153 and *Satamedia Oy* C-73/07.

to the scope of the legal protection of journalistic activities. So far, there is no published case dealing with this type of problem. However, Danish courts are likely to make substantive rather than formalistic decisions, and it is likely that genuine journalism will be protected, no matter whether the actual journalist is a professional or not, entailing that the privilege of reporting on matters of public interest will be granted also to non-professional participants.[52] On the other hand, claims of journalistic activities are not likely to be accepted if the claims are not substantiated by genuine activities such as thorough research, comprehension of public interest, and including diverse views and opinions from the various factors involved.

52. An unpublished decision by the Copenhagen city court provides the right to protection of sources for a person, not being a professional journalist and not covered under the Danish act (decision 19 May 2016, SS 4-12426/2016).

Chapter 2. Journalists' Rights

§1. Independence

108. There are no statutory rules protecting the independence of the journalists similar to the constitutional rules protecting the independence of judges (section 64 of the Constitution). However, the Guiding Rules for the Ethics of Journalism (dealt with more detail in Chapter 6) contain the following provisions:

It is a violation of the Ethics of Journalism to prevent the legitimate publication of information which is of essential importance to the public. Similarly, it is a violation to comply with outsiders' demands for influence over the content of the mass media if such compliance may raise doubt as to the freedom and independence of the mass media. To require a journalist to perform tasks contravening the Ethics of Journalism is in itself a violation of the Ethics. Besides, journalists should not have tasks imposed on them that are contrary to their conscience or convictions.[53]

109. The rules are reasonably clear, but they are hardly operational. First, the rules are found in the Guiding Rules for the Ethics of Journalism, which as the name indicates are not binding but only guiding. Second, the Press Council, which is authorized to make decisions in relation to Ethics of Journalism, rarely accepts cases in which the complainant is neither mentioned nor depicted in the media. Consequently, the Press Council has never dealt with complaints relating to the *prevention* of publication of information, and it is difficult to imagine a complaint in which the complainant is mentioned and is able to point out undue influence.

§2. Confidentiality

110. Breach of confidentiality is a criminal offence according to the Danish Criminal Code (CC), section 152–152f. However, it is not unlawful for journalists to publish information obtained by a breach of confidentiality, unless it concerns a person's strictly private life (subsection 2) or if the information is confidential because of its importance to the safety of the state or the protection of state defence (subsection 3). In a case a member of the Regional Council forwarded information on public expenses in relation to placing of a young person in foster care. The journalist used the information for public discussion in relation to the expenses in such cases, but did not reveal anything personal. The member of the Regional Council was sentenced, but the journalist was not even prosecuted – obviously, as she had done nothing unlawful.

111. If there is a breach of confidentiality, section 152e provides two defences: (1) The disclosing person is under an obligation to forward the information. This is only relevant for legal obligations. (2) The disclosing person acts in order to lawfully safeguard public interests or the interest of himself/herself or other persons.

53. The Press Council has published its English version on www.pressenaevnet.dk.

Obviously, the second defence will be invoked by journalists. In a Copenhagen District Court judgment of 4 December 2006, a journalist and the editor were acquitted for having passed on information from a person employed by the Defence Intelligence. The employee was sentenced to four months imprisonment for the disclosure of material in relation to the motives for going to war in Iraq in 2003,[54] but the District Court found that the journalist's publishing of the information was acceptable as it constituted a lawful safeguard of public interests.

§3. Protection of Journalists and Their Sources

I. Introduction

112. Throughout the 1990s a series of statutory changes were passed. In 1991, the MLA came into force expanding the scope from printed media to all media, and as a consequence included journalists working in the broadcasting media, also in relation to protection of sources. Statutory provisions in the AJA were changed in order to streamline the protection of journalistic sources from only being exceptions to the duty of giving evidence in court to cover also seizure, search and edition (the obligation to hand over documents to the court). In addition, the protection was expanded and now includes due considerations as to the importance of the protection of sources, not primarily as a privilege for journalists, but as a prerequisite for a free flow of information.

113. Presently, the main problem is the linkage between protection of journalists and affiliation to the MLA. In order to seek protection of his/her sources under Danish law, the journalist has to work for a media under section 1 of the MLA, i.e., either: (1) newspapers etc. printed in Denmark; (2) broadcasting media with a Danish broadcasting authorization or registration; or (3) other types of media that have registered with the Press Council. The situation for these non-included media is dealt with below, Chapter 3 §2.

II. Evidence in Court

114. According to Danish law, nobody is under a legal obligation to give information to the police, except for indicating name, address and identification number when asked. Before a court of law, the opposite prevails: according to section 168 of the AJA, everybody must give evidence if no exemptions are available. Apart from the general ban on self-incrimination, the following groups have certain privileges: civil servants with an obligation to observe professional secrecy (section 169), priests, doctors, lawyers and legal mediators (section 170), close relatives, (section 171), *and* journalists (section 172).

---

54. *UfR* 2006.650.

115. The wording of section 172 is rather complicated. Subsection 1 deals with 'editors and editorial employees' – i.e., journalists – working for Danish printed media (*see* MLA, section 1(1)). *First*, they are exempted from giving evidence as regards who is the source of a piece of information, who is the author of an article and who is the photographer. The exemption is independent on the actual publishing – a journalist may receive information and decide not to make any publication – but in case of publishing, it is a condition for the exemption that there is no indication of the source, the author or the photographer. There is a connection to the MLA: if an author or a photographer is anonymous, he/she is not liable according to the MLA and the editor (or others) is not required to pass on their identity. In return, the editor is responsible for any unlawful content. *Second*, editors etc. are exempted from giving evidence as regards who is on the picture or who is mentioned in an article if the persons in question were promised anonymity. In case of publishing, it does not matter whether there is any agreement as to anonymity as long as the identity is not disclosed through the publication. The idea is that before the eventual publication, there must be an agreement of anonymity between the journalist and the person in order for the journalist to be exempted for giving evidence. In case of publishing, the protection is widened. A journalist who has made a research on, say, vandalism[55] can thus before publication be ordered to give evidence as regards his/her sources, if he/she has not promised not to disclose the identity of the source. A professional journalist will, of course, be sure to give this guarantee. After publication, it is merely sufficient that the source is not identifiable in the newspaper.

116. Subsection 2 deals with 'editors and editorial employees' working for authorized or registered broadcasting media. The regulation is very close to the one regarding editors etc. connected to printed media, with some nuances. *First*, not only authors of texts but also authors of works are included in the group of protected sources. This relates to the fact that there may be many authors involved in a TV programme, not only text writers and photographers. *Second*, the identity of those taking part in a programme shall not be revealed when anonymity is guaranteed. If the programme has been published, it is, however, a condition for the exemption to give evidence *that* the identity is not indicated and *that* the broadcasting station has made reasonable efforts to conceal the identity. In case a station has promised anonymity to an interviewee and the station makes a mistake by indicating the name or showing the person directly on the screen etc., the editor and journalists are *not* exempted from giving evidence as to the further identification of the person even if he/she was guaranteed anonymity beforehand.

117. Subsection 3 expands the exemption to other persons who have knowledge of the identity by virtue of their being employed by the broadcasting station or otherwise engaged. Thus even cleaners and bell boys are exempted from identifying the journalists' sources.

---

55. This was the case in *UfR* 1986.340/3H in which a journalist actually ended up being detained for his refusal to give evidence. This happened before the various changes of the rules.

118. According to subsection 4, the exemption mentioned in subsections 1–3 also applies to media under the MLA, section 1(3), i.e., media that are neither printed nor broadcasting media, but other types, such as Internet based, on the condition that they are registered with the Press Council.

119. Subsection 5 circumscribes the scope of the exemption. If it is: (1) a question of a serious offence; (2) with a maximum penalty of at least four years (leaving defamation, privacy violations, hate speech, blasphemy, etc. out of reach as the maximum penalty is much lower); (3) if this particular evidence is crucial; and (4) if the interest of the case obviously outweighs the media's interest in protecting its sources, then the court may require the editor (journalist, bell boy, etc.) to give evidence anyway. All four conditions must be fulfilled. Since the enactment of this version of the statute, no journalist has been required to give evidence as regards his/her sources.[56] Danish national law is in accordance with European human rights, with its emphasis on the protection of journalists' sources except in cases of 'overriding requirement in the public interest'.[57]

120. According to subsection 6 of section 172, the court can require journalists etc. to provide evidence in cases of breach of confidentiality, unless the source or the journalist wanted to reveal issues of public interest. When journalists get a hold of information obtained through a breach of confidentiality, they can only be required to disclose the source if the purpose is private, e.g., the person passes on the information in order to be paid, spreads rumours about a colleague, etc. In *UfR* 2002.1580V, a journalist was required by a District Court to provide evidence as to who had passed on confidential information about the expenses in relation to youths in foster care (*see also* Chapter 2, §3 above). As the issue obviously was of public interest, the High Court exempted the journalist from giving evidence. A similar outcome took place in *UfR* 2011.1329H, in which an employee closely connected to the Minister of Defense leaked info on upcoming deployment of Danish special troops in Iraq. The leak did not appear to have the purpose of informing the public, still the Supreme Court held that the issue was of general interest to the public and hence the involved journalists did not have to reveal anything related to the matter.

III. Seizure, Searches and Orders to Produce Documents Before the Court

121. According to AJA section 804, a person who is not suspected of anything unlawful can be required to hand over material to the court if the material can serve

56. According to a decision made by the Eastern High Court, 12 Sep. 2002, a journalist was not required to give evidence, in a case in which he had published articles on Danish Jews on 'death rolls' by extremists. The Court, quashing the decision by the District Court, found that the police had other means of investigation (Condition No. 3 above). In *UfR* 2015.2423H dealing with an interview on a TV station the Supreme Court held that the journalists involved were the only ones with sufficient information for the police (condition No. 3 above), but that the interest of the case did not outweigh the media's interest in protecting its sources.
57. *Goodwin v. United Kingdom*, 27 Mar. 1996, 39 and 45.

as evidence (and in some other situations that are not particularly relevant for journalists). However, if information will be disclosed which the person is not under an obligation to disclose, *see* AJA sections 169–172, the court cannot make such an order. Thus, a media is not required to hand over material, such as original recordings, if the journalist or others could not be ordered to give evidence. In the case mentioned above, *UfR* 2011.1329H, it was contested whether a journalist had the obligation to hand over an audio file. As indicated, the Supreme Court found that this was not the case.

122. In *UfR* 2002.2503H, a journalist had worked undercover in order to disclose information on Danish sex tourists engaging in sex with children. The programme was transmitted on the national broadcasting station, DR, with the title 'The paedophile Danes', with some of the participants blurred when appearing on the screen. As some of the participants seemed to be engaged in criminal activities, the police wanted to see the original recordings in order to be able to identify the relevant persons. DR refused and the case ended up before the Supreme Court. The Court emphasized the distinction between participants who were promised anonymity on the one hand and the involuntary participants on the other hand, persons who did not know that they were being filmed, *see* AJA section 171(2). According to the ethics of journalism, persons being recorded secretly should have their identity concealed when the recordings are transmitted (*see* Chapter 6, §5), but the fact that DR acted according to the ethics of journalism and blurred the dubious participants did not bring these under the protection of section 172. Accordingly, the Supreme Court ordered DR to hand over those parts of the original material that did not reveal the identity of the ones actually promised anonymity. As regards these persons, the Court did not apply section 172(5), but as a matter of course accepted the journalist's right of protection of sources. An important ingredient of the Court's argument was the relationship of trust. Between the ones secretly filmed and the journalist, there was no such relationship, but as regards the ones openly interviewed, they trusted the journalist's promise to conceal their identity, and the Court respected the importance of protecting this kind of trust when dealing with media reporting.

123. In an earlier case, the Eastern High Court had similar considerations. In *UfR* 2000.1005Ø, riots broke out in a part of Copenhagen, and journalists and photographers located themselves among the rioters in order to report on the incidents. As the situation involved several criminal acts, the police wanted the photos and recordings for further investigation. The Court, however, rejected the claim arguing more generally that in order for news reporting in such situations, it was essential that the reporters were not seen as reporters for the police. Obviously, section 172 did not apply directly as there were no agreements or promises involved. However, in contra distinction to *UfR* 2002.2503H, the option of taking photos and making recordings during the riots required some kind of trust relationship between the media reporters and the participants, otherwise the reporters would not be able to be present and do the reporting. In *UfR* 2002.2503H, there was no such relation between the media reporters and the suspected paedophiles, on the contrary.[58]

124. In a more recent case, *UfR* 2009.75Ø, a journalist infiltrated the prostitution environment, and with clear guarantees of anonymity he participated in a programme, transmitted by DR. The police charged a person appearing in the film and required the entire material handed over. The Court concluded *that* the person fell within the scope of section 172(2)(2) and *that* subsection 5 ought to be considered. It was a serious crime with a maximum penalty of more than four years. However, the Court found that the promised anonymity had been a precondition for the journalist's activities and that his identity should not be revealed. As the police had required the entire material, the claim was rejected.

125. As for *search* and *seizure* the same rules apply. The police have a right to search for and to seize material – with or without court warrant as the case may be – but they do not have the right to search for material falling under section 172, and they do not have the right to seize such material. If the police searches locations belonging to a section 172 person – after all journalists may as anybody else be involved in criminal activities – the person involved may require all seized material to be presented before a court which must screen the material as to whether it contains protected information before the police has the right to examine it (section 807(3)).

126. In a highly exposed case, a weekly magazine had obtained access to info from the Danish credit card company processing transactions from almost all Danish credit cards, thereby acquiring knowledge of the whereabouts of famous actors etc. as well as members of the royal family. In *UfR* 2015.1249H, the Supreme Court accepted the search and seizure and rejected the claim made by the media company[59] that the information was of public interest, a claim that was indeed ill-founded.

IV. Obstinate Witnesses in Court

127. Persons who are required to give evidence before a court or persons who are required to hand over material to the court may be sanctioned if they do not abide by the court order. Section 178 provides for a range of measures including fines, being fetched by the police, compensation for superfluous expenses, current daily fines up to six months and imprisonment up to six months. Since the changes

58. Here Danish law seems to give a better protection of journalists than European human rights. At least the Commission did not find a similar case covered by Art. 10, decision 18 Jan. 1996, Appl. No. 25798/94.
59. The matter falls outside the scope of the Media Liability Act: It is not a matter of media content but of actions prior to publication.

of the rules in the 1990s, no sanctions have been applied to journalists, but previously imprisonment and daily fines were used – to no avail.[60]

V. When the Media Does Not Fall within the MLA

128. In various situations a journalist does not have statutory protection in relation to protection of his/her sources, as this protection is linked to the MLA. Thus, journalists writing books rather than newspaper articles, journalists working for foreign media rather than Danish ones, and journalists working for an Internet media not registered with the Press Council do not enjoy the rights according to section 172 of the AJA.

129. Prevailing law in these situations is not clear. On the one hand, the Supreme Court has previously decided that the statutory provisions, then protecting only journalists attached to printed media, could not be expanded as to include journalists from broadcasting media.[61] On the other hand, the ECHR has since been incorporated into Danish national law on par with other statutes, and European human rights law is rather clear: freedom of expression includes protection of journalists' sources and protection against (undue) search,[62] and the Court does not distinguish between periodicals and books when freedom of expression and the role of the press are at stake.[63] Only if there is an 'overriding requirement in the public interest', a journalist may be ordered to give evidence etc.[64]

130. There may be a distinction between cases in which the journalist cannot help but being outside the scope of the MLA (book writers, journalists working for foreign newspapers and broadcasting stations) and cases where the media has the option to register, but has in fact chosen not to. In the last-mentioned situation, the media has chosen between two legal options, and it seems fair to require the journalist to abide by the standard rules of giving evidence rather than by the ones especially drafted for the media. In the other situation in which there is no way for the journalist to be included, weight must be given to Article 10 of the ECHR, freedom of expression and the protection of the media, including concealing its sources unless there are overriding requirements in the public interest. Whether the national courts in such cases technically will argue for an expansive interpretation of the statutory rules, argue from the basis of Article 10 or argue more freely from basic legal principles remains to be seen.[65]

---

60. *UfR* 1987.29H (imprisonment); *UfR* 1988.315H (daily fines).
61. *UfR* 1986.340H.
62. *Goodwin v. United Kingdom*, 27 Mar. 1996, *Voskuil v. the Netherlands*, 22 Nov. 2007, and *Tillack v. Belgium*, 27 Nov. 2007.
63. *Chauvy and others v. France*, 29 Jun. 2004, 68.
64. *Voskuil v. the Netherlands*, 22 Nov. 1997, 65, and similarly Recommendation No. R(2000) 7 on the right of journalists not to disclose their sources of information, Principle 3 (a).
65. As mentioned above Ch. 1, 'The Journalists' Profession', the City Court of Copenhagen has applied the expansive approach.

§4. Journalists Working under Cover and Other Journalistic Methods

131. In quite a few cases, Danish courts have been presented with the task of deciding whether and to what extent it was a mitigating factor that the culprit was a journalist who, in his/her attempt to obtain information, found it relevant or necessary to break the law. Journalists cannot always get the relevant and correct information by interviewing, and putting questions such as: 'Do you sell illegal commodities?' probably will not bring about any information. Journalists have been quite creative, inventing fake identities including forging documents such as passports and birth certificates, entering into private locations in order to take photos, carrying knives in airports, and buying illegal explosives and firearms.

132. There are at least seventeen published cases dealing with this intricate question. In the following sections the courts' central considerations will be highlighted.

133. From the case law it is evident that information on *issues of general public interest* will lead to considerations of acquittal or conviction without penalty. This is hardly contested: how asylum seekers are treated upon arrival,[66] demonstration against large traffic constructions,[67] the security situation in airports and elsewhere,[68] all are issues of public interest. The courts will assess whether in fact the issue is of genuine public interest or whether it merely is in the interest of the journalists or of a curious and inquisitive public. Private information on well-known people may appear awfully interesting but is normally not of any genuine public interest.[69]

134. The courts engage in a *balancing of interests*, freedom of expression and information on the one hand and the various interests involved on the other. In *UfR* 2010.1859H the Supreme Court argues as follows: 'In the balancing of the interest of freedom of speech against other interests ("hensyn"), such as the protection of private life, care must be taken that no such barriers are constructed which will prevent the media in a reasonable fulfilling of its role as public organ of information and control.'[70] Even though balancing cannot provide any precise result – the balancing does not involve decigrams, but loosely identifiable factors – it is a useful and operational tool: large public interest is weighing heavily, whereas only a slight public interest does not add much. *UfR* 2012.2328H dealt with the issue of a hidden

66. *UfR* 1990.71H.
67. *UfR* 1994.988H: Journalist's trespassing of the minister's garden and *UfR* 1999.1675H: Journalist's trespassing of a private island. In both cases the journalists covered demonstrations at the private locations. The demonstrators were convicted and the journalists acquitted.
68. *UfR* 2008.671H. Journalist's carrying of a knife in Copenhagen airport in order to point out security problems. The majority of the Supreme Court held the action to be criminal but meted out no sanction. Two dissenting judges voted for acquittal.
69. *UfR* 2008.1565H: A well-known football coach relation to 'booze and women' were private matters and not of genuine public interest; *UfR* 2015.1249H: The whereabouts of famous actors and members of the royal family were private matters and not of genuine public interest.
70. Authors' translation.

camera in a kitchen where the residents carried out illegal trade of dogs. The infringement was not heavy – the kitchen served as salesroom and nothing very private was going on – but on the other hand, illegal dog trade is not a highly important issue either. The Supreme Court was divided, three voted for acquittal and two for a (minor) fine. On the contrary, gross violations of privacy, such as broadcasting the washing of an elderly's bottom, is unacceptable even though the theme of the broadcast 'how are the elderly treated at public elderly institutions' is of general public interest. And vice versa, when the infringement on privacy is low: photos taken of a person at a private place but doing nothing personal, and the theme is of general public interest, *UfR* 2010.1859H (pictures inside a car, the theme being the reception of alcoholics at an alcoholism treatment institution). Or when the photographer trespasses private property at an uninhabited small island in order to cover a demonstration with many participants, *UfR* 1999.1675H. The intensity of the interference is also relevant. A prior injunction is more intense than a sanction meted out afterwards, *UfR* 2010.1859H.

135. All cases involving forgery have led to convictions, also when the forgery was carried out in order to provide the journalist with a convincing identity when working under cover. In *UfR* 1990.71H, a journalist forged a passport in order to act as an asylum seeker. The journalist managed to show unacceptable procedures and treatment of the asylum seekers, and the court accepted the public interest. Still, the journalist was convicted, the idea being that the trust in public documents is weighing heavily on the balancing scales. However, the sanctions were lenient.

136. Actual danger is also relevant. In *UfR* 2007.1673Ø, two journalists bought illegal fireworks in order to show how easy it was. After buying the explosives, they drove directly to the police and were presented with a charge. Regardless of the fact the case falls under freedom of information, but it is dangerous to drive around with illegal explosives, which is why it is prohibited in the first place. The case was taken to the ECtHR, which confirmed the sentence right away. The case was rejected as 'manifestly ill-founded', cf. *Mikkelsen & Christensen v. Denmark* 24 May 2011. Other cases involving weapons do not involve danger: taking a knife from a restaurant in the airport and carrying it to the gate (in order to point out a security problem) is not dangerous (*UfR* 2008.671H) and neither considered as dangerous is buying weapons without proper permission (*UfR* 2009.920Ø).

137. In these types of cases, the courts often consider whether the journalistic method was *necessary*. This is not a straightforward consideration and the judges may disagree as to whether the journalistic activity was necessary in order to provide the relevant information.[71] However, the consideration is relevant, and for the journalists it entails that they have to consider whether the planned activity is necessary for providing the relevant information or whether it is more the actual fun of using hidden cameras, microphones etc. which is driving the activities. The ECtHR

71. In *UfR* 2008.671H the judges disagreed as to whether it has been necessary to actually carry the knife from the restaurant to the gate in order to point out the security problems.

has emphasized that it is not for the courts to make editorial decisions.[72] Still, it appears to be relevant for the courts to assess whether in fact the activity, carried out by the journalist, is necessary in cases where the journalists are on the fringes of acting criminally and where the courts may accept freedom of information as a valid defence. To the extent that the journalists have in fact tried in other ways to obtain the relevant information but to no avail, the Danish courts are more likely to accept the journalistic necessity as a relevant parameter. This necessity test is carried out in relation to the various components of the case. In *UfR* 2012.1788H the Supreme Court appeared willing to accept the necessity of showing recordings made by hidden camera, based on the fact that the journalists had approached the director of the institution in order to make an interview, but were rejected. However, the showing of an elderly having his private parts washed was not necessary in order to bring out critical information as to how the elderly were treated at the institution.

138. It has been debated[73] whether initiative is relevant. In some cases journalists are merely reporting what is going on, such as reporting from ongoing demonstrations,[74] while in other cases the initiative comes from the journalists.[75] In one case, the initiative was decisive. Some journalists researched how it was possible to obtain passports and drivers' licences based on false information and easily forged documents. The issue was publicly debated, but nothing was done and politicians even denied that it was a problem. The journalists therefore took the initiative to obtain the public documents based on false information. After acquiring the documents, the journalists posited them in a locker with the editor and later they handed over the documents to the police. After the publishing, the procedure was changed, making it more difficult to obtain passports etc. based on unreliable information. Nevertheless, the journalists were sentenced, the main argument being exactly that the activities were initiated by the journalists. According to the present authors, this judgment is not convincing, and later judgments from the Supreme Court also indicate that the question of who is taking the initiative is not relevant. This approach gives a better protection of active journalism: investigative and active journalism ought to be protected on the condition that it is carried out in respect of the involved and with due regard to the ethics of journalism. If legal protection of journalism were only for passive and merely reporting journalism, this could result in less relevant information to the public.

---

72. *Jersild v. Denmark* 23 Sep. 1994, pr. 31.
73. Vibeke Borberg, 'Mediernes brug af skjult kamera på privat område' [*The Media's Use of Hidden camera on private locations*], *UfR* 2014B.258; Sten Schaumburg-Müller 'Om retlig beskyttelse af aktiv journalistik – En kommentar til UfR 2014B.258 om mediernes brug af skjult kamera på privat område' [On Legal Protection of Active Journalism – A Commentary to the Media's Use of Hidden Camera, *UfR* 2015B.9-14.
74. *UfR* 1994.988H; *UfR* 1999.1675H.
75. *UfR* 2007.1673Ø (illegal fireworks); *UfR* 2008.671H (knife in airport); *UfR* 2008.1055Ø (fake passports and drivers' licences); *UfR* 2012.1788H (recordings from an institution for elderly).

139. Two published cases[76] deal with the issue of journalists having to obey the orders of the police. In both cases, the journalists were convicted. Journalists do not have a special licence that exempts them from having to abide by the law or police orders. On the other hand, the forwarding of relevant information may require the presence of journalists and photographers. In the above-mentioned cases of journalists and photographers covering demonstrations held in private locations, the media workers were acquitted for charges of unlawful trespassing.[77] In a similar case with a photographer covering a demonstration at the office of the Refugee Board, the court emphasized that the photographer did not take active part in the demonstration and that he obeyed police orders without any trouble.[78] As long as police orders acknowledge the importance of the presence of media workers, the journalists and photographers also have to obey the orders. If, on the other hand, the police had ordered the media workers to leave the scene, thereby hindering the media coverage, the situation would be different. Such a police order would violate Article 10 ECHR, and media workers not obeying the order should not be punished.

140. Summing up, Danish courts are engaged in a highly considerate balancing of interests when dealing with active journalism, and to the present authors' assessment Danish case law convincingly complies with ECtHR case law relating to Article 8 and Article 10 ECHR.

76. *UfR* 2005.1145Ø; *UfR* 2008.251Ø.
77. *UfR* 1994.988H and *UfR* 1999.1675H.
78. *UfR* 2008.2738Ø.

Chapter 3. Journalists' Liability

§1. General Information on the Liability System

141. Limitations in freedom of speech are largely regulated by criminal law.[79] The Criminal Code has provisions criminalizing incitement to, and public approval of, certain acts facilitating terrorism e.g., by means of propaganda, intrusion of private life, dissemination of private information, individual defamation and group defamation. In relation to court case reporting, the AJA has provisions criminalizing i.a. the taking of photos during court sessions. As for advertising, the MPA also criminalize violations. Some issues are conflicts between two subjects rather than issues between the public and a possible criminal offender. Consequently, the area is a mixture of criminal prosecution and civil procedure and of criminal law and private law.

142. As for the procedure, Danish law provides three ways of criminal procedure. *First*, prosecuting by the public prosecutor, which is by far the most common way of dealing with criminal acts. Danish procedural law does normally not accept private prosecution of crimes. The public prosecutor takes the decision whether to prosecute and has the right as well as the obligation to prosecute criminal acts. *Second*, some crimes are under conditioned public prosecution, implying that the act must be reported to the police in order for the police and the prosecution to take action. Crimes relating to intrusion of private life are under conditioned prosecution (Criminal Code section 275). In practice, also the prosecution of group defamation, which is not considered propaganda (*see* below Chapter 3, §6), is conditioned on someone reporting the crime. *Third*, there is the option of private criminal prosecution which is an anomaly in Danish criminal law. However, defamation cases are as a point of departure under private prosecution, and in intrusion of private life cases the offended may choose to prosecute the case privately rather than to report the case to public authorities. Private prosecution mainly follows the rules of civil procedure instead of criminal procedure, the main difference being that one party (or both)[80] may receive a penalty. The private parties may in fact choose to desist from criminal prosecution and merely file a private suit against the offender. In this case, of course, the case cannot result in any criminal sanction.

143. According to section 19 in the general part of the Criminal Code, Danish criminal law distinguishes between intended and negligent acts. As a point of departure, only intended acts are penalized under the Criminal Code, whereas acts under any other statute such as the AJA or MPA are criminally sanctioned even if they are not intended, but only carried out with negligence. Most of the media-related acts, such as libel, privacy infringements and hate speech, are under the Criminal Code

79. Sten Schaumburg-Müller, *Presseret* [*Media Law*] (Jurist- og Økonomforbundets Forlag, 2003); Knud Aage Frøbert & Jørgen Paulsen, *Medieansvarsloven med kommentarer* [*The Media Liability Act with Commentaries*] (Jurist- og Økonomforbundets Forlag, 2007).
80. In *UfR* 2009.614V, both parties claimed penalty and compensation from the other because of mutual accusations.

and thus require intent in order to be sanctioned by criminal law. Under section 21 attempts are penalized in the same manner as committed crimes.

144. According to CC, section 23, anyone who has contributed to the act in question by 'instigation, advice, or action' can be punished. Danish law does not as a point of departure distinguish between main actors and side actors, and disseminating unlawful expressions comes under the section. However, *first*, the MLA normally exempts media from section 23 (*see* below §2 on 'Media Liability'), and only in cases in which the maximum penalty is at least four years, section 23 is applicable to media matters. In *UfR* 2009.1453H, six persons were convicted for financing terrorism by collecting money for the Columbian Fuerdas Armadas Revolucionarias de Columbia and the Palestinian the Popular Front for the Liberation of Palestine. Section 114c carries a maximum penalty of six years, and thus the special media liability rules do not apply. *Second*, the media have certain liberties when reporting (in contradistinction to forwarding views themselves).[81] In cases where the media is not covered by the MLA and when the information or the view is not merely reported, but forwarded, section 23 applies with its rather extensive coverage of possible accomplices. The courts may, however, have a tendency to limit the verdicts to the more directly involved.[82]

145. In private law, a person is as a point of departure liable for his/her negligent tortious acts and the distinction between intended and negligent acts is of little importance. If several persons are involved in the act, they will all be liable and the victim can recover the total claim by any of the persons involved. Section 26 of the Compensation for Damages Act provides tort compensation for unlawful acts, infringing on any person's peace or honour.[83]

§2. Media Liability

I. The Complicated Regulation of Media Liability

146. For a long time, the printed media had its own statute, *inter alia*, providing for a special liability regime. In 1992, a new MLA[84] came into force, setting up a generally clear and well-functioning media liability system. The details, however, are (too) complicated, and there are problems with the scope of the act.

---

81. *See*, e.g., *Jersild v. Denmark*, 24 Sep. 1994. Jersild was convicted according to s. 23 of the Penal Code, but the European Court of Human Rights found that the conviction was a violation of Art. 10 as he was merely reporting, not propagating the unlawfully expressed views.
82. In *UfR* 1988.411V a poster was found unlawful. The printer, however, was charged under s. 23 but acquitted.
83. In *UfR* 1969.233Ø, DR broadcasted a television documentary on prostitution. The interviewed persons were anonymized albeit unsuccessfully, and one of the participants claimed compensation. As the then prevailing Act required intent in order to be liable for these kinds of damages, the claim was rejected – whereupon a new bill was passed, making compensation for negligent acts possible.
84. Presently the Consolidated Act No. 914/2014 with later amendments. An unauthorized English version of the Act is available at the Press Council's web page http://www.pressenaevnet.dk/media-liability-act.

147. Roughly, the main idea is that there are two principal actors, the author and the editor. The author who, e.g., makes a racist remark, writes a statement supporting terrorism, has an unlawful picture published or produces a radio broadcast defaming another person, is liable when not anonymized. If the content is anonymous, the editor is liable. If the author is not anonymous, the editor is often co-liable. As a point of departure, nobody else can be held liable, even though they have participated in one way or the other. Thus, the person who reads out an unlawful statement, the newspaper vendors and the signal carriers are not liable even though they may have contributed to the unlawful act by disseminating unlawful expressions. Explicitly publishers or other owners of media are not liable for the content of the media (with some restricted exceptions, *see* below).

148. To be more specific: if the identity is known, those who utter a statement, such as interviewees and journalists on radio and TV when actually talking, as well as the writer of a text, are liable for the content (sections 14 and 10). This is rather easily handled when dealing with the printed media: anonymous writers and anonymous interviewees are *not* liable. Only if their identity is revealed with their consent, they are liable. Otherwise, the editor functions as the stand in, having strict liability for the content of the article. And conversely, if the identity of the one making an oral statement or of the writer is disclosed to the public with their consent, they will be liable, not the editor.

149. However, the editor may be liable anyway together with the one uttering a statement and the author, if the author is an employee of the newspaper or if the editor had some knowledge of the article (section 13). Thus, the editor, apart from the strict liability in cases of anonymous content in printed press, has a kind of expanded liability which does not follow the usual requirements of intent and negligence.

150. Legally speaking, a photographer is the author of the photo: if photographers consent to the photograph being published and to the publication of their name, they will be liable (section 9(2)). Conversely, if they have not consented to the publishing of the picture or have not consented to their identity being revealed, they cannot be held liable. In such cases, as with anonymous writers, the editor will be liable, his/her knowledge and deeds notwithstanding.[85]

151. Generally, the editor is liable for any anonymous content; i.e., not only anonymous articles or letters to the editor (which in practice are never anonymous) but also headlines etc. In *UfR* 2001.237Ø, the court had issued a prohibition of revealing the name of a suspect in a specific case. A journalist wrote an article respecting the prohibition, but the sub-editor put a photo of the suspect on the same

85. *UfR* 1974.775B is illustrative: A young girl was murdered, and a rather explicit nude picture covered the front page. The photographer was not indicated (probably being a friend who had not consented to the publication of what appeared to be a private picture). The editor was on holiday and knew nothing of the matter, yet he was sentenced to fourteen days prison. It is noteworthy that prison sentences are very rare in freedom of speech cases, and that the editor did not appeal the verdict passed by a lower court.

page. Seen in isolation, neither the article nor the photo was unlawful, and consequently neither the author nor the photographer was liable. The sub-editor is not among the possible subjects in the MLA, and therefore the editor was held liable for disclosing the identity against an order from the court.

152. It should be noted that each newspaper or broadcasting company has only one editor who has this special expanded liability. There may be many sub-editors or even editors of the culture section, editors of the opinion section, etc., but there is only one editor in relation to liability. This editor must be indicated, either in printed form or registered with the Press Council (sections 3 and 5).

153. When dealing with *electronic* media, the question of anonymity becomes much more difficult. In principle, the same rules apply: only the author and the editor may be liable, always at least one, and the author only if he/she is not anonymized. However, the details are complicated. When is a person appearing on the radio or especially on the TV screen anonymous? When his/her name is left out? (On TV that is clearly insufficient), or if the face is covered or blurred? (He/she may be easily recognizable anyway) or must the voice as well as the appearance be distorted? (Sufficient but maybe not necessary). The MLA provides some very detailed rules, distinguishing between live reporting of public meetings and current events, other direct programmes, and indirect – i.e., edited – programmes.

154. As regards live reporting of public events, the standard liability rules prevail (section 20(2)). This entails that, say, a demonstrator making unlawful remarks is the one liable, even if his/her identity does not appear. Other participants may be included according to the Danish legal conception of complicity, cf. section 23 CC mentioned above. However, European human rights law has to a large extent excluded media workers from liability when they are only doing their job of reporting, *see Jersild v. Denmark*, 24 September 1994. The editor does not have a special position in this situation and can only be made liable according to the standard rules.

155. As regards indirect programmes, the wrongdoer is regarded anonymous: (1) if the person cannot be identified; (2) if the person has not consented to his/her remark being broadcasted; or (3) if the broadcasting station has promised anonymity *and* has taken measures to secure it (section 18). As regards direct programmes (apart from the live transmissions of current events), the one expressing an unlawful statement can only escape liability if the broadcasting station has promised anonymity *and* has taken measures to secure it (section 20(1)), equivalent to the third option in section 18. In situations in which the person making the statement is not liable, the editor is vicariously liable. Thus, it is easier for an interviewee to avoid being held liable in edited programmes, and correspondingly easier for the editor to be responsible. The rationale is that the station is in a better controlling positing as regards edited programmes. The editor can be held responsible also if the person has given incorrect information on his/her identity.

156. Besides, the editor may be co-liable in cases in which he/she or the station has acted reproachfully, but is not liable according to traditional legal standards. For example, if an interviewee is promised anonymity, but is in fact exposed fully recognizable, the interviewee will be liable for his/her unlawful accusations etc. as there are no exemptions available (*see* above), but so will the editor. Besides, and similar to the situation as regards printed matters, the editor may be liable if a statement is made by an employee and the editor knows about it (section 21).

157. Writers of texts are liable similarly to the situation as regards printed matter. If they have consented to text being published and their identity being revealed, they are liable. If not, the editor is (section 17).

158. Noteworthy is that the journalist as such does not carry any liability. Only as an 'author', the journalist may be liable under the MLA.

159. The liability system includes some fall back clauses: if the author cannot be held liable because they cannot be sued in Denmark or because they are mentally ill, the editor will automatically be responsible. The same applies to the publisher if the editor is either not domiciled in Denmark or not sane. The last situation is obviously exceptional, and as far as the present authors are informed, there have been no examples of the publisher being liable.

160. More practically important are the provisions making the publisher (and the station etc.) immediately responsible for the payment of any fines or compensations decided under the MLA (sections 16, 30 and 32). Thus, complainants who have been granted compensation can demand the amount to be paid by the publisher or the station, no matter who is actually liable according to the media liability rules. The publisher will in turn have recourse to the legally liable subject. In practice, this implies that compensation for unlawful writings or remarks made by known authors – in which case normally only the author is liable – may be recovered directly from the publisher.

161. It is not explicitly stated in the MLA whether injunctions should be directed at the editor or the publisher. In *UfR* 2014.462H the Supreme Court held that injunctions should be directed at the publisher. However, in *UfR* 2018.651H, the court changed its mind and held – more in line with the media liability system – that the editor is the correct addressee.[86]

162. Summing up: the overall approach restricting the group of possibly liable persons to very few and, conversely, expanding the liability of the editor, fits well to the needs of the media and to the need of the general public. However, sometimes and especially when dealing with electronic media, the rules are so detailed and complicated that very few would know how to deal with the situation in a legally correct way.

86. The decisions are thoroughly discussed in Trine Baumbach, 'Medieansvar eller redaktøransvar i forbudssager – har det nogen betydning' [*Media Liability and Editor's Liability in Injunction Cases. Does It Have Any Importance*?], *UfR* 2018B.36.

II. The Scope of the MLA

163. The MLA applies to three groups: (1) domestic periodicals; (2) DR and TV2 and other stations with broadcasting permissions (either authorization or registration); and (3) any other printed or electronic material with news reporting characteristics (section 1). The two former groups are automatically covered by the MLA and cannot opt out whereas the latter group must report itself to the Press Council in order to be covered by the MLA (section 8).

164. Thus, newspapers and magazines published in Denmark are covered, whereas foreign newspapers etc. are not. Radio and TV stations with a permission to broadcast from Denmark are covered, others are not. This implies that television stations broadcasting to a Danish audience, i.e., broadcasting in Danish, do not come within the scope of the Act if they do not broadcast from Denmark or do not have the permission to do so.

165. As for liability, this is straightforward. A Danish newspaper and a Danish broadcasting company fall under the Danish MLA, whereas foreign actors do not. However, falling under the MLA carries other privileges and special regulation, and it is problematic – legally as well as substantially – that foreign media are treated less favourably than Danish ones.

166. Media falling within section 1(3) may come within the scope of the Act, provided that they register with the Press Council. Besides, they must have the characteristics of news reporting, which implies that they must be edited. Thus, web pages which do not have the mixed character of reporting do not come within the scope. It does not have to be specifically *news* reporting, but the content must be of an edited, mixed character, just like the traditional newspapers and radio and TV stations. Most Danish newspapers and all broadcasting stations have web pages registered with the Press Council. If the web pages have blogs or similar open spaces, these parts will not be covered by the MLA. At the time of writing, October 2018, 988 media have registered under the MLA, compared to 289 in December 2009.

167. It is an open question of how commentary boxes with direct access are treated legally. On the one hand it may be argued that this type of content is out of the editor's control and therefore simply does not fall under the MLA.[87] On the other hand it may be argued that if the media is under the MLA this applies to the entire media.[88] Even in this situation, it is unlikely that the editor will be strictly

87. This is the approach taken by the Press Council, *see* below Ch. 6.

88. Søren Sandfeld Jakobsen & Sten Schaumburg-Müller, 'Pressenævnets kompetence' [*The Jurisdiction of the Press Council*], *Juristen*, 2013, No. 4, pp. 185–193. Trine Baumbach, 'Anonyme, uredigerede debatindlæg – skal ingen bære ansvaret?' [*Anonymous Debate – Nobody's Liability*?], in Nis Jul Clausen et al. (eds), *Ikke kun retsfilosofi – festskrift til Sten Schaumburg-Müller* [*Not Only Legal Philosophy. Festschrift to Sten Schaumburg-Müller*], (Jurist- og Øjkonomforbundets Forlag, 2016), pp. 57–72.

liable for anonymous content. Rather, the situation is somewhat similar to synchronic reporting,[89] in which case the ordinary complicity rules apply. Presently, the MLA itself does not offer a solution and, as of yet, there is no case law dealing with the matter.

168. It is probably the case that web-based media not operating from Denmark are not able to register This makes sense in relation to liability but less in relation to the special media privileges (protection of sources etc.), which formally are not guaranteed by Danish statutory law.

169. Summing up on the scope of the MLA, the special media liability regime does not apply to a host of media: foreign newspapers, foreign broadcasting stations, unregistered web pages, web pages that do not have real media content and journalists writing books.

170. As mentioned, falling under the MLA is not only relevant for the assessment of liability, it is also decisive in a range of other situations:

- The Press Council, which gives opinions in relation to ethics of journalism, only has authority to deal with media under the MLA. Media that are not covered, do not have to bother with the Press Council – but may, of course, have to face court proceedings as the alternative (*see* Chapter 6).
- There is a special right under the MLA, sections 36–40, for reply (*see* Chapter 4). Only media under the Act have this obligation.
- The provisions in the AJA dealing with protection of sources, restrictions in search, seizure and obligations to produce documents etc. in court are all connected to the status as media under the MLA. Thus, if not covered, media cannot invoke any Danish statute in order to protect their sources, at least not directly (*see* Chapter 2, §3).
- The media have special rights in relation to court cases. If the court is considering meetings in camera, any present media reporter has the right to protest, and if the court in fact does decide to proceed in camera, the media can appeal this decision – provided that the media comes under the MLA (*see* Chapter 5 §2),
- The media have special rights in relation to access to court material. The special rights are contingent on being covered by the MLA (*see* Chapter 5 §2).
- Finally, there are special exemptions and rules for running databases with personal information (*see* Chapter 3 §4). These rules only apply to media under the MLA.

III. Commercials and Other Special Features of the MLA

171. Besides media liability and the obligation for media to comply with ethics of journalism (*see* Chapter 6), a few special features ought to be mentioned.

89. MLA s. 20(2) mentioned above 'I The Complicated Regulation of Media Liability'.

As for commercials, the group of persons who may be liable is restricted to the advertiser, the advertising agency and the editor. According to section 27(1)(1), anyone who has inserted an advertisement in a media under the MLA is liable according to general liability standards. This implies that the advertising person or company is liable for negligent acts in relation to tort compensation and for intended acts as regards trespassing of the Criminal Code. The same applies to those having assisted, section 27(1)(2), meaning that the advertising agency may also be responsible. However, others who may have been involved in the process, such as printers, newspaper vendors, etc., cannot be held liable under this section. The editor may also be liable for commercials, but as a point of departure only according to general standards of liability (section 27(2)(1)). The editor has an explicit duty to pass on name etc. of the advertiser (section 4), and if s/he does not pass on this information when required, he/she will be liable for the content of the advertisement even if s/he did not have any knowledge, let alone participated in its creation (section 27(2)(2)). As for broadcast commercials, special rules pertain in addition to the MLA, *see* Part V.

172. According to section 28, criminal prosecution in relation to anything appearing in a media (covered by the MLA) must be submitted to the Director of Public Prosecution (DPP) ('Rigsadvokaten') for approval – the idea being that prosecution is an infringement of the freedom of speech and therefore is a serious decision. In practice, the provision may work in favour of uniformity rather than reticence as regards the prosecution of journalists.

173. The meting out of the sentence has attained special attention by the legislator. In general, the sentence must be set according to section 80 of the Criminal Code, which requires consideration on 'the seriousness of the offence and information of the offender'. As liability under the MLA is partly strict liability, the criterion 'information of the offender' is hardly relevant. Instead, the MLA requires consideration of the circulation or prevalence of the media in question and the possible profits from the criminal act (section 26(2)). There is no equivalent statutory rule as regards meting out compensation. According to case law, compensation in these kinds of cases is standardized lump sums at a rather low level, varying in accordance with the nature of the offence.

§3. Defamation

I. Sections 267–275

174. The sections 267–275 in the Penal Code, dealing with defamation and the protection of personal honour, are founded on a basic distinction between charges or allegations on the one hand and terms of abuse on the other.[9091] Charges deal with

90. Gorm Toftegaard Nielsen, Thomas Elholm & Morten Niels Jakobsen, *Kommenteret straffelov. Speciel Del*, [*The Criminal Code. A Commentary. The Special Part*] 11. udgave, Jurist- og Økonomforbundets Forlag 2017. Søren Sandfeld Jakobsen & Sten Schaumburg-Müller, *Medieretten* [*Media*

allegations of facts such as 'he is a bank robber' whereas terms of abuse are abusive words with no reference to facts, such as oaf, lout, etc. It has legal implications whether a word is categorized as an allegation or a term of abuse. The distinction is in principle logical and easily manageable. However, neither words nor reality is purely logical, and besides the distinction does not correspond well with the similar distinction in European human rights case law between allegations of fact and value judgments.[92]

175. As a consequence, Danish courts have preferred not to follow the wording of the defamation section literally, but rather aimed at reaching substantively correct judgments. After the incorporation of the ECHR into Danish law, the Courts often times state that the defamation sections must be interpreted 'in the light of the ECHR', thus reaching decisions that are in accordance with ECHR Articles 8 and 10 and case law from the ECtHR. (*See* below for more details).

176. In 2017, the Criminal Code Commission ('Straffelovrådet') produced a report suggesting that the wording of the defamation sections be updated in order to keep up with present-day case law and the actual needs of balancing the various interests at stake rather than relying on a philosophical position abandoned a long time ago – that of logical positivism – claiming that it is always possible to distinguish between words referring to something real and words without this particular reference. 16 May 2018, a bill, largely based on the suggestions made by the Commission, was presented to the *Folketing*, the Danish Parliament. It is likely that the statute will be changed much in accordance with the bill. In the following, the still prevailing sections of the Criminal Code will serve as point of departure, noting that even with a change in the wordings, the substance of prevailing defamation law will very much remain as it is.

177. Section 267 runs as follows: 'Any person who violates the personal honour of another by offensive words or conduct or by making or spreading allegations of an act likely to disparage him in the esteem of his fellow citizens shall be liable to a fine or to imprisonment for any term not exceeding four months.'[93] Thus, the section provides the distinction between 'offensive words and conduct' and the 'making or spreading of allegations' and, second, lays out as a point of departure that

---

Law] Jurist- og Økonomforbundets Forlag, 2013. Trine Baumbach, *Medieret. Frihed og ansvar* [*Media Law. Freedom and Liability*], Karnov 2017.

91. The Danish terms are 'sigtelse' and 'ringeagtsytring' respectively. There is hardly any precise translation of the words. In the following, the English terms 'charge' or 'allegation' and 'terms of abuse' are chosen as the most adequate.
92. *See*, e.g., *Lingens v. Austria*, 8 Jul. 1986, 46, 'In the Court's view, a careful distinction needs to be made between facts and value-judgments. The existence of facts can be demonstrated, whereas the truth of value-judgments is not susceptible of proof.' This distinction is not handled so easily, either. In *Pedersen and Baadsgaard v. Denmark*, GC 17 Dec. 2004, nine judges held the words in question to be allegations of facts and eight judges found that they were value judgments.
93. The translation from Malene Frese Jensen et al., *The Principal Danish Criminal Acts*, 3rd edn. (DJØF Publishing, 2006), uses the term 'allegation' for 'charges'. It should be noted that it is not equivalent to the term 'allegation of fact' in European human rights law.

both are unlawful. Offensive conduct could be showing contemptuous signs or spitting,[94] and offensive words are set on a par with conduct. When dealing with words, the categorization as either offensive words (terms of abuse) or allegations (charges) is important in relation to the subsequent sections.

178. Section 268 deals with 'malicious allegations' and increases the maximum penalty to two years imprisonment. The section only applies to charges. A forwarded allegation that a person is a bank robber with the knowledge that this is not the case falls within the scope of section 268, whereas it is not possible 'maliciously' to claim that somebody is an oaf. Section 268 is often invoked, but less often applied by the courts. In *UfR* 2002.2767Ø a person made allegations of forgery and fraud in letters and on the Internet against several civil servants, some of whom had been involved in the person's child custody case. He was sentenced to imprisonment for sixty days. Prison sentences are very rare in defamation cases.

179. Section 269 provides for exemptions if the charge is either true or: 'if the issuer of the allegation in good faith has been under an obligation to speak or has acted in lawful protection of obvious public interest or of the personal interest of himself or of others'. It is noteworthy that the exemption only applies to charges, not to terms of abuse. The idea is that terms of abuse cannot be true or false, and hence they are unlawful. In contradistinction, charges can be true, and obviously true allegations are not criminalized. The scope for freedom of speech is larger; however, in cases in which the speaker is in good faith, i.e., he/she believes the statement to be true even if it is not, *and* s/he had reasons to forward the charge, such as protecting public or private interests. Subsection 2 provides that: 'punishment may be remitted where evidence is produced which justifies the ground for regarding the allegations as true'. In other words, in cases in which the allegations are not true and there may not be sufficient interests involved, the person who has produced the charges may have the sentence remitted if s/he had reasons to believe that the allegations were true.

180. Thus, the statutory regulation of defamation is largely centred on 'truth': if words cannot be true or false, words like 'oaf' or 'lout', the courts merely have to ascertain whether the words are abusive, and if they are, they should be punished. If the words can be true or false, words like 'bank robber', the defendant must either establish the truth or establish that he/she believed them to be true or at least had good reasons to believe so.

181. However, there are two sets of problems with this approach. *First*, judges are not linguists and not primarily interested in analysing language, rather they engage in judging whether words ought to be spoken out loud or not. Even though the distinction between 'terms of abuse' and 'charges' is fundamental, the courts often try to avoid it, and if they actually apply the distinction, this is not always done in a fully convincing and coherent manner. In *UfR* 1958.1182H the Supreme Court had troubles categorizing several words in a literary review debate, in *UfR*

94. A lot of spitting may amount to assault, *UfR* 2003.2245Ø.

1991.269H the expression 'dingy mole activities' referring to a political opponent in a debate was held to be a charge, and even a true charge, and in *UfR* 1999.1910Ø alleging that a book was 'full of lies' was not a charge against the author or even terms of abuse, but categorized as comments on a book not on a person. As for the two last-mentioned cases, the results – acquittal – are convincing, but the categorizations are not. In *UfR* 1991.269H the remarks were made in a political debate and ought to be accepted.[95] However, it is difficult to see how the plaintiff's action, propagating a no in the Irish referendum in 1990, is truly a 'mole' activity ('mole' usually referring to internal spies) and even more so a 'dingy' one. In *UfR* 1999.1910Ø, a known author and instructor had made a critical review of a book written by a leading member of Hell's Angels during his imprisonment as he was convicted for murder. In a literary review there must be some room for hard critique, but it is difficult not to categorize 'lie' as a charge, and it is difficult to understand how a book can be full of lies without implying that the author is the liar.

182. Second, focus on truth does not fit well with the approach by the ECtHR. In *Unabhängige Initiative Informationsvielfalt v. Austria*, 26 February 2002, the Court noted that: '"the degree of precision for establishing the well-foundedness of a criminal charge by a competent court can hardly be compared to that which ought to be observed by a journalist when expressing his opinion on a matter of public concern" (p. 46), or in other words, to require the same standards for establishing truth in a court of law as when dealing with journalists' newspaper writing and political debate may unduly restrict freedom of speech. The European Court, therefore, focuses on relevance and reasonableness rather than truth. By the employment of the term "value judgment", the Court in cases of public interest protects remarks which are the author's subjective value judgment or comment on factual situations. Thus, the Court has accepted "unlawful" and "neofascist" as value judgments,[96] expressions which with a strict reading of the Danish statutes would be charges'.[97]

183. Besides, 'terms of abuse' are as a point of departure unlawful, and there is no statutory backing for the courts to consider whether a term of abuse is a comment based on facts.

184. Danish courts therefore often face a difficult task when dealing with defamation cases, trying to avoid the wording of sections 267 and 269 and to align the result with the ECHR. *UfR* 2003.2044 may be illustrative. The Danish People's Party, since 2002 parliamentary support for the minority government, has a critical stance towards especially Muslim immigrants and is regularly accused of being racist, an accusation the party vehemently opposes. In 2000, during the campaign in relation to the Euro referendum, a politician against the Euro was asked why she did not cooperate with the Danish People's Party, and she replied that she did not

95. The result is perfectly in line with European human rights case law. The words are obviously value judgments, forwarded in a political debate on a public issue.
96. *Vides Aizsardzibas v. Latvia*, 27 May 2004, and *Karman v. Russia*, 14 Dec. 2006, respectively.
97. *UfR* 1965.914Ø, 'semi sadist' as a remark on the behaviour of some army officers towards recruits put forward in a debate was found to be untrue charges and therefore punishable.

want to cooperate with the party because of the party leader's racist attitudes. Filing a suit, the party leader claimed that she was not a racist and the words amounted to defamation. The lower courts found that the party leader was, in fact, not a racist, and consequently convicted the political opponent. The Supreme Court, being aware of the case law from the European Court,[98] had to avoid conviction, as the remark obviously amounted to a value judgment put forward by a politician in a political debate regarding public issues. The Court stated that the remarks were not 'unduly' offensive referring to the public content of the debate and the fact that the party leader herself had been rather provocative in her statements.

185. Even though Danish statutory law as regards defamation does not easily fit into the legal terms of European human rights law, Danish case law generally harmonizes well with European human rights, and for the past approximately fifteen years case law from the European Human Rights Court is taken into consideration, either explicitly or implicitly. In some areas the protection of freedom of speech has been strengthened as a result of the European Convention and the concomitant case law, not, however, as a marked shift, but rather as a strengthening of trends already in existence.

186. Besides the issue of 'truth', there is the issue of level. Not any defamatory statement is criminalized. As for charges, expressions leading to conviction are either charges of criminal behaviour of a certain level or charges of highly unprofessional behaviour. Thus, if a person is charged by another person of murder, a public official of corruption or a journalist of inventing his or her stories, they are above the criminal level. On the other hand, charges for driving without light on the bicycle or of not being very good at one's job will normally not suffice.

187. As for terms of abuse, there are very few cases, which no doubt is connected to the fact that prosecution as a point of departure is private. As stated, a certain level has to be reached, and it may also be important whether the terms of abuse are used continuously or only in a quick oral exchange.

188. In the next paragraphs a few special areas will be highlighted:

189. *Literary critique* has for a long time had special liberty, and so far there are no convictions even when the review made attacks on the author's character such as in *UfR* 1969.47H, 4–3 vote in the Supreme Court ('he is using the experiments in the Nazi concentration camps as a pretext to write about perversion and sadism'), and Eastern High Court judgment of 19 November 1984 ('he is glorifying his own lust for incest' accepted in a review on a book on Freud).

190. *Satire* is also viewed with leniency – and a smile. There are very few cases (lawsuit is private, *see* above §1, and it is therefore for the potentially offended to

98. European case law was not cited by the defendant's lawyer before the lower courts.

initiate court proceedings). As an example, the High Court rejected the claim that the Mohammed cartoons were offensive to the plaintiffs, various Muslim organizations, *UfR* 2008.2302V.[99]

191. Apart from the tradition for satire, it is now very difficult, if not impossible, for *organizations* to succeed in defamation suits. In earlier case law the police union and a group of army officers have succeeded in winning defamation suits,[100] but more recent case law has rejected the claims, arguing that the offensive remarks were not directed at any particular person, but aimed at raising critique of public relevant issues.[101]

192. Public and political issues have enjoyed the protection of the courts for a long time, even if case law is not totally coherent, with statutory backing in section 269 ('lawful protection of obvious public interests'). In *UfR* 1938.576V the then Minister of Justice was heavily criticized, but the Court acquitted except for one count, an accusation for high treason, arguing that harsh political debate was normal; and the above-mentioned *UfR* 1991.269H also acquitted a sharp remark made by an eloquent Foreign Minister in a political debate. There may have been a tendency to accept critique 'downwards' more than 'upwards', and there certainly are examples of unimpressive judgments: in *UfR* 1949.922H the police issued an order against the handing out of leaflets criticizing the British colonialism, and the order was accepted without any consideration as to freedom of speech even when the situation showed no sign of disorder, let alone rioting; and in *UfR* 1940.158Ø seizure of a newspaper very critical towards the government was accepted also without any freedom of speech considerations whatsoever. More recent judgments tend to involve freedom of speech aspects more seriously (*see also* Part I), and they are more neutral as to the relative status of the speaker and the offended.

193. In a highly profiled case, *UfR* 2015.3106H, a historian made public charges against a journalist, claiming that he served as an agent for the KGB. Obviously, the issue was of public interest, the journalist had participated in the public debate and consequently had to be more thick skinned. And finally, the charges were not totally made up. The journalist had in fact had contacts with the KGB; however, the journalist claimed that this was a natural part of his job as a reporter on security issues during the cold war. Based on these arguments, the High Court acquitted the historian. However, the Supreme Court came to the opposite conclusion, basing the decision on the facts *that* the historian had access to secret files which allegedly proved that the journalist was an agent, and *that* the historian did not present the journalist with the relevant material, thus rendering him unable to defend himself.

99. *See also* §5 below as regards blasphemy.
100. Eastern High Court judgment 17 Oct. 1986 (a special branch of the police was criticized as 'semi fascists' and a 'behaviour as an army of occupation') and *UfR* 1965.914Ø (commanding officers criticized as 'semi sadists').
101. *UfR* 1999.509Ø, 'the police unable to control their mad dogs'; *see also UfR* 1999.122H in which the Court argued that because allegations were forwarded towards a named policeman rather than the police in general, the statements were unlawful (*Pedersen and Baadsgaard v. Denmark*, GC 17 Dec. 2004, the majority arguing along the same lines).

The Supreme Court explicitly referred to the case law of the ECtHR in which the media enjoys special protection under the condition that they abide by ethics of journalism, including the principle of contradiction. According to the Supreme Court, there is a similar wide protection for academic researchers who have a right to publish their findings. However, when presenting charges against other persons, the ones charged must be able to defend themselves, including having access to the relevant data. Besides being interesting in itself – probably the only transitional justice case before Danish courts[102] – the case also shows that the Supreme Court actively makes use of concepts and ideas developed by the ECtHR.

194. Lawyers and especially defence lawyers have a leeway, particularly in the courtroom. After all, their job is to defend their clients. In *UfR* 1951.1106Ø, the defence lawyer was charged with defamation as he alleged that the Danish Railways accepted deaths and wiped off the liability on the level crossing keepers. The Court acquitted, arguing that he as a defence lawyer was taking care of public interests. In *UfR* 1999.1572H, a lawyer wrote an opinion to his client finding the conduct of a treasurer unlawful as the person was mixing his own economy with that of the association's. The letter was quoted at the general meeting and reported in a newspaper. The lawyer was acquitted as he was merely advising his client; the newspaper, however, was convicted for disseminating the allegations.

195. The *reporting of the media* does enjoy a certain leeway,[103] depending on the set up. Correct and neutral reporting from the courtroom is always acceptable (provided, of course, that the court has not issued a ban on reporting, *see* below Chapter 5, §2). However, the way it is done plays a part. In *UfR* 1979.1028H, a person charged with drug dealing referred to the investigating police officer's wife as a prostitute, with no connection at all to real life. A newspaper reported the case under the headline: 'Police Officer: My Wife is Not a Prostitute'. The newspaper was convicted according to section 264d (protection of privacy).

196. In another highly profiled case, *UfR* 2014.1540H, ROJ TV, a TV station broadcasting in Kurdish, was closed. The courts went at length to make a proper distinction between on the hand reporting from the Kurdish part of Turkey, including violent clashes between PKK and Turkish forces, and on the other hand propaganda for PKK, which is held to be a terrorist organization. The courts found that the entire broadcasting, and not only isolated broadcasts, was indeed propaganda, a fact corroborated by close financial connection between the PKK and the TV station.

197. Section 270(1) prescribes that if an allegation is 'unduly offensive', it may be sanctioned even if it is true, and subsection 2 makes it possible to prevent the

102. On Transitional Justice and the ECtHR, *see* Eva Brems, 'Transitional Justice in the Case Law of the European Court', 5 *The International Journal of Transitional Justice*, 2011, pp. 282–303.
103. Now case law from the European Human Rights Court emphasizes the importance of press protection, *see*, e.g., *Jersild v. Denmark*, 24 Sep. 1994. This approach was known also in Danish case law, although less developed.

defendant from producing evidence supporting his/her allegation. Fortunately, this section has been applied very rarely. Sanctioning offensive but true expressions which do not violate any other law is against European human rights.[104]

198. Section 271(1) prohibits the production of evidence in favour of allegations against persons who have already been acquitted for the same charge in a court of law. According to a decision from the Supreme Court, the same applies if the police have dropped the charge because of the state of the evidence, *UfR* 1993.356H. In *UfR* 2004.1773H a man was acquitted for having sex with children, and right after the judgment, a mother of one of the children claimed that she wanted to expose him as a paedophile. The quote was on the headlines in a tabloid newspaper which was acquitted as it merely quoted the expressions and thus reported an opinion (the public watchdog principle).[105] The prosecuting lawyer made the mistake of not including the author of the charge in the court case but merely chose to sue the editor. Had the author been included, she would probably have been convicted. And in that case the offended person could recover damages and costs with the media (*see* above Chapter 3). Section 266c criminalizes acts when persons after a judgment continue to advance the allegations. Apparently, this section has never been activated in a criminal charge.

199. Section 271(2) provides that in certain cases the fact that a person has been convicted for a criminal offence should not be mentioned, especially if the case is old. The provision has not been used for the last fifty years, and in *UfR* 1955.912H the Supreme Court found that the discussion of an eleven-year-old forgery case against a politician was still relevant.[106]

200. Section 272 provides that if the offensive remarks are retaliatory, they may not be sanctioned. Obviously, a person who is provoked by offensive remarks has more room for giving his/her version. The section covers 'charges' as well as 'terms of abuse'. The principle has been applied also in cases relating to privacy. In *UfR* 2008.1565H, some football players were interviewed on TV and they told about their previous coach's relation to women and alcohol. The Court found that such information is private (under section 264d), but acquitted as the interviewed were responding to verbal attacks made by the football coach.

201. Section 273(1) provides a special option for the offended, namely that: 'if a defamatory allegation is unjustified, a statement to that effect shall, at the request of the injured party, be included in the sentence'. This sanction (in Danish 'mortifikation') is rather unique and, to the present author's knowledge, only prevalent in Danish and Norwegian defamation law. It is possible to invoke only this section, i.e., without claiming compensation or punishment, and the court may apply this section even in cases when neither punishment nor compensation is meted out. The option is only available as regards charges, not terms of abuse.

104. *See*, e.g., *Jerusalem v. Austria*, 27 Feb. 2001.
105. For some reason the one who actually made the statement was not sued.
106. *See Schwabe v. Austria*, 28 Aug. 1992, with a similar reasoning.

202. Section 273(2) provides that the offended may be rewarded a lump sum in order to publish the judgment or an account of the judgment. This payment is different from the payment as compensation for tort and damages.

203. Finally, section 274 makes it clear that the previous articles are relevant even if the offended was dead at the time, and section 275 provides for private criminal prosecution as a point of departure in defamation cases (*see* above §1 as regards private and public prosecution). If the offended person is a civil servant and the charge or terms of abuse relate to his/her job, the public prosecutor may take action.

II. Special Groups

204. According to section 110d, the maximum penalty in relation to a number of crimes, including defamation and intrusion of private life, may exceed the maximum prescribed in the various sections by one half if the victim is the head of state or the head of a foreign diplomatic mission. The section, which requires public prosecution, has not been applied since before World War II. In a case from 1934, some persons delivered a note to the German charge d'affaire criticizing the then Nazi regime, *inter alia*, 'down with the Nazi's bloody horror regime' for which they received a penalty according to section 110d. In a more recent case, *UfR* 1984.346H, the editor of a newspaper which had accused the Ugandan charge d'affaire for being involved in mass murdering was sanctioned according to section 267. The section is problematic. Criticizing heads of state and other countries will often be a part of a public discussion and therefore ought to be better protected from sanctions rather than having the penalty extended.

205. The same goes for section 115 which prescribes the redoubling of the maximum penalty if the person is either the king or the head of the government. The section has never been applied, and persons holding important public offices ought, in fact, to be more thick-skinned rather than having special protection from offensive criticism.

206. According to section 121 'any person who attacks a public servant with insult, abusive language or other offensive words or gestures while they are executing their office' is liable to fine or imprisonment not exceeding six months. It is not the general critique which is criminalized, but the offensive deed or expression while the person is doing his/her job.[107] The section does not distinguish between charges and terms of abuse, and journalists hardly have a special leeway. In *UfR* 2008.251Ø, a journalist was punished for critical remarks to police in action after a football match (however, not according to section 121, but for violating police regulations). In gross cases, spitting is regarded as a violent attack (section 244 and *UfR* 2003.2245Ø).

107. The distinction between general critique and interference with the execution of the office is relevant, *see*, e.g., ECtHR *Janowski v. Poland*, 21 Jan. 1991.

207. Section 193 renders it criminal to disturb various public services such as public means of transportation, public mail services, public supply of gas, water and electricity, including the disturbance of radio and television. Newspapers etc. are not covered. In *UfR* 2001.1187Ø, a number of persons who disturbed the news programme on a national channel with the effect that the programme was cancelled for twenty minutes were sentenced to ten days imprisonment. The special protection of radio and television dates back to the time of monopoly.

III. Concluding Remarks

208. The Danish law on defamation works reasonably. There is room for freedom of speech, and mainly downright incorrect and gross accusations are punished. Case law from the ECtHR is integrated either explicitly or – more often – implicitly.

209. However, the wording of the statutes is problematic. As regards defamation, the distinction between charges and terms of abuse – a distinction introduced in 1930 in the heydays of logical positivism – has never worked well. With the case law from the ECtHR and the differing distinction between allegations of fact and value judgments and the protection of value judgments regarding issues of public interest with some factual basis, the wording of section 267 is genuinely misleading. On 16 May 2018, the Minister of Justice presented a bill to the Danish Parliament, the *Folketing*, including an updated version of the provisions regarding defamation.[108] The bill was not adopted by the end of the update of this publication.

210. In addition, the expansion of the maximum penalty in cases of defamation of heads of state etc. is not in line with European human rights law. Sections 110d and 115 have not been applied since the 1930s and ought to be abandoned altogether.

§4. Privacy

I. Some Special Features of Sections 263–264d of the Penal Code

211. Sections 263–264d of the Danish Penal Code criminalize acts in two ways, one by an objective criterion and the other by a content-related criterion.[109] Some

108. L 240 of 16 May 2018. The bill is based on report from the Criminal Law Council 1563/2017 on violation of peace and privacy.

109. Baumbach, Trine, Medieret. Frihed og ansvar [*Media Law. Freedom and Liability*], Karnov 2017. Jakobsen, Søren Sandfeld & Sten Schaumburg-Müller, Medieretten [*Media Law*] Jurist- og Økonomforbundets Forlag, 2013. Jakobsen, Søren Sandfeld & Sten Schaumburg-Müller, Mediejura for journalister og andre mediearbejdere [*Media Law for Journalists and Other Media Workers*] Jurist- og Økonomforbundets Forlag, 2016. Nielsen, Gorm Toftegaard, Thomas Elholm & Morten Niels Jakobsen, Kommenteret straffelov. Speciel Del, [*The Criminal Code. A Commentary. The Special Part*] 11. udgave, Jurist- og Økonomforbundets Forlag 2017. Schaumburg-Müller, Sten,

sections simply criminalize the very act of, e.g., opening a letter, of tapping a telephone, of trespassing on private ground, etc., no matter whether in fact any private information has been revealed. Other sections criminalize the dissemination of genuinely private information, no matter whether in fact letters have been opened, telephones have been tapped, etc.

212. In addition to the distinction between content-related and content-unrelated (or objectively described) crimes, it will be relevant to distinguish between the primary and the secondary act: the primary act consists in the actual reading of the private letter, the actual recording of a telephone conversation, etc., and the secondary act is the dissemination of the obtained information. The distinction is important for the understanding of what is actually being criminalized, and especially important in relation to the MLA (*see* above §2) which only covers the secondary acts, the dissemination of the information in the media. Thus, a photographer making an unlawful photo (the primary act) will be liable for this act (and others could be parties by instigation), the MLA notwithstanding, whereas the printing of the photo in the newspaper (the secondary act) is covered by the MLA, implying that the liability is restricted to a very limited number of actors and dependent on anonymity, etc.

213. Finally, it is noteworthy that all descriptions of the crimes under sections 263–264d require the act to be 'wrongful', indicating that in some cases it may not be wrong to open letters, tap telephones, shoot photos, etc.[110] Obviously, if the potential 'victim' has consented to the act, by accepting that another person reads his/her letter or enters his/her apartment etc., the act is not wrongful and consequently not criminal. But wrongful is a broader concept than consent, and in some cases considerations on freedom of speech, discussion on public issues and dissemination of information on issues of public matter may overrule the protection of privacy. In these cases, the court must assess the 'wrongfulness' of the act by weighing[111] the interests at stake, the protection of privacy and the public's interest in being informed. In case law, e.g., minor trespassing of private property criminalized under section 264 will be accepted if there are public issues at stake.[112]

'Hypotetisk samtykke og privatlivets fred' [*Hypothetical Consent and Protection of Private Life*], in Nis Jul Clausen, Annette Kronborg, Nina Dietz Legind & Bent Ole Gram Mortensen (eds), Festskrift til Hans Viggo Godsk Pedersen, Jurist- og Økonomforbundets Forlag, 2017, pp. 495–510.

110. The Danish word is 'uberettiget'. One may consider whether the better translation is 'unlawful' or 'wrongful'. In a translation of the Danish criminal acts the term 'unlawful' is employed. (Malene Frese Jensen et al., *The Principal Danish Criminal Acts*, 3rd edn. (DJØF Publishing, 2006). The present author tends to prefer 'wrongful' while it indicates that the sections require an extra consideration which does not follow automatically from existing law.

111. A constitutional scholar, Peter Germer, has vehemently argued that freedom of speech cases should not be decided by unpredictable weighing, but ought to be regulated by clear-cut rules. In case law, weighing is unavoidable, and according to the present author, it also gives a better protection than very strict rules, provided, of course, that the weighing is done within rather fixed limits and according to express standards. (Peter Germer, *Statsforfatningsret* [*Constitutional Law*] (Jurist- og Økonomforbundets Forlag, 2007), 348 f.

112. *UfR* 1994.988H (journalists' entry into the garden of the Minister of the Environment), *UfR* 1999.1675H (journalists' entry upon an uninhabited, artificially made island) and *UfR* 2008.2738Ø (photographer's entry into the office of the Refugee Board). *See* below.

II. Sections 263–264c: Objective Criteria

214. According to section 263(1)(1), anyone 'wrongfully' depriving someone of or opens his/her letter, telegram or any other sealed communication shall be liable to punishment. Here the criminalization is unrelated to the content and unrelated to any publication. The mere fact of opening the letter etc. is a criminal act, provided that it is wrongful. Since it is regulated in the Criminal Code, wrongfulness requires intent. If someone opens another's letter by mistake, this will not be criminal. However, as soon as he/she realizes that this is not his/her letter, he/she must stop reading; otherwise, he/she has the required intention to read the letter (*dolus subsequens*).

215. According to section 263(1)(2), the same goes for anyone obtaining access to hiding places such as drawers, bags, etc. The mere looking into another's bag is criminalized, provided the nosing is 'wrongful'. Checking customers' bags in order to avoid shoplifting will not be regarded as wrong as long as the checking is proportional to the aim.

216. According to section 263(1)(3), the secret listening to or recording of private (i.e., closed) conversations with the aid of equipment is criminalized. Thus, bugging and telephone tapping are criminalized. If the person doing the recording is himself/herself part of the conversation or the telephone conversation, the act is not criminal.[113] However, the secondary act, the revealing of the content of the lawfully recorded conversation, may still be criminalized, but not under this section that only relates to the primary act. The wording of the section also implies that public speeches or conversations are not protected. A student recording the lecture at the university is not doing anything criminal if the lecture is publicly accessible. There may, of course, be local by-laws dealing with these issues, but even if by-laws rule out recording of, say, a public meeting, the infringement of this precept does *not* render it criminal under section 263. Reversely, one cannot claim that one has a *right* to record if the recording is not criminalized under section 263.[114]

217. Section 263(2) criminalizes the 'access to another person's information and programmes designated for use in an information system'. Arguably, unauthorized access to computers could be covered under subsection 1(2), but in 1985 the present subsection was introduced in order to be sure that unauthorized access to computers was clearly criminalized. It is noteworthy that the maximum penalty for hacking according to this subsection is one and a half years, compared to the traditional privacy offence's six-month maximum.

113. *UfR* 1980.670/2Ø: Journalists had taped a telephone conversation of which one of the journalists was part. All journalists were acquitted.
114. *UfR* 1972.601H.

218. Section 263(3) expands the maximum to six years under aggravating circumstances, and the subsection explicitly mentions any systematic or organized violation or violations in order to exploit trade secrets. There are several recent cases.[115]

219. Section 263a criminalizes the dissemination of passwords and even the obtaining of passwords in cases of information systems of public importance or systems which contain personal information (subsection 3). The obtaining and passing of passwords to pay systems are criminalized in section 301a (in the chapter on property crimes).

220. Section 264 criminalizes wrongful trespassing on 'not freely accessible places'. The section has been relevant in a number of cases when journalists or photographers have trespassed on private property or similar not freely accessible places in order to cover a story, following demonstrators either immediately as they enter or subsequently entering an office or the like when a demonstration is taking place. In the late 1980s, two cases were decided by the Supreme Court, and the Court ruled that the fact that the person was a media reporter did not play any role as for the criminal part of the act (but to some extent as regards meting out the sentence).[116] The Court was not unanimous, and in 1994 the Supreme Court reached the opposite conclusion, stating that the journalist did not trespass 'wrongfully' taken into consideration that the entering into a garden was not severe *and* that the purpose was news reporting.[117] Obviously, this is not a carte blanche for journalists to enter any private place, but it does give media reporters the option to follow demonstrators when they are going into gardens, closed offices and other not freely accessible places that are not intimately private. The courts weigh the interests, and as long as the trespassing is not of major importance, the consideration for the free flow of information weighs heavier.[118] Media reporters entering into private homes, bedchambers, etc. are not likely to be acquitted and must have very good reasons to do so in order to outweigh the interests of private life.

221. There is a draft bill on its way through Parliament.[119] Compared to the existing provisions, the significant changes are: (1) Installing GPS in order to check other persons' whereabouts will be criminalized; (2) for several provisions it will be an aggravating factor if private information is disseminated through the Internet; and (3) there is a re-ordering of the provisions, so that, e.g., the criminal act of opening letters is not the first to be mentioned.

115. UfR 2018.993V; *TfK* 2018.2034Ø; *UfR* 2018.1787H.
116. *UfR* 1987.934H and *UfR* 1987.937H.
117. *UfR* 1994.988H, *UfR* 1999.1675H and *UfR* 2008.2738Ø.
118. In a recent decision of 1 Nov. 2018, the Eastern High Court acquitted journalists for entering a restaurant when it was not open, the purpose being researching on the restaurant's problematic activities. Prior to the trespassing, the journalist had made many unsuccessful attempts to contact the owner. (Judgment of 1 Nov. 2018, unpublished at the time of writing).
119. L 240 of 16 May 2018. The bill is based on suggestions by the Criminal Law Council, report 1534/2017.

222. Section 264 is actually divided into two subsections: besides criminalizing the trespassing, subsection two criminalizes the failing to leave 'another person's land' when asked to do so. The reason for this is the fact that it may be difficult to know whether a place is actually freely accessible in the legal sense and one may have a lawful purpose for entering, e.g., a plot of land, but not for staying when asked to leave. Thus, it is lawful to enter into the front yard of a house, ring the bell or knock on the door. If nobody is home and you leave, you have done nothing unlawful. And sometimes it is not easy to recognize whether a place is freely accessible. The line between the front yard which is not freely accessible in a legal sense and the sidewalk which is publicly accessible may not be distinguishable.

223. The distinction between freely and not freely accessible places may not always be clear. As a rule-of-thumb, places to which access does not require permission are freely accessible. Thus, shops, restaurants, the reception at hotels, doctors, lawyers, etc., the corridors of schools and other public institutions are 'freely accessible' during opening hours, whereas kitchens at restaurants, hotel rooms, lawyers' offices and classrooms are not freely accessible, and trespassing or the failure to leave when asked may be a criminal offence.[120] It is irrelevant whether there is cover charge, e.g., to concerts, bars etc. The criterion is whether the place is generally open to the public.

224. In addition to the Criminal Code there may, of course, be by-laws or local rules dealing with the accessibility. Thus, private shops, restaurants, etc. are freely accessible, but the owners may put rules or restrictions such as dress codes in restaurants and 'no bags' in shops.[121] Violations of such rules are not criminal and section 264 does not cover such situations.

225. Section 264a criminalizes anyone taking a photo of a person who is located at a not freely accessible place. It is the location of the depicted that is relevant. Where the photographer is located may be relevant under section 264 (*see* above), but not section 264a. The idea is that people in public places must accept being photographed. Section 264a deals only with the primary act, the shooting of a photo. The secondary use, dissemination of photographs, is dealt with by other sections (264c and 264d, *see* below), and the shooting of a photo may be fully legal, but the distribution clearly criminal. As a point of departure, section 264a does not bother about the content of the picture. As long as the person is located in a place not freely accessible, he/she is protected by section 264a, and vice versa: as long as the person is located in a public place, he/she must accept being photographed.

226. Similar to the other sections, 264a requires the act to be 'wrongful', and consent renders lawful the taking of a photo of a person in a not freely accessible

120. *UfR* 2006.1584Ø Greenpeace. Rooftop not freely accessible. *UfR* 2009.696V Police station not freely accessible outside office hours.

121. Such rules may not be discriminatory according to the Consolidated Act No. 626 of 1987. *UfR* 2003.2438V sanctioned the proprietor of a pizza joint who had put up a sign informing his clients that he did not want to serve German or French customers.

place. Consent does not have to be explicit, tacit consent suffices, e.g., in situations where a photographer is shooting pictures at private or closed parties. In some cases it may require active rejection in order to be protected by section 264a. Consent does not automatically cover the secondary use. One may agree to a private photo, but not to its ending up on the front page of a tabloid newspaper.[122] Not only consent renders the taking of a photo lawful. There may be situations, equivalent to the photographer following the demonstrators into a garden etc., in which the shooting of a person may be legal even if he/she is not located in a freely accessible place. Obviously, photographing burglars on the job will be lawful even if they perform their work in a not freely accessible place such as a private home. Persons who unlawfully are located in a not freely accessible location are not protected by section 264a.[123] Also situations with a strong public interest may render the taking of photos lawful. Thus, a photo of a boozing politician who is strongly against alcohol may be lawful even if he/she is drinking on a not freely accessible location.

227. As in section 264 the question arises of the demarcation of a 'freely accessible place'. As a point of departure section 264 and 264a cover the same areas. If the place is not free to the public, the trespassing and the shooting of photos will be covered. Some places are obviously not freely accessible, but may cause problems in relation to photos. Thus, balconies are not freely accessible, but taking photos including persons on their balconies may be legal especially if the person is not the chief motive.[124] In other situations, such as a person entering into a private garden in order to call on the persons living there, the access is lawful, but taking pictures of persons in the garden will not be legal – as a point of departure and provided the person has legal access to the garden.

228. Proprietors of restaurants and concert halls may, of course, set out conditions for customers such as the prohibition of making recordings and photographs. Violation of such rules does not activate the Criminal Code, but is primarily a civil law matter, and the proprietor can expel the trespasser and may demand compensation.

229. Section 264c criminalizes the secondary use of information obtained illegally according to sections 263–264a. As the preceding sections, 264c disregards the content of the information, but only considers the act of obtaining the information. This implies that once information, including pictures, is obtained unlawfully, the further use is also unlawful, no matter the content. (The opposite is not the case.

122. This was probably the case in *UfR* 1974.775B: A young woman was murdered and a rather explicit nude picture covered the front page. The picture seemed to be taken by a friend, i.e., with her consent, and in that case did not fall under s. 264a. However, obviously, the dissemination of the picture was unlawful, *see* below regarding s. 264d.

123. *UfR* 1981.364Ø: Policemen, lawfully searching a house, are covered by s. 264a.

124. *UfR* 1981.379Ø: From a hotel balcony a plain clothes police officer was taking photos of persons participating in a demonstration. From another balcony another person took pictures of the photographing policeman. This person was charged of violating s. 264a, but was acquitted by the Court.

Even if information or pictures are obtained legally, the further use may be unlawful, *see* below regarding section 264d.) Section 264c rarely appears in case law, probably because it is natural to consider the content of the published information, rather than merely looking at whether the obtaining of the information, including taking pictures, was illegal per se. However, in a highly profiled case, several subsequent editors of a weekly magazine were convicted of i.a. use of material gathered in violation of section 263(3). At least one editor had paid a source to provide the magazine with information of the whereabouts of celebrities and members of the royal family, illegally exploiting access to the Danish credit card system. The activities rendered it possible for the magazine to send out photographers on the relevant locations. All editors involved accepted the convictions which included various degrees of suspended and unsuspended prison sentences.[125]

III. Section 264d: Content-Related Criteria

230. Section 264d provides that 'any person who unlawfully forwards information or pictures concerning another person's private life or other pictures of the person in question in circumstances which can obviously be expected to be withheld from the public' is liable to criminal sanctions. The section also applies to deceased persons. Thus, section 264d deals with the content of the information, not with the geographical or any other spatial demarcation, and the section deals only with the secondary use. It is immaterial for the application of section 264d whether the primary use, the obtaining of the information or the photo was unlawful.

231. The sanctions are fines and imprisonment up to six months. In 2018 a second paragraph was added, adding the possibility for imprisonment up to three years. The harsher penalty is meant to be used in cases of dissemination to a wide audience, e.g., via the Internet, and with aggravating circumstances such as unconsented sexual content.

232. It may be considered whether the second part of §1, 'other pictures of the person in question in circumstances which can obviously be expected to be withheld from the public', plays an independent role. Pictures which can be withheld from the public cannot be public, but must be private in some sense. At any rate, the sentence emphasizes that the publication of pictures gives a harsher exposure than the mere piece of information. As an example: it would normally be completely unproblematic to publish the information that a person has been killed in a car accident. But publishing a picture from the accident with blood, bones, intestines etc. will be punishable according to section 264d. And case law provides some good examples of pictures that 'obviously' ought to be withheld from the public: a plastic surgeon taking pictures in relation to liposuction should not publish the pictures afterwards (*UfR* 1991.194/2Ø), and an ex-husband should not upload explicit nude pictures of his former wife, especially not with offensive remarks (*UfR* 1999.177V – prison sentence).

125. Unpublished judgment by the city court of Glostrup, 24 Nov. 2016.

233. *Consent* is relevant, one can obviously consent to the dissemination of information or pictures that are of private character, and consent can be tacit. However, it is important to scrutinize the scope of the consent. Even a tacit consent has its substance, and agreeing to the taking of a private photo does not imply agreeing to it being published. Girls who let their boyfriends take nude pictures etc. have not automatically consented to anything but letting the boyfriend have the picture.[126] However, once they have consented to the publication, it is no longer private and consequently beyond the protection of section 264d.

234. Consent may not be decisive. First, in order to be criminally sanctioned, the act must be wrongful or unlawful, and it may be lawful even without consent of the victim. Thus, the information that, say, a minister has a heavy alcohol problem may (according to the circumstances) be published even if addiction to alcohol is of a private character. Public interest may overweigh private interest, or put more precisely: circumstances, such as the person in question is a politician and a minister, may render the issue public even if it is private in the first place. Second, consent may not suffice. In *UfR* 1975.1008Ø a film was made showing the deteriorating health and final death of a drug addict. He had consented to the recordings and the publication, in fact approved of it as he wanted to send a warning to potential addicts. However, his family protested and the Court issued an injunction. The decision is not beyond critique as the Court did not consider the public interest (warning against abuse of narcotics), which ought to have been weighed against the private interest. On the other hand, death is a serious matter not least for the surviving family, and the section explicitly protects pictures of deceased persons.

235. *Death* is sensitive and to some extent private. The publication of pictures of dead bodies will as a point of departure be covered by section 264d (*UfR*1982.244Ø, conviction for showing a corpse after a fire), but even more neutral pictures may fall within the scope of section 264d. In *UfR* 1991.549H, the Supreme Court sentenced a weekly magazine for having published pictures of a woman looking at the sea in which her husband had just drowned. Obviously, the taking of the picture was legal – the woman was at a freely accessible place. But the publishing of the picture and the story was, just as obviously, a violation of section 264d. In certain cases even the information may be unlawful: in *UfR* 1998.1936V the spouse of a Member of Parliament was fatally ill, and his terminal diagnosis covered the headlines of a local newspaper. The mere message that the spouse of a member of Parliament was ill and that the member of Parliament had leave to take care of him would be acceptable and in the public interest, but the way in which the diagnosis was exposed made it unlawful.

236. *Private relations and affairs* currently give rise to lawsuits. As a point of departure amorous affairs and breaking up relations are private. 'Lovers' indicating the names and faces of the couple on the cover of a weekly magazine held to be a violation of section 264d (*FED* 2001.2520Ø). The case is interesting because the defendants argued that the boundaries for publication of what used to be considered

126. *See* transfer of copyright, *see* Ch. 7.

private had changed considerably. However, the Court emphasized that this was to some extent the case for matters of public interest, but not for plain prying interest.[127] Even press coverage of a separation in a case where the plaintiff had previously given interviews on private affairs and the information could be gathered publicly by the Land Registry ('tingbogen'), the Court held the information to be private under section 264d. The popular saying: 'If you are invited for the wedding, you can also come for the funeral', does not have backing from the courts. Consent to being interviewed is consent to the interview in question, not consent to the dissemination of private information, and even if the mere information is publicly available, it may still be an offence to publish it in an easy to read tabloid version. In *UfR* 2008.1565H, the Supreme Court held remarks of 'too much alcohol and too many dames' in relation to a football coach to be private, but in the actual case the defendants were acquitted. The Court found the remarks to be acceptable retort made to heavy criticism advanced by the coach himself.

237. *Other unacceptable encroachments*: The courts do not hesitate to employ section 264d when needed. A man had uploaded an invitation on the Internet pretending it was from a young girl, 'Hey cheery guys' with invitations to different kinds of sex. He had invented a name, very similar to a real-life girl who received various proposals from interested men. The uploader was sentenced two weeks imprisonment and required to pay tort compensation (*UfR* 2001.2573Ø). Lately, there have been a lot of cases dealing with dissemination of nude pictures and sex videos. In the so-called 'umbrella' case, more than 1,000 youngsters have been charged with unlawful dissemination of sex videos. Since the participants in one of the videos were under 18 years, section 235 of the Criminal Code, dealing with child pornography, is relevant. So far, at least one case has been published, UfR 2018.2438V, resulting in a rather lenient sentence of five daily fines of DKK 500 (approx. a total of EUR 335). The disseminated version was made blurred, it was difficult to recognize the participants including their age, and there was consent to the recording, although not to the dissemination.[128]

238. *Criminals*: The fact that a person is sentenced is not private. The mentioning of the sentence and dissemination of name is therefore not private. (As regards press coverage during trial, *see* Chapter 5, §2.) Pictures from the prison, however,

127. This is very much in line with the case law of the ECtHR. A politician who 'inevitably and knowingly lays himself open to close scrutiny of his every word and deed by both journalists and the public at large' (*Lingens v. Austria*, 8 Jul. 1986, 42) must be more thick-skinned; but the publication of private affairs without public interest is not protected under Art. 10, *see* as example *Campmany y Diez de Revenga v. Spain*, 12 Dec. 2000.

128. Other recent judgments: UfR 2018.2970V Nude pictures to mother, 20 days suspended prison sentence; TfK 2018.1052Ø nude pictures sent to various persons, suspended prison sentence and tort compensation DKK 15,000; TfK 2018.672V explicit nude pictures to friends and relatives, 3 month prison sentence and compensation DKK 20,000; U2018.567V sexual intercourse filmed and briefly uploaded, suspended sentence and tort compensation DKK 20,000 to each of the two persons involved.

are unlawful, as the persons are located at a not freely accessible place. The High Court has chosen to cite section 264d, indicating that the serving of a sentence is a private matter (*UfR* 1987.859Ø).

239. Business matters are generally not seen as private. Danish law, of course, offers protection of industrial secrets, but the protection is mainly directed at competitors and employees, not the media. In a District Court decision, a company unsuccessfully sought an injunction against the publishing of an article revealing the company's purchase prices,[129] and higher ranking courts seem to be reluctant to protect business by means of section 264d.[130]

240. Associations have sought protection from section 264d, but it has apparently become more difficult to obtain it. In *UfR* 1982.750H, the Supreme Court issued an injunction against a TV programme showing the initiation rites of the Free Masons. The story was a dramatic reproduction, based on a newspaper article, and thus there was no hidden camera involved and no trespassing of section 264a (unlawful photographing of persons on not freely accessible locations, *see* above). The decision has been criticized in scholarly works, and it has been argued that the injunction was violating the ECHR, Article 10, as the information was already out.[131] At any rate, there has been no violation of section 264d in relation to associations since, and case law has been reluctant to grant associations as such protection in relation to the media.[132]

241. It is understood that business enterprises and associations enjoy protection in relation to, e.g., search of offices etc. Here they are 'private' on a par with individual persons. But in relation to section 264d and the media's passing on of information and pictures, associations and commercial enterprises are hardly private.

IV. Personal Pictures: Between Civil and Penal Law

242. Taking photos of persons located in a not freely accessible place are covered by criminal law, CC section 264a, and based on section 264d the dissemination is criminalized if the content is private and/or ought not to be disseminated. Pictures may also have a commercial value, and the unauthorized use of personal pictures may be protected under civil law. Besides, pictures may fall under personal data protection, *see* below subsection V. There are no statutory rules in civil law protecting personal pictures, but legal principles and case law are guiding the matter and have created a protection.

129. Aarhus District Court, decision 31 Mar. 2004.
130. As examples, *UfR* 1989.1146S, *UfR* 1992.385H and *UfR* 1994.292H.
131. *The Observer and others v. United Kingdom*, 26 Nov. 1991 (The Spycatcher) and *Bluff! v. the Netherlands* 9 Feb. 1995.
132. *UfR* 1999.509Ø (critique of the police), *UfR* 2001.953Ø (comment on the bikers 'Bandidos' in a prison), both cases relating to s. 267, subs 4 below.

243. The commercial use of photos in advertising etc. is only allowed with the consent of the depicted person. This was stated in *UfR* 1965.126H, in which an actor could prevent the use of his picture in commercials and had the right to tort compensation as the use had been unlawful, contrary to 'basic legal principles'. Since 1965 there have been quite a few cases in which pictures of publicly known persons such as actors, musicians, football players, etc. have been used without the consent of the depicted. In *UfR* 1989.1146, the Commercial Court laid down that the principle covers all persons, not only publicly known persons whose pictures usually will be of a larger commercial value.

244. The same goes for use of personal photos in political campaigns. In *UfR* 1986.728/2Ø, a union ran a campaign proposing a thirty-five-hour week and made use of quotes and pictures from publicly known persons who had somehow supported the idea. However, they had not consented to being part of the union's agenda, and the use of their pictures was found unlawful. In *UfR* 1989.1146SH, a newspaper ran a slogan 'you cannot be everybody's friend' in order to indicate its critical role as a public watchdog. The campaign even included pictures of persons whose business had been critically dealt with by the newspaper. In this connection, the pictures were unlawful. Obviously, when dealing with the business of the persons in question as a part of the current press coverage, pictures can be included without problems. Running a campaign is different, however, and the depicted do not have to accept this particular and to some extent offensive use of their pictures. In *UfR* 1988.411V, members of a political party put up posters with the wording 'Wanted – Bank Robber' and with a partly distorted picture of the president of the board of one of the major Danish banks. On the poster, the depicted person looked somehow like a vampire. The Court emphasized the importance of political freedom of speech and remarked that it was not clear from the poster that the message was political, a point that was partly accepted by the accused. The authors of the poster were fined.[133]

245. Publishing a picture with no relation to the text may be unlawful when the combination of text and picture is somehow misleading. In *UfR* 1973.730B, an article covered the issue of crime among immigrant workers, and a photo was added showing some Greek immigrant workers with connection neither to crime in general nor to the actual story. The Court found the picture unlawful, but did not cite the section which covers unfounded accusations (section 267, *see* §3 above). In *UfR* 1998.170Ø, a newspaper published a letter to the editor regarding the amount of compensation in rape cases, and the newspaper printed a picture from a theatre performance, a half-naked rape-like scene, used as press release. Even though the picture was released and the newspaper had informed the readers that the picture was 'from the archives', the Court found the printing unlawful as it was totally unrelated to the issue and printed without consent.

133. Interestingly, the printer was acquitted. Printing of posters does not fall within the scope of the Media Liability Act (or the then prevailing Press Act), and the printer had taken part in the act. However, the Court indirectly applied the media liability principles going for the central actors. (*See* §2 regarding media liability.)

246. *Nude pictures* have been the subject of quite a few cases. In the 1980s the offensive context seems to be decisive. In *UfR* 1986.405Ø, a well-known singer was bathing topless from a deserted beach, and the pictures were printed in a soft porno magazine presented as if the singer had consented to the publishing. The Court particularly stressed the importance of the context, arguing that the beach was freely accessible (section 264a being inapplicable) and that it could reasonably be expected to appear topless, indicating that section 264d did not apply either. However, the context in which the pictures were published was offensive, and she was granted compensation. Similar cases with nude pictures involve invented interviews and look-a-likes, and the courts have granted compensation even if the pictures had already been published (*UfR* 1989.511Ø, *UfR* 1989.981Ø and *UfR* 1998.160Ø).

The recent trend is not to accept the publication of nude or semi-nude pictures without consent. In UfR 2010.2448H, the Supreme Court has found the publication of a TV hostess bathing pregnant and topless unlawful leading to a tort compensation of DKK 75,000. However, it did not fall under the Criminal Code: not section 264a as the depicted was located in a freely accessible place, and neither section 264d, as bathing topless and highly pregnant was not particularly private. A recent proposal for the amendment of the criminal code suggests that this situation will fall under section 264d.

V. The Personal Data Act

247. The GDPR,[134,135] Article 85(1), provides that 'Member States shall … reconcile the right to the protection of personal data … with the right to freedom of expression and information, including processing for journalistic purposes … ', and in §2 it is indicated that the Member States shall provide for exemptions or derogations chapter by chapter (except for Chapter 8).

248. The Danish legislature passed a new act, the DPA,[136] to supersede the older Personal Data Act from 2000 which again was enacted in order to suit the older EU Directive. As regards media, the DPA on the one hand provides for a general exemption for journalistic personal data processing, i.e., without any distinction regarding the many rules and provisions in the GDPR (except for Articles 28 and 32, *see* below). On the other hand, the exemption is divided between various categories that neither fit neatly with the categories of the GDPR nor with EU law in general. DPA section 3 provides for five different exemptions which are related to freedom of expression and the media. All the provisions are copy-pasted from the previous act.

134. Henrik Waaben & Kristian Korfits Nielsen, *Lov om behandling af personoplysninger med kommentarer* [*The Personal Data Act: A Commentary*], 2nd edn. (Jurist- og Økonomforbundets Forlag, 2008).
135. Regulation (EU) 5419/2016 of the European Parliament and of the Council on the protection of natural persons with regard to the processing of personal data and on the free movement of such data, and repealing Directive 95/46/EC (General Data Protection Regulation).
136. Act No. 502/2018, enacted just in time 23 May 2018.

249. First, according to DPA, section 3(1), the Act does not apply if this would result in a violation of freedom of speech and freedom of information. The subsection refers to Article 10 of the ECHR and the EU Charter Article 11, and it serves as a reminder that freedom of expression must be taken into consideration. In principle this is fine, although somewhat strange in a legislative act to remind the readers of other prevailing acts. In practice, it may turn the weighing in favour of freedom of expression vis-à-vis protection of private life. The Danish Data Inspection Board ('Datatilsynet') has decided some cases, citing the provision.

250. In one case, the Danish People's Party's webpage published the names and districts of 3,218 persons who were granted Danish citizenship, including comments that some of them were criminals. As the names were already published in connection with the granting of citizenship, this publication was not violating the Act, and the comments fell within the protected area for freedom of speech.[137] In the second case, a company had published the name, position and workplace of a public employee working for the Danish Working Environment Service and commented his visit to the company. The Board found the mentioning acceptable, as it was a part of a public debate. The Board did not go into any consideration as to the protection of reputation which is also part of Article 8, and the Board did not make any weighing of the rights involved in the respective articles – of which only Article 10 is mentioned in the Danish act.

251. In a later case, 'The Black Register'[138] ran an open webpage featuring names, job title, work phone of public servants under the headings 'neglect of duty' and 'abuse of power'. Sometimes also date of birth and political affiliation was added to the personal data. The Board dismissed the case, referring to what is now the DPA section 3(1), arguing that it was part of a public debate with a mere voicing of opinions. According to the assessment of the present authors, the Board failed to engage in a proper weighing of the relevant rights involved. According to the case law from the ECtHR, there is a difference between criticism of public authorities and charges against an individual public servant.[139] (Danish Courts to have a better grasp of the weighing; *see* above Chapter 3, §3).

252. Second, according to section 3(4), the Act does not apply to media databases if the databases are covered by the Media Data Bases Act (MDBA)[140] (*see* below subsection 4.6). Most, if not all, Internet media are databases. In order to fall under the MDBA the media must:

(1) Register with the Press Council as a media under the MLA (MLA sections 8 and 1(3). The registration serves the purpose of acknowledging the registrant as a media under the act.

137. DT 2000-216-0005.
138. DT 2011-215-0874.
139. *See ECHR Pedersen & Baadsgaard v. Denmark* 17 Dec. 2004 [Grand Chamber].
140. Act No. 430/1994 with later amendments.

(2) Feature mixed content similar to traditional media, MLA section 1(3). This implies that e.g., blogs with focus on beauty products etc. will not fall under the MLA, and as a consequence not under the MDBA, either.
(3) Register with the Data Inspection Board, as regards internal databases for purely editorial use.
(4) Once again, register with the Press Council (this time the registration relates to the MDBA) as regards open databases – in fact most Internet-based media. In addition, the open database must be registered with the Data Inspection Board.

It follows from the requirements 1–4 that if a media has missed one of the registrations or if the media does not live up to the content requirements in the MLA, then the media database is not exempted from the personal data regulation.

253. Third, according to section 3(5) and 3(6) databases solely consisting of information gathered from media under the MLA are exempted. This makes sense. What has been published in media under the MLA has already been under both editorial scrutiny and liability under the Criminal Code and Danish law in general. Besides, publishing under the MLA implies that the media must act according to ethics of journalism and that the Press Council is competent to receive complaints. Thus, material which has already been published does not fall under the personal data regime only because it is gathered in a database. The exemption does not cover Articles 28 and 32 of the GDPR (*see* below).

254. Fourth, according to section 3(7), the Act does not apply to manual archives with extracts from published newspapers etc. if the purpose of the archives is purely journalistic. Also in this case GDPR Articles 28 and 32 apply. It is difficult to see how this exemption can play any part, the general exemption taken into consideration, *see* immediately below.

255. Fifth, according to section 3(8) any other processing of personal data with purely journalistic purposes is exempted from the GDPR – apart from Articles 28 and 32 GDPR. Applying this exemption presupposes that none of the above-mentioned exemptions apply. This implies that when dealing with media databases, section 3(4–6) applies, not section 3(8). One may question whether this broadly formulated exemption lives up to the requirements in Article 85 GDPR, according to which the Member States must balance the involved rights *and* consider the respective rights under the GDPR in relation to processing personal data for journalistic purposes.

Articles 28 and 32 of the GDPR apply in most cases when journalistic activities are involved, except when the situation falls under the MDBA. Article 28 deals with the data processor and is relevant especially if personal data processing is outsourced. Article 32 deals with 'Security of processing', and it is relevant also for media to live up to security requirements.

VI. Media Databases Act

256. This Act applies to information databases either attached to or itself constituting a media. Thus, the Act does not apply to all kinds of databases, such as, private databases dealing with genealogy or public administrative databases with information on patients etc.

257. The Act distinguishes between three types of databases: (1) unedited publicly accessible databases; (2) editorial databases for internal use; and (3) other edited publicly accessible databases.

The *first category*, the unedited publically accessible databases, is covered neither by the Media Databases Act, section 1(2), nor the DPA, section 3(4) and (5). The idea is that the context of such databases has already been published in a media and therefore regulated by all the relevant statutes and provisions, the Penal Code, ethics of journalism, etc. In order to fall within this category, it is a requirement that the material has previously been published in a media under the MLA, mainly implying that it has to be a Danish media (*see* further details above in §2). If this requirement is not fulfilled, the database falls under category 3.

258. In order to fall within the *second category*, editorial databases for internal use, the database must be registered with the Data Inspection Board (section 3). The registration from one media house will include all the internal bases connected to that media. Access to this type of database must be restricted to journalists, the journalists must not use the database(s) for other purposes than purely journalistic, and safeguards must be in place in order to block access for unauthorized persons and prevent non-journalistic use of the contained information. If the database is not registered, it will fall within the DPA provided that it contains information in relation to persons which is very likely to be the case. If one were to follow the requirements of the GDPR and the DPA it would be impossible to run a media database. The non-fulfilment of the security safeguards is criminally sanctioned, and if no precautions have been taken whatsoever, the database will not fall within this privileged category. If the requirements are fulfilled, there are no restrictions as to the processing of personal data. Publishing of such data follows the standard rules, such as the Criminal Code and the Guiding Rules for the Ethics of Journalism.

259. The *third category*, edited and publicly accessible databases, must be registered with the Data Inspection Board as well as the Press Council, section 6, and there must be a person responsible for the database, section 7. If the database is not registered, it will fall under the (journalistically impossible) rules of the GDPR and the DPA rather than the more favourable rules of the Media Databases Act. As the information is publicly accessible, it must not contain information that cannot legally be published, section 8(1), or information of which publication will infringe ethics of journalism, section 8(2). Besides, private information, i.e., on race, religion, colour of the skin, political or associational affiliation, health, social problems or abuse of alcohol or narcotics, must be deleted after three years, unless public interest outweighs the interest in personal data protection, section 8(3) and (4). Persons mentioned in a publicly accessible database under the Act can require the media to delete, correct or update information that is wrong or misleading, and it is particularly mentioned that new administrative decisions, acquittals in court, or the prosecutor's decision to stop criminal proceedings must be updated upon request from the person involved in the proceedings, section 9.

260. Failure to comply with a request can be brought before the Press Council. So far (November 2018), it seems that the Press Council only has received one complaint under the MDBA.[141] The Press Council rejected the claim for deletion, arguing that the person in question had himself participated in public debates and voiced his political opinions. Consequently, his political views could not be considered 'private' under MDBA section 8(3) and ought not to be deleted (section 8(4)).

261. Instead of making a claim of deletion etc., the person involved has a right to reply similar to the right to reply according to the MLA (*see* Chapter 4).

262. Finally, as regards the third category, a person may require those responsible for the database to inform him/her whether he/she is in fact mentioned, section 11, and the responsible must take steps to secure that the information included in the databases cannot be changed by unauthorized intruders.

263. The MDBA dates back to 1995 and is not updated on contemporary technology, nor on contemporary law. Most Internet-based media serve as databases and consequently fall under the Act. The requirement of deletion rather than e.g., correction, anonymization or denotification could amount to an infringement of Article 10 ECHR if it were followed verbatim. So far, the Press Council has not made any decision as to the deletion of correct information, and exactly because it is a Press Council, it is not very likely to happen except in very extraordinary circumstances.

§5. Offences Against Public Peace

I. Blasphemy

264. The blasphemy clause was repealed in 2017. The last conviction dates back to 1938, and in legal terms the repeal does not make much difference. For info on the blasphemy section we refer to the 2010 edition of the present volume.

II. Offences Against Public Peace

265. According to section 100, 'any person who by public statements incites enemy action against the Danish state or who brings about an evident danger of such action shall be liable to imprisonment for any term not exceeding six years'. Subsection 2 of the section provides that a person who by public statement incites to intervention by a foreign power in the affairs of the Danish state can be punished

141. Decision 17-70-01075 'The extremist extremism researcher'.

with up to one year of imprisonment. The section has not been invoked and is normally understood to cover only genuinely dangerous situations. However, the wording covers a wider area.

266. Section 102 provides that a person who in times of war or enemy occupation assists the enemy by word or deed can be punished with up to sixteen years of imprisonment. Assistance includes propaganda in favour of the enemy, subsection 2(4). The section is adapted to traditional warfare and is not well suited for contemporary wars, let alone 'war against terrorism'.

267. Section 136(1), which is placed under the heading 'Offences against Public Peace and Order' and requires public prosecution, prescribes that anyone 'who publicly incites others to an offence' can be punished with a maximum penalty of four years. The provision is invoked in cases of violent attacks being followed up by further incitements. For a long time there were no published judgments. In *UfR* 1938.407Ø, some kind of fireworks or explosives had been ignited at the Prime Minister's residence, and a newspaper commented 'why the H ... didn't they use more dynamite'. In the tense atmosphere of the 1930s with widespread political violence throughout the continent, the case was prosecuted and the editor sentenced to four months imprisonment. The section was not applied until 2007 when a person pretending to support the 'Ungdomshuset'[142] had the following at his webpage: 'Make a Smash Hit. Kill a Fascist' arguing that the Minister of the Interior would be an obvious target for attack. The Minister is responsible for immigration issues and at her private residence her car had previously been vandalized. The person was also convicted of illegal possession of firearms (*TfK* 2007.774Ø). Since 2016 there are now seven published cases. The advent of the Internet and the menace from terrorism have activated the provision. One example: in *UfR* 2017.351V a person commented violent attacks on mosques in France following the terrorist attack on the premises of the magazine Charlie Hebdo: 'Great. They can get a taste of their own terror. Go on attacking!' (authors' translation). The person was sentenced to thirty days suspended imprisonment.

268. Section 136(2) criminalizes any publicly expressed approval of acts contravening provisions in Chapter 12 'Offences against the Independence and Safety of the State' and Chapter 13 'Offences against the Supreme Authorities of the State'. After the terrorism amendments, in section 114–114e of the Criminal Code, section 136(2) now also covers the public approval of various acts of terrorism. According to the wording of the provision, approval of terrorism, also against international organizations and against foreign public authorities, is criminalized, no matter the character of these authorities. Authors have argued that approval of attacks on suppressive regimes does not fall within the scope of 136(2), an understanding which is in accordance with Article 10 of the European Human Rights Convention. Until recently, there were no (published) convictions solely with reference to section 136(2), but that seems to be changing. In *UfR* 2018.383Ø a person was convicted

142. 'Ungdomshuset' [the 'Youth House'] in Copenhagen, for many years the cause of many controversies between youngsters who wanted to have a place of their own and the authorities.

for approval of the 2015 terrorist attacks in Copenhagen. The terrorist was lauded for having a heart of gold and being a hero,

269. Section 266a, in the chapter on Offences against Personal Honour etc. provides that: 'any person who, in circumstances other than those covered by sections 136 and 266 of this Act, makes public statements aimed at provoking acts of violence or destruction shall be liable to a fine or imprisonment for a period not exceeding one year'. The section has apparently only been applied once in a District Court decision.

§6. Group Defamation (Hate Speech)

270. Section 266b(1) runs as follows: 'Any person who, publicly or with the intention of wider dissemination, makes a statement or imparts other message[143] by which a group of people are threatened, insulted or degraded on account of their race, colour, national or ethnic origin, religion, or sexual inclination shall be liable to a fine or to imprisonment not exceeding two years.' Subsection 2 provides that: 'In determining the punishment it shall be considered a particularly aggravating circumstance if the conduct is of propagandistic nature.' The term 'hate speech' is misleading in the sense that 'hate' is immaterial. The section criminalizes threats, gross insults and degrading remarks towards specific groups. Hate is not criminalized.

I. History

271. The section was added to the Penal Code in 1939 in order to provide protection for people of certain beliefs and origins who were victims of severe persecution. According to the knowledge of the present authors, Denmark was the first country to penalize public derision of vulnerable groups. In 1971, it was altered in preparation for Denmark's ratification of Committee on the Elimination of Racial Discrimination (CERD), the UN Convention on the Elimination of All Forms of Racial Discrimination. CERD Article 4(a) requires that the Member States 'with due regard to the principles laid down in the Universal Declaration', *inter alia*, 'shall declare an offence punishable by law all dissemination of ideas based on racial superiority or hatred, incitement to racial discrimination'. During the preparation for CERD, the intricate relation to freedom of expression was on the agenda, and it is not quite clear to what extent the 'due regard' clause circumscribes the obligation to punish the dissemination of racist ideas. At any rate, according to the travaux préparatoires in relation to the altered section 266b expressions forwarded as part of scientific activities or as part of a serious debate should not come within the scope of the provision. Besides, not too gross expressions should also be left unprosecuted.

143. In Malene Freese Jensen et al., the term 'information' is used. The Danish term 'meddelelse' is not only of informative character, but may cover other forms of communication, including communication of non-verbal character.

272. In 1987 'sexual inclination' was added. 'Sex' is not included, implying that gross sexual insults are not covered by the section. Prosecution for insulting sexual groups is rare, and in *UfR* 1990.636V the Court acquitted the author of a letter to the editor with the words: 'homosexual activity is the most repulsive kind of adultery'. The accused defended herself with quotes from the Bible, and the Court, consisting of three professional and three lay judges, was divided 3–3 with three judges arguing in legal detail as to why the remarks must fall within section 266b. Recently, in *TfK* 2018.901V, an imam received a suspended prison sentence of seven days for his expressed views on homosexuality: 'It's like eating your own shit, like paedophilia' (authors' transcription).

273. In 1995, a second subsection was added stipulating that it is an aggravating circumstance if the statement or message has the status of propaganda. The provision was added in order to avoid that Denmark would be a sanctuary for the dissemination of racist propaganda.[144]

II. Prosecution

274. Prosecution is public. In practice, the police and the prosecution only handle cases reported to the police, i.e., conditioned public prosecution (*see* above §1). This may be seen as a result of the considerations for freedom of expression, the 'due regard' clause in CERD Article 4 and the emphasis in the Danish travaux préparatoires that only remarks of a more gross character should be prosecuted. By awaiting reporting from the public, the prosecution also ensures some kind of popular legitimacy when deciding to prosecute in cases which often involve politicians.

275. Only statements and messages made *in public* or *with the intention of wider dissemination* fall within the scope of the section.

276. Remarks made in private are not criminalized, and a person who makes a statement which is insulting towards a group because of race etc. with no intention of wider dissemination cannot be punished. In *UfR* 2012.2361H a person was acquitted for making remarks which contentwise obviously fell under the scope of section 266b. However, there was no proof of intention to disseminate. The person knew that he was talking to a journalist, but did not know (or claimed not to know) that the remarks were meant for dissemination and not only for background. Similarly, in *TfK* 2018.135/2V, expressions falling under section 266b were not considered to be criminal because of the lack of intent to publish: the expressions were uploaded on a closed Facebook account and deleted as soon as he realized that the expressions were shared.

---

144. In *UfR* 1988.788V, extradition of a German national denying Holocaust was rejected by the Court. Denial of Holocaust is not criminalized in Denmark.

277. On the other hand, remarks made in private may be criminal if open to the public. In *UfR* 2010.335Ø, the owner of a bench in a private garden, visible from public area, with inscriptions: 'Nur blankes' and 'Kaffer nie' was convicted with a fine and confiscation of the bench.

278. The statement and messages are only criminalized if they are insulting etc. towards *a group*. The group does not necessarily have to be a minority, but so far in practice this has always been the case.[145] Insults against an individual are regulated by sections 267 ff., but the courts have applied section 266b in cases of jeering even only to one or a few persons. The relevant criterion seems to be whether the insult covers the group and not just the particular individual, in which case section 267 is relevant. In *UfR* 2007.1468Ø the Court sentenced a participant in a football match who yelled 'black swine' etc. to a player from the opposite team, and in *UfR* 2007.1679Ø a man was sentenced for uttering 'Paki spawn' to some children of Somali origin waiting at a bus stop. *UfR* 2016.3536Ø backs up the previous case law.

279. Leniency in cases of retaliation is not as relevant as when dealing with section 267. However, in some cases, it may play a part if the remarks are forwarded as part of a heated debate in which the one making the statement felt provoked. Some decisions from the DPP not to prosecute point in this direction, and even though the insulted group has not been part of the exchange, it seems reasonable to give some weight to a preceding heated discussion. There is a difference between words uttered during a heated debate and the totally unprovoked insults.[146]

280. Not only verbal statements come within section 266b but also other types of *messages* may be sanctioned. In *UfR* 1994.993Ø, the burning of a cross outside a shelter for newly arrived refugees was considered to be a violation of section 266b.

281. As regards the question of which kinds of words fall within the criminal category, case law is rather clear in cases of comparison with animals like rats and pigs and when using the metaphors of diseases such as plague and cancer. This makes sense as the understanding of groups of other people as subhuman, as dangerous animals or diseases that ought to be fought down may be dangerous. History is sadly filled with examples of verbal de-humanization of groups often followed by more active persecution and even genocide. On the other hand, accusations of misuse of the social system and criminality in general do not normally fall within section 266b. Allegations of serious crimes committed by the particular group are covered, however. In *UfR* 2003.1947Ø, accusations of mass rape, serious violence,

145. The DPP has rejected to prosecute a Muslim imam for calling the Danes 'infidel'. However, the decision not to prosecute is not based on majority considerations, the term is simply not particularly degrading.
146. In Art. 10 cases, the ECtHR has regularly pointed to the preceding heated debate in support of freedom of expression.

etc. were found to be a violation of section 266b, and a call for setting up concentration camps for certain groups (*UfR* 2004.734H) or calls for downright extinction (Eastern High Court judgment 27 June 2006 'wipe them out') are criminalized, with imprisonment as the sanction. In *UfR* 2003.1428Ø and *UfR* 2007.1471Ø, the leader of Hizb ut Tahrir[147] was sentenced to prison for pamphlets against Jews: 'Kill them wherever you find them', the last mentioned judgment being the first one under section 266b to impose unconditioned imprisonment. One might consider applying section 136, public incitement to crimes, with a maximum penalty of four years compared to two years in section 266b. At any rate, the courts do impose prison sentences for such kinds of serious threats.

III. Propaganda

282. The more systematic dissemination of group degrading remarks etc. requires heavier punishment according to the second subsection of section 266b, and the courts have imposed prison sentences in a number of cases: uploading on the Internet, *UfR* 2004.734H, distribution of pamphlets, *UfR* 2003.1428Ø and *UfR* 2007.1471Ø, posters, *UfR* 2003.1947Ø, public advertising of a meeting (Eastern High Court judgment 30 September 2004) and radio programme (Eastern High Court judgment 27 June 2006). In a case, a former politician who had to appear before the court charged with trespassing of section 266b gave an interview outside the court building in which he reiterated his opinion. For this he received seven days imprisonment.

IV. Perspectives and Problems

283. It is not easy finding the balance between the protection of freedom of expression and the prevention of gross group defamation. Danish law is reasonably well balanced, accepting insulting remarks made in debates while being harsher on the more systematic dissemination of hate speech, not accepting remarks that compare certain groups to diseases or infestants and even including jeers against persons belonging to certain groups under section 266b.

147. Hizb ut Tahrir is a legal association in Denmark. According to s. 78 of the Danish Constitution, associations can only be dissolved by a court of law if they employ violence or aim at attaining their object by violence. The DPP has assessed that an application for the dissolution of the organization is not likely to be successful.

Chapter 4. Right to Reply

284. The default rule is that there is no right to reply. The editors are the ones responsible for the content of the media, and consequently the editor, or whoever is acting on behalf of the editor, is making the decision as to the content of the media. However, there are some exceptions.

285. Section 273(1) of the Penal Code provides that 'if a defamatory allegation is unjustified, a statement to that effect shall, at the request of the injured party, be included in the sentence', and subsection 2 provides that the offended may be rewarded a lump sum in order to publish the judgment or an account of the judgment. This is not a direct right to reply. A newspaper being convicted in a defamation case cannot be ordered to publish the verdict. However, the newspaper or any other defendants can be ordered to pay the plaintiff money in order to enable him/her to advertise the result of the judgment.

286. According to section 36 of the MLA, 'requests for reply in the mass media to information of a factual nature which might cause anyone significant financial or other damage, and which has been published in a mass media, must be heeded, except where the correctness of the information is unquestionable'. The Press Council has competence to order the media to bring a reply. The reply can only be given to a factual statement, and the reply must only comment on the factual content. In principle, it is easy to distinguish between a piece of factual information and a comment.[148] In practice, however, the classification depends on the context, and the Press Council may use the classification to avoid an order to reply.[149] Besides, the injured party often has difficulties in restraining himself/herself to factual corrections.[150] Please note that this possibility of reply only applies to media under the MLA (*see* Chapter 3, §2 above).

287. The right to reply according to section 36 is not the same as the media's responsibility to rectify on its own motion according to the Guiding Rules. If the media has actually (and timely) corrected an incorrect piece of information, the Press Council refuses a reply.[151]

288. A media running a publicly accessible database may also be required to bring a reply, *see* section 10 of the MDBA. The obligation is similar to the one according to the MLA. So far, no one has made use of this particular right to reply.

289. Pursuant to the Broadcasting Act section 44(3), the Radio and Television Board makes decisions regarding the right to reply in relation to factual information

148. *See* the distinction between 'charges' and 'terms of abuse' in s. 267 and the ECtHR's distinction between allegations of facts and value judgments.
149. 85/1992 dealt with an article about the fire resulting in the deaths of hundreds of people on the ferry Scandinavian Star. 'K had tax reduction for DKK 42 millions' was classified as a comment, not a very convincing classification, but the ship owner did not carry much sympathy.
150. 2009-6-790.
151. 2006-6-367 and 368.

provided in advertisements. Right to reply presupposes that the information might cause anyone significant financial or other damage, and that the correctness of the information is not unquestionable. The Board can impose on an owner of a programme service licence or registration to broadcast a reply. The Board can decide on the reply's content, form and placement.

Chapter 5. Access to Public Information

§1. Public Documents and Meetings

I. The Freedom of Information Act

290. Access to information about the public administration's activities, decisions and procedure is vital for the press' ability to elucidate attempts to abuse power and inappropriate administrative measures.[152,153]

291. The first limited act on access to information in Denmark was adopted in 1964. In 1970, the Parliament approved the Act on Access of the Public to Documents in Administrative Files. The 1970 law was replaced in 1985 by the Freedom of Information Act.[154] The law was revised and modernized in 2013.[155]

292. The purpose of the Act is to ensure transparency among authorities in order to support, *inter alia*, freedom of expression and information and the media's dissemination of information to the public, cf. section 1. According to section 2, the scope of the Act is very broad, as it applies to 'all activity exercised by the public administration'. This includes all administrative authorities, regardless of whether they belong to the central government, regional or local government, and whether they are general administrative authorities, special boards or councils or other special management units, such as the national central bank (Danmarks Nationalbank) and the state-owned public service broadcaster, DR. The Act also applies to private companies of which 75% of the ownership interests belong to Danish public authorities, cf. section 4. However, this does not apply to listed companies and their subsidiaries.

293. The Act does not apply to the courts or legislators. Documents relating to criminal justice or the drafting of bills before they are introduced in the Danish Parliament (Folketinget) are exempted. Authorities who orally receive information of importance to a pending case have an obligation to prepare a written note of the information, *see* section 13(1).

---

152. Sandfeld Jakobsen & Schaumburg-Müller, *Medieretten* [*Media Law*] (Jurist- og Økonomforbundets Forlag, 2013), Ch. 11.
153. *See*, *inter alia*, Jon Andersen, *Forvaltningsret* [*Administrative Law*] (Karnov Group, 2017). Sten Bønsing, *Almindelig Forvaltningsret* [*General Administrative Law*] (Jurist- og Økonomforbundets Forlag, 2018). Karsten Revsbech, *Forvaltningsret. Almindelig emner* [*General Administrative Law*] (Jurist- og Økonomforbundets Forklag, 2016). A brief English description can be found in Børge Dahl, Torben Melchior & Ditlev Tamm, *Danish Law in a European Perspective* (Thomson Publishing, 2002), pp. 149 et seq.
154. Act No. 572 of 19 Dec. 1985.
155. Act No. 606 of 12 Jun. 2013.

A. The Right to Access

294. The main rule of the Act is section 7(1), which provides 'everyone' with a right to demand documents that are subject to administrative casework or procedure. The right is primarily used by journalists but also private individuals and organizations make use of the Act.

295. The notion of 'documents' is interpreted widely, encompassing not only physical documents (papers) but also electronic documents, e-mail, tapes, microfilm, etc. What is decisive is that the information can be stored and retrieved. It is, however, a requirement according to section 9 that a person demanding access is able – at least broadly – to identify the documents or case he/she wants to examine.[156] Further, the request for access can be denied if it requires an 'undue use of resources', cf. section 9(2). If the person requesting access can prove a special interest in the documents, which is often the case for the media, access can rarely be denied with reference to section 9(2).

296. The concept of 'administrative casework or procedure' is also broad and covers both pending and already decided cases, as well as documents which do not relate to a specific case where a legally binding decision will be made, but relate to operational activities carried out by public institutions in general, such as the operation of a hospital, teaching, etc. Documents which are solely received by the authority for storage or archive, or material such as teaching material, booklets, etc., are not covered.[157]

297. Besides the right according to section 7(1) to demand access to documents in general, section 8 provides a person whose personal information is included in a document within a public authority with the right to access to that information. This right is supplemented by a similar right according to the Data Processing Act[158] Chapter 9.

156. In Case 2001-0619-501 a journalist was denied access to 'all documents covering the period 1 January 1996 to 19 January 2001' from a commission under the Ministry of Transportation. The Ombudsman agreed that the journalist's request was not sufficiently identifiable. Likewise, the Ombudsman in Case 1996–2735-401 agreed that a journalist's request of access to 'all documents regarding accidents or technical errors with relation to medical equipment' was too broad.

157. In Case 1993–2357-401 the Ombudsman accepted that the Ministry of Defence denied access in a booklet which had caused public debate. The booklet had been used in connection with teaching, but had not been included in an administrative file or been subject to administrative case work.

158. Act No. 429/2000, implementing Directive 95/46/EU on the Processing of Personal Data.

B. Exceptions

298. Chapter 4 of the Act (sections 19–35) contains a number of exceptions to the main rule of access in section 7(1). The exceptions can be categorized in exceptions that concern access to all documents in certain types of cases, access to certain types of documents and access to certain information contained in documents (but not the rest of the document).

299. Criminal cases, cases regarding preparation of legislation before Parliament and cases regarding employment in the public sector are examples of cases which as such are exempted from access, cf. sections 19–21. With regard to documents, due to considerations to the administrative decision-making process, section 23 exempts internal documents, e.g., recommendations from civil servants to ministers and minutes of proceedings. The exemption regarding recommendations from civil servants to their minister covers the entire ministry, i.e., also recommendations from subordinate authorities within the ministry, cf. section 24. This rule is highly controversial as it provides the government with plenty of opportunitie to deny the media's access to documents in important political cases.[159] Records, documents and minutes of the Council of State and meetings between ministers, correspondence between authorities and outside experts in drafting laws or for use in court proceedings or deliberations on possible legal proceedings, as well as material gathered for public statistics or scientific research are also documents which are exempted in their entirety according to section 27.

300. However, notwithstanding sections 23–24 and 27 information in such documents which regards factual circumstances is subject to access in accordance with the main rule in section 7(1), *see* section 28. Hence, such information must be extracted from the relevant documents which are exempted from access.[160]

301. Further, pursuant to section 30, information in documents related to the private life of an individual or an undertaking's or organization's trade or business secrets is, subject to a specific assessment, exempted. The rest of the information in such documents must be disclosed in accordance with the main rule on access.[161]

---

159. In a letter to Parliament of 6 Oct. 2016 the Ombudsman pointed out that s. 24, which was introduced in 2013, has led to considerable restrictions on the right to access.

160. In Case 2014-14 the Ombudsman stated that although a memo from the civil servants to the minister within the Ministry of Taxation contained political considerations and recommendations covered by s. 24, the vast majority of the memo consisted of factual information which could not be exempted.

161. In Case 1996–2429-301 a journalist was denied access to documents in the Ministry of Business regarding certain loans to private shipyards. The Ombudsman stated that the decision was not based on a specific assessment, and that the Ministry had failed to assess whether there was information in the documents which was not exempted from the right to access and thus should be extracted and made accessible to the journalist.

302. Access to information can also be restricted to the extent it is deemed necessary, subject to e.g., considerations relating to the security of the state and defence of the realm, protection of foreign policy, law enforcement, taxation and public financial interests, *see* sections 32–33.

303. Section 35 stipulates that the right to access under the Act is limited by the rules regarding professional secrecy of public servants.

C. *Access to a Wider Extent than Required*

304. It should be noted that the exceptions to the main rule on access to information are minimum rules in the sense that the authorities can provide access to a wider extent than stipulated in the exceptions, *see* section 14, unless this will conflict with the rules on professional secrecy.

305. The authorities are obliged to consider in each case whether access to a wider extent than stipulated can be provided. The Parliamentary Ombudsman, who supervises and controls the legality of the public administration's decisions and activities, has stated that this obligation is considerably strong with regard to the press' requests for access to information.[162]

D. *Complaints Regarding Denied Access*

306. Pursuant to section 37(1), an authority's decision on access to information can be brought before the authority which is competent to handle complaints regarding the substance matter of the case from which the request on access is derived.

307. Pursuant to section 36 requests regarding access shall, as a main rule, be decided within seven days, and if this deadline is exceeded the authority must inform the requestor of why and when a decision is expected. In practice, it happens very often that decisions regarding access are delayed, thus making it difficult for notable journalists to obtain access in due time.

162. *See* the Ombudsman's Annual Report 1998, 403, where it was stated that even though the journalist had not correctly identified the documents which he requested access to, the authority should have considered access to a wider extent than stipulated by the act. In Case 2016-30 the Ombudsman did not find reason to criticize the national public service broadcaster, DR's decision not to offer access to a wider extent than required in documents regarding the financial situation concerning one of its radio programmes.

E. The Parliamentary Ombudsman

308. Decisions regarding access to documents can also be brought before the Parliamentary Ombudsman. The Ombudsman was established in 1955 by virtue of section 55 of the Constitution which provides for an ombudsman. Detailed rules are set forth in the Ombudsman Act.[163]

309. The Ombudsman controls all parts of the administration on behalf of the Parliament.[164] He/she is, however, independent of Parliament in the discharge of his/ her functions. Any person can lodge a complaint with the Ombudsman against a public authority, *see* section 13. The Ombudsman can also start its own investigations, *see* section 17. The Ombudsman decides for himself/herself whether he/she wants to investigate a case or not, *see* section 16. Thus, as opposed to the courts the Ombudsman is not forced to take up a case.

310. The Ombudsman's legal review encompasses an assessment of whether any authorities or persons falling within his/her jurisdiction act in contravention of existing legislation or otherwise commit errors or derelictions in the discharge of their duties, *see* section 21. Accordingly, the Ombudsman not only deals with traditional legal problems, but also with 'proper administrative behaviour', which is a broader concept covering also *inter alia* the administrations considerateness, openness and the avoidance of unsuitable bureaucratic routines in the public administration.[165] He/she shows a far greater impetus towards the administration than the courts, and he/she works with a far greater degree of flexibility.

311. The Ombudsman has no power to impose formal sanctions. Hence, he/she cannot alter or repeal an authority's decision on access to information, or order public authorities to act. According to section 22 he/she can only review decisions and issue his/her opinions and recommendations, e.g., that requested documents be released or that the authority justify its decisions better. His/her recommendations are, however, generally followed by the administration.

II. The Administrative Procedures Act

312. It should be noted that the Administrative Procedures Act[166] also contains rules on the access to documents. These rules are fairly similar to the rules of the Freedom of Information Act. However, the rules in the Administrative Procedures Act, as the Act as a whole, only apply to cases in which an administrative decision is made, and only for *parties* to the specific case (as opposed to 'anybody' covered

163. Consolidated Act No. 349/2013. An English translation of the Act can be found on the Ombudsman's website www.ombudsmanden.dk.
164. *See* ss 1 and 7 of the Ombudsman Act.
165. In Case 1990-967-23, the Ombudsman criticized that it took an administrative body more than six months to answer a request regarding access to documents.
166. Consolidated Act No. 433/2014.

by the Freedom of Information Act). Moreover, the rules on the access of parties to information are more far-reaching because the exceptions are not so extensive. This is due to fact that a party involved in a specific case against a public authority in general has a more substantial interest in getting access to the documents in the case compared to someone who is not involved in the case.

III. The Act on the Re-use of PSI

313. In addition to the right to access to information under the Freedom of Information Act, the Act on the re-use of public sector information (PSI)[167] provides the public, including the press, with certain rights with regard to access to information developed in the public sector. The Act implemented the requirements set forth in the EU Directive on the re-use and commercial exploitation of PSI[168] and was adopted in June 2004. The purpose of the Directive and the Act is to enhance the re-use of public authorities' information resources.

314. The Directive supports the two key pillars of the internal market: transparency and fair competition. It sets minimum rules for the re-use of PSI throughout the EU. It encourages Member States to go beyond these minimum rules and to adopt open data policies, allowing a broad use of documents held by public sector bodies. The Danish transposition Act obligates public authorities to publish a table of documents and databases which are made accessible for re-use.

315. The difference between the right to access under the Freedom of Information Act and the PSI Act is that the Freedom of Information Act only provides right to information in documents which are identified, whereas the PSI Act gives right to access to 'mass' information.

316. However, the PSI Act does not extend the access to information under the Freedom of Information Act. This means that the exceptions to the right to access under the Freedom of Information Act, *see* above, also apply to information covered by the PSI Act.[169]

IV. Access to Public Authorities' Meetings

317. Besides access to documents, access to information in the public sector can be achieved via access to meetings held in public authorities. As opposed to documents there are no general rules on the public, including the press' access to meetings in the public sector. In the absence of such general rules the starting point is that unless an express rule authorizes access to specific meetings held in the public sector, no right to such access exists.

---

167. Act No. 596 of 24 Jun. 2005.
168. Directive 2003/98/EC, as amended by directive 2013/37/EU.
169. *See* the preparatory works to the PSI Act.

318. The principle of extended access in the Freedom of Information Act section 14, cf. above, does not apply to public sector meetings. As an example of an express rule on access to meetings, town council meetings in municipalities are open to the public.

§2. Court Hearings and Documents

I. Court Hearings

319. Court hearings are open unless decided otherwise by a statute or according to a statute, section 28a of the AJA. When delivering judgments and passing sentences, the court is always open, section 28a(2).

320. By statute the following types of cases are held in camera: divorce and child custody cases, section 453; paternity cases, section 456m; and cases concerning adoption without consent, section 475g.

321. The presiding judge may exclude certain persons from attending otherwise open court hearings: if the courtroom is overcrowded, section 28b(1), (in which case the court ought to leave room for the media representatives) and persons under the age of 15 and persons whose behaviour is inconsistent with the dignity of the court, section 28b(2), may be required to leave the courtroom. The presiding judge may also exclude persons if their presence is likely to interfere with witnesses giving evidence, section 28b(3). These provisions are hardly relevant to the media.

322. The court may decide to sit in camera for the sake of orderliness in the courtroom, in consideration of the relation to foreign powers, and if an open court may be excessively humiliating or offensive, section 29(1).

323. In civil cases the court may decide to sit in camera when asked to do so by a party and if the party has an interest in secrecy and no public interest weighs against, section 29(2).

324. In criminal cases the court may make the decision to sit in camera if the accused is under 18, if special officers are giving evidence (the special officers, e.g., being agents working in disguise), if a public hearing may put someone in danger and if a public hearing may prevent information coming forward, section 29(3). When considering to hold sittings in camera, the court must consider the pros and cons, and not merely satisfy itself that, e.g., the accused is under 18.[170] In some cases the accused does not want to give information when the media are present, a difficult situation to handle for the courts. On the one hand it is not for the accused to decide whether the media should be excluded, and on the other hand the presence of the media in the pre-trial phase – especially if the accused is considering making a full confession – may prevent the confession. In two – special – cases, the

170. *UfR* 2004.658V.

high court has decided in favour of sittings in camera, in one case the accused was mentally unstable, in the second the accused had killed his mother.[171]

325. After the pre-trial phase sitting in camera is an exception, and at any rate the court must consider whether other means are sufficient to obtain the goal, such as reporting and identification ban, section 29(4) and (5).

326. When considering a decision to sit in camera, the court must hear the pleas from the media present, section 29c, and the media have the right to appeal against the decision if representatives from the appealing media were present at the hearing (section 393(2) as regards civil cases and section 968(2) as regards criminal cases). These rights pertain only to media under the MLA, i.e., mainly Danish media.

327. In criminal cases dealing with sexual offences, the victim may require the court to sit in camera when he/she is giving evidence, section 29a. If the victim so requires, the court must clear the courtroom, in these cases there is no room for the discretion of the court.

328. In some special cases, namely cases relating to guardianship and administrative detention, the courts may also decide to sit in camera (sections 462 and 473). In these cases the media have no right to plead against the decision, but have a right of appeal if present when the decision was taken.

II. Recordings and Pictures from the Court

329. According to section 32(1) of the AJA, there is a general prohibition of audio as well as video recordings (including the taking of photographs) during court hearings, and the publication of such unlawful recordings is also unlawful.[172] The court may as an exception allow for recordings. The courts are reticent to give permission (e.g., *UfR* 2009.613V), and permission has so far only been given in a few cases in which the participants had willingly appeared in the media in interviews, shows, etc. The permission to record will be restricted to recording of the professional participants from stationary cameras, *UfR* 2001.1255H. The court also has the power to prohibit persons from bringing cameras, computers, and cell phones into the courtroom during hearings, section 32(3) and (4). Obviously, cell phones can be used for communicating to waiting witnesses, but even participating lawyers etc. may be prevented from bringing their computers (*UfR* 2005.2436H) and so may representatives of the media. Drawings are not included in the ban, but the court may in concrete cases prohibit the actual drawing as well as its subsequent publication, section 32a.

330. Visual recordings are generally prohibited in the court building, section 32(2), but the president of the court may give his/her permission. This is rarely, if

171. *UfR* 2001.908V and *UfR* 2001.1373V.

172. The publication comes within the Media Liability Act, the recording does not, *see* Ch. 3, §2.

ever, given in relation to shooting photos of persons involved in court cases. The publication of unpermitted visual recordings is equally unlawful. Audio recordings from the court building are not prohibited – and they are probably uninteresting.

331. According to section 32(6), visual recordings outside the courtroom – a freely accessible place and therefore not covered by section 264a in the Penal Code (*see* Chapter 3, §4 above) – are now also prohibited in relation to persons on their way either to or from a court hearing and if the person is either charged with a criminal offence or is a witness in a criminal case. The persons themselves may consent, in contradistinction to recordings inside the building where permission from the court or the president is required. Pictures of the professional participants are allowed, and the provision does not cover civil cases. The publication of an unlawfully made photo is also unlawful, and even the negligent publication of an unlawful photo is criminalized.[173]

III. Other Reporting from Court Hearings

332. According to section 129a of the Penal Code, 'any person who publishes versions which he/she knows to be untrue or false quotations or communications on facts given in court sittings ... shall be liable to a fine or imprisonment for any term not exceeding two years'. This section appears never to be applied.

333. Sections 1016a to 1017d deal with the public commenting on criminal cases. Section 1017(1) requires the press coverage of criminal cases to be 'objective and honest' (why this only applies to criminal cases is not clear to the present author). It is, however, a rather general wording, and the provision does not carry any specific sanction. On the other hand, the provision may be conceived as a general legal principle. In *UfR* 1979.1028H, the accused in a criminal case asserted that the wife of the leader of the investigations was a prostitute, which was, of course, flatly refused by the officer. A tabloid newspaper made the headline: 'My wife is not a prostitute', which was sanctioned according to the Penal Code section 264d on privacy. The underlying idea is that the reporting of a criminal case should not be distortive.

334. Section 1017(2) criminalizes the public dissemination of incorrect information on current criminal cases as well as comments that are likely to influence the decision of the court. The section seems not to have been applied since *UfR* 1982.1022H, in which a tabloid newspaper on the front page at the day of the verdict in a jury case had the text: '(Name) ought to be acquitted'. The newspaper was sentenced, with the slightest majority in the Supreme Court. Three out of the seven judges voted for acquittal, referring to the fact that the case had been widely debated, and that considerations for the free exchange of views ought to prevail.

173. In *UfR* 2005.2578V, a professional photographer received a fine of approximately EUR 1,500 for violating s. 32(6).

Seen in retrospect, the minority's vote is now prevailing law and it may be questioned whether the statute is, in fact, prevailing Danish law.

335. According to section 1017b, the identity of victims in sex cases must never be revealed to the public either before, during or after trial. The same applies to lay jurors – a provision less comprehensible, taken into consideration that jurors are appointed partly from local municipality party lists. According to 1017d, the public dissemination of criminal cases must anonymize victims, witnesses and the accused. The provision was altered in 2004 in connection with a broader access to criminal cases.

336. In some types of cases the names and identity of the persons involved must not be published. This applies to divorce and child custody cases, section 453; paternity cases, section 456m; and cases regarding adoption without consent, section 475g.

337. In practice, the decisions of the courts play an important part as to the reporting and especially the public identification of persons involved in court cases.

338. According to the AJA, section 29d, the reporting from a court sitting in camera is prohibited, no matter the content of the information. Sitting in camera may follow from statutory provisions or from concrete decisions by the court, and the reporting ban prevails in both situations. The only exception is when the decision to exclude the public has been taken because of disorderliness in the courtroom. In such cases, the court ought to exclude the disorderly elements and not the media. The situation is different from disclosure of information from the administration. Here, the media can report even when the information has been obtained through a breach of confidentiality (Penal Code section 152d, and Chapter 2, §2 above) unless the information is strictly private or relates to state security. Reporting from courts sitting in camera may also result from a breach of confidentiality, e.g., by the lawyer, but the media have no special reporting right, and the reporting is prohibited no matter its content.

339. The court may also issue a reporting ban, but only in criminal cases and mainly if the accused is under 18, section 30–30b. Reporting bans are rather uncommon. Normally, courts decide to sit in camera or order an identification ban (*see* below).

340. Interestingly, the court must hear the opinion of the media before making the decision, section 30b, and the media have the rights to make an appeal against it, section 968(2). These rights only apply to media under the MLA and the right to appeal a decision for the court to sit in camera only if the media (not necessarily the particular journalist) were present at the hearing.

341. According to section 31 and 31a, the court can issue an order not to publish the names of the accused or other persons involved in a criminal case. It is an identification ban, not merely a name ban,[174] and the court has to consider the pros and cons: the safety of involved persons and the damage of a publication on the one hand and the importance for the society on the other. If the involved person holds a responsible post, he/she is less likely to be protected, section 31(3), and the more serious the crime, the less likely is an identification ban.[175] Similar to the reporting ban, the media have a right to be heard when the decision is about to be taken, and the media have the right to appeal, 'media' meaning media under the MLA. The right to appeal is continuous, section 31a(2): under changing circumstances, the reason for the ban may not prevail.

342. When reporting, the media have an obligation to check on an eventual identification ban, section 32b(2), and the media[176] may be sanctioned for violating a ban that they did not know.

343. In guardianship cases (dealing with persons who cannot handle their own affairs) and cases relating to administrative detention (mainly involving mentally disturbed persons), the court may decide that the name and identity of the involved must not be revealed, sections 462 and 473 respectively. In these cases the media do not have a right to be heard before the decision is made. In fact, the court will often sit in camera in these kinds of cases, and the media have the right to appeal against this decision only if they were present at the actual court hearing.

IV. Court Documents

344. Access to documents must be distinguished from the use of the documents, such as reporting, copying, etc.

345. The holders of rights to access to court documents are divided into three categories: the general public, persons with a specific interest and media, AJA section 41. As for the media, the special rights only pertain to media under the MLA, i.e., mainly Danish media. If access is open to everybody, this will of course also include the media, no matter its status under the MLA. The media may also obtain access indirectly through the party.

346. *Everybody* has access to the conclusion of a judgment when requested within a week from the passing of the judgment, section 41a. This section neither provides any right to copies nor access to the whole judgment including evidence etc.

---

174. *UfR* 1988.365H: A newspaper reported that an unnamed football coach of a team in a provincial town was charged. The newspaper received a fine.
175. *UfR* 2010.1427H. The Supreme Court upheld a ban on publishing a name of a celebrity who had been charged with position of drugs, even though the name had appeared on a web page before the injunction. The Court argued that publishing of the name had no general interest.
176. As to which person(s) will be held liable, *see* Ch. 3, §2 on the Media Liability Act.

347. According to section 41b, everybody has access to a copy of a judgment or decision except: (1) special types of cases such as divorce, custody and paternity cases; (2) criminal cases more than one year old; (3) decisions (different from the final judgment) in current criminal cases; (4) evidence given in camera; and (5) evidence in case of reporting ban. However, the access may be restricted if: (1) necessary for state security; (2) if required because of prevention or detection of crimes; and (3) if the judgment contains private information *and* if the private interests weigh heavier than the public information interests. Note that the reporting which reveals the identity of sexual crimes victims and parties in criminal cases is never allowed, section 1017b and 1017d. The above applies also to most written documents presented before the court, section 41c.

348. Access to court documents for the general public was expanded significantly in 2004. Now access has become the point of departure.

349. Persons with a specific interest, including victims in criminal cases, have as a point of departure access to all documents of a court case, section 41d(1). The group includes parties and lawyers, but not persons who are going to give evidence. Access does not comprise documents in relation to mediation, section 41d(2), or 'working documents', such as papers produced by the court, the lawyers or the prosecutor for their own use, the voting record or letters within the police and prosecution. Besides, the access may be limited by a decision by the court, section 41d(3): (1) if another party has his/her access limited by statute; (2) if state security considerations carry more weight; (3) if private information carries more weight; or (4) if considerations for prevention and detection of crimes carry more weight.

350. Access for the *media*, section 41f, includes: (1) the right to browse through judgments of the previous four weeks; (2) indictments; (3) 'helping' documents during court hearings such as sketches of the scene of the crime; and (4) in civil cases all other documents during the court hearing if the parties consent. The media also have access to criminal judgments more than one-year old, section 41b(2)(3). This right also applies to legal researchers.

351. The material must only be accessible for journalists and is only supportive for journalistic work, section 41f(6). Thus, e.g., a copy of a criminal judgment acquired under section 41f(1) can be used as a support when reporting on the case, but the journalist may not quote long passages, let alone print the whole judgment, and according to an Executive Order (546/2004) section 7, the media must keep this kind of material in a separate locked closet in order to prevent unauthorized access.

Chapter 6. Press Council and Ethics of Journalism

§1. Introduction and Institution

352. According to the MLA, section 34, the content and conduct of the mass media shall be in conformity with ethics of journalism.[177,178] When the bill was presented to the Parliament, a set of Guiding Rules for the Ethics of Journalism[179] was attached which was a slightly altered version of a private set of rules adopted some decades earlier by most newspapers. The Guiding Rules were originally made for the printed media, and even though the MLA applies to all kinds of media (*see* Chapter 3, §2), the Guiding Rules were not changed to fit also the broadcasted media. The Guiding Rules were, however, modernized in 2013, not least due to the advent of the online media. Despite its name, the Press Council handles complaints from all media under the MLA including broadcasting media with the exception of radio and television commercials which fall within the competence of the Radio and Television Board.

353. The Guiding Rules are, as the name indicates, not binding as a statute, but only guiding. However, the Press Board often – and apparently increasingly in recent years – cites a guiding rule if applicable. Ethics of journalism, however, covers a larger area than the Guiding Rules, and the Press Council has set up its own case 'law' without backing in the rules, especially as regards the use of hidden camera. The rules pertaining to hidden camera have been 'codified' with the 2014 update.

354. The Press Council can only: (1) make decisions as to whether the media has acted in accordance with the ethics of journalism; (2) require the media to publish the decision; and (3) direct the media to bring a reply (as for this right, *see* Chapter 4 above). The Council cannot impose fines, require compensation to be made, let alone punish the media, and it cannot make decisions as to whether the Penal Code or any other law has been violated, all of which are a matter for the courts. All it can do is to express its views and require the media to publish it. A media that does not publish the view of the Press Council or publish an ordered reply is liable to punishment, a situation dealt with by the public prosecutor and the court. A media that does not follow the content of the decisions from the Press Council only faces the hassle of publishing the view by the Council that the media is violating ethics of journalism.

---

177. Sandfeld Jakobsen & Schaumburg-Müller, Medieretten [*Media Law*] (Jurist- og Økonomforbundets Forlag, 2013), Ch. 8; Lambert & Gjessing, Medieansvarsloven med kommentarer [*The Media Liability Act with Comments*] (Jurist- og Økonomforbundets Forlag, 2017). Baumbach, *Medieretten Medieret. Frihed og ansvar* [*Media Law. Freedom and Liability*] (Karnov, 2017).
178. The translation at the Press Council's web page uses the term 'sound press ethics'.
179. An English version of the rules can be found on the Press Council's web page www.pressenaevnet.dk. The Press Council's translation is 'Press Ethical Rules'. Some years back the Council employed the term 'National Code of Conduct'.

355. The Press Council can only handle complaints which fall under its power. Thus, complaints against media that do not fall under the MLA (*see* above Chapter 3 §2 section II) will be rejected. As regards unedited comments the 2013 revision of the Guiding Rules provides that they do not fall under the power of the Council, and as a result the Council has rejected complaints in relation to unedited online comments.[180] However, it is an obligation for the media to have internal complaints procedures in place in relation to the unedited comments. It would amount to a violation of the Guiding Rules if a medium does not have clear complaints procedures. So far, the Press Council has not received complaints as to the lack of proper complaint procedures.

356. The advantage of the Press Council is its relatively swift and costless procedures. A complaint has to be made within twelve weeks, and the medium has to answer within four weeks. In comparison court procedures often last more than a year at the first level. Even though it is an option according to the MLA, the Council rejects oral hearings including hearing of witnesses, and as a consequence it regularly rejects claims if they cannot be substantiated. No doubt the Council has found it more important to deliver swift decisions. Engaging in oral hearings will not only prolong the cases in question, but also burden the Council and make its general processing of cases much slower.

357. It is possible to file a petition dealing with the same case both to the Press Council and to the court. The bodies may make different decisions because the Press Council decides as to whether the media has acted in accordance with ethics of journalism and the court whether it has acted according to the law. Sometimes the results coincide, but there is no automatic accordance.

358. The parties to a complaint before the Press Council are on the defendant's side simply the media. On the plaintiff's side, complaints are only accepted if the person, company or association is identifiable in the media. This implies that complaints on behalf of others are not accepted (except, of course, in cases when the identified person has authorized someone else to make the complaint). Thus, an employer cannot lodge a complaint if an employee is mentioned,[181] nor can a union automatically lodge a complaint on behalf of a member.[182] There are some exceptions: first, close relations can complain in cases of reporting about a deceased person, and second, parents are the relevant persons when children or even youngsters are mentioned. As for children and youngsters, the Press Council is rather strict requiring the involvement of the parents.

359. Besides, the requirement that the person etc. is identifiable in the media implies that more ideally driven complaints are not accepted, including consumers complaining about incorrect information. The Guiding Rules for the Ethics of Journalism also include provisions against the hindrance of publication of relevant news

180. 2018-80-0216 among several others.
181. 2008-6-676.
182. *PÅ* 1999, 5.

and against susceptibility to undue influence. However, such complaints will normally not be handled by the Council as no identifiable person, company or association is likely to make a complaint. The MLA, section 34, requires the media to act in accordance with ethics of journalism as regards the content of the media as well as its conduct. However, complaints about the conduct of the media which have not resulted in the complainant being identifiable in the media are rejected by the Press Council.

360. The Council has the power to handle cases on its own motion. This option has only been used once in a series of cases dealing with private pictures of the Danish Crown Prince. The Royal House never engages in legal procedures – the Queen is sacrosanct according to the Constitution section 13 and cannot be held liable for her acts – and the Press Council decided to intervene in the case in which the Guiding Rules had obviously been violated. Otherwise, the Council does not initiate proceedings on its own motion. This position has been criticized, also by the Parliament, as a result of which the Press Council in 2015 decided to be more open to initiate proceedings on its own motion in the future. However, this still remains to be seen in practice.

361. In sum, the Press Council has in certain areas restricted its own activities even though these activities are provided in the statute: it does not hold oral hearings, it rejects complaints if the complainant is not identifiable in the media and it does not take up cases on its own motion. The reason for this is probably that the Council fears to be disregarded by the media. Besides the power to require the publishing of its decision, the Press Council has no means of power and must rely on its decisions being convincing and acceptable among the media. So far this seems to be the case. By and large most media follow the general principles emerging in the case 'law' of the Council. But they do not have to, and this may be the reason why the Council is reluctant to be too active in its approach.

362. Several larger media houses have their own complaints procedures and some even codes of conduct. Some have a 'readers' editor' who receives complaints and even may take up questions on his/her own motion. The phenomenon is rather new in Denmark, and presently there is no research comparing the various approaches etc. Apparently, these local institutions have not limited the number of complaints to the Press Council.[183]

§2. Correct Information

363. The Guiding Rules for the Ethics of Journalism have a preamble called 'Fundamental Views' and are divided into three sections: (1) correct information; (2) conduct violating ethics of journalism, mainly dealing with questions of privacy; and (3) court reporting.

183. The number of complaints for the last ten years is around 130–170.

364. The media have an obligation to bring correct information, and incorrect information is regularly criticized by the Council. As stated above, only persons (companies etc.) who are identifiable in the media can lodge a complaint. The requirements for correctness vary according to the seriousness of the information. Incorrect information in relation to police charges etc. is regularly criticized,[184] whereas the Council decided not to criticize the term 'immigrant' in relation to a person born in Denmark and holding Danish citizenship.[185] The obligation to forward information that is correct goes together with the obligation to verify or at least to make a genuine research. The more reliable the source, the less reason for further verification, and of course the more serious allegations, the more need for verification and thorough research.[186]

365. The obligation to present information to those criticized and let them give their view ('contradiction') is a standard requirement and according to the present author's judgment an area in which the Press Council has succeeded in changing the general behaviour of the media. As an example, a headline in a tabloid newspaper ran 'X Municipality stinks' with a critical article concerning the Department for Family Matters. No one from the department was interviewed, and the Press Council criticized.[187] As another example, a newspaper ran stories indicating that a municipality's treatment of a person's case has led to that person's suicide. No one from the municipality was given the chance to comment on the accusations, which were largely undocumented. The Press Council expressed serious criticism.[188] Also information passed on by an interviewee must be checked if it contains allegations,[189] and the media is not exempted from the obligation to check itself when information is passed on from other media.[190] The Press Council is not very formal as to the requirements regarding how the contradiction is done as long as it is done.[191] Often persons do not want to comment, and the relevant criterion is whether the media has given them a chance to do so.[192] Sometimes persons are difficult to reach, and the Press Council emphasizes that genuine attempts must be made and the person must have some time to answer.[193] Often the person in question has certain requirements for speaking to a journalist, such as not this particular journalist or not this particular media etc. For the Press Council, the important thing is that the person has had a chance to give his/her comment. If that option is given,

184. Decisions 2008-6-622, 624 and 634, 2010-6-0947, 12-70-00260 and 16-70-01060 as examples.
185. Decision 2008-6-242.
186. Decision 8/2003: A detained person had the same name as a person known from a TV show. The media presented the information as if the known person were detained, and was, of course, criticized for not having checked the information. *See also* decision 2010-6-1018 and 2017-80-0002.
187. 68/2003.
188. 2017-80-0002.
189. 2007-6-464.
190. *PÅ* 2007, p. 20.
191. 2006-6-452. 11-70-00175 and 14-70-00628.
192. *See also Bergens Tidende v. Norway*, 2 May 2000. The ECtHR found it part of ethics of journalism that the criticized person was given an opportunity to present his views. In the actual case, the plastic surgeon did not make use of this option, for which the newspaper was not to blame.
193. 135/2002 and 11-70-00183. This rule was codified in the 2013 revision of the Guiding Rules.

the media is not criticized.[194] Sometimes it may be questioned who is the relevant person to comment. It is not sufficient to contact the company if a named person is criticized.[195]

366. In case of incorrect information, the media has an independent obligation to rectify. The rectification must be swift[196] and conspicuous.[197] It is also a requirement that there be a certain connection between headlines, contents bills, pictures and the actual article. In a programme on organic poultry farming, pictures were showed from non-organic farming where the chickens have less space etc., and the Press Council criticized. If illustrations are used that have no connection with the actual case, which is often the case, this must be indicated one way or the other. If it is not, the illustration will be criticized as misleading.

367. In cases of defamatory comments, the Press Council is very much in line with the ECtHR: even harsh comments are accepted if they have a factual background and the subject is of public interest, and the reporting of other persons' comments is accepted if it is obvious that they are particular persons' comments.[198] Editorials, reviews (often restaurant reviews) and letters to the editor have large room for commenting as they express the personal views of the authors. Here the Press Council does not require contradiction or the like.[199]

§3. Privacy

368. The Guiding Rules for the Ethics of Journalism stipulate that information which can infringe someone's right to privacy shall be avoided, unless clear public interest requires publication. In the preamble of the Guiding Rules, the importance of the media's news reporting is emphasized, and the Press Council gives much weight to issues of public interest.[200] Especially when the behaviour of the persons in question is reproachful, the media have more leeway. As examples: three brothers shared lottery tickets, and when their lot was drawn, two of them tried to deprive the third, reportedly backward brother, of his share. The story was covered including their names and the Press Council accepted, even though one could question whether the names of the ones involved were of public interest. However, the Council criticized the publishing of their addresses.[201] In another case, two shoplifters were discovered by the department store detective followed by a television crew.

194. 2004-6-114, 2005-6-268/269, 2008-5-645 and 2018-80-0143.
195. 2005-6-261.
196. 2006-6-366, one month not acceptable.
197. 2008-6-653 and 12-70-00216, where the display of the rectification was found not to be sufficiently conspicuous. In 2010-6-1023 it was criticized that the media had rectified an error in the online version of an article, but not the printed version. *See also* 15-70-00905.
198. 2004-6-155, 'ass lickers' accepted as comments from interviewed person's on other persons' behaviour.
199. 2004-6-102 (restaurant review), 2006-6-329/30 (editorial) and 2008-6-670 (letter to the editor).
200. 2006-6-426, the reporting of violence problems in families in the public interest. So is information about political groupings and their members' political views, 11-70-00131 and 11-70-00133.
201. 2003-6-99.

The incident was broadcasted and the persons were rather easily identifiable even when their eyes were barred. However, the Council, which in other cases is quite demanding as to the effectiveness of anonymity, did not criticize the television station.[202] It should be noted that defamatory information is also covered by the rule regarding privacy in the Guiding Rules.[203]

369. Genuinely, private affairs such as love affairs and child custody cases are conceived of as private, and the media will be criticized if they do not respect the privacy.[204]

370. Suicide is a sensitive matter, and the Press Council is rather strict. If close relations lodge a complaint, the Council will criticize even when the feature is a story told by friends.[205] There may be a generation gap: if the friends of a young suicide find release by telling the story, and the parents complain, the Press Council upholds the contention of the parents (the Council members being of the parents' age). Suspicions of suicide, reporting of suicides not including any personal approach and the filming of suicidal candidates are not accepted. In a case, a television station broadcasted the carrying away of a surviving suicide and justified its action by arguing that neither she nor her brother, who was present, protested. This was, of course, not accepted by the Council.[206] In a television programme concerning suicides among teenagers, a specific girl's name was made public against the family's will. The Press Council criticized.[207]

371. Often the disputed question is whether the identity of a particular person may be revealed. In cases of critique of public administration, leading officials must accept that their names are mentioned, whereas the names and identity of rank and file of public officials are normally protected. In other cases, the degree of reproachfulness plays an important part, and victims are better protected than perpetrators (*See also* below as regards reporting from courts etc.). If a person has identified himself/herself publicly or if the identity is already known, the Council usually does not censure the identification.

§4. Reporting from Courts

372. A whole section of the Guiding Rules is devoted to court and police reporting, an area in which the media's obligation to report may well infringe on the presumption of innocence and the right to privacy. The rules require a reasonably balanced reporting and a follow-up on the result. In the initial stages, this implies that the accused person's plead must be included. Only when the person has been

202. 111/1996.
203. *See*, e.g., 2009-6-0812 regarding a media's reporting without consent of a picture from a private arrangement where plaintiff applied a nazi symbol.
204. 119/2002, 15/2003, 11-70-00104 and 11-70-00126.
205. 2004-6-86.
206. 2005-6-266.
207. 15-70-00838.

convicted, the media may refer to the person as guilty. When the case has found its solution, especially of course in cases of acquittal or the police wavering charges, this information must appear if the media covered the initial stages, even though it is not a selling story anymore.

373. After judgment, the name and identity of the convicted may be released. Until then it is more problematic; the more important the case, the more the Press Council is likely to accept disclosure of identity.

374. The guiding rule to avoid the mentioning of a person's family history, occupation, race, nationality, creed or membership of organizations has created some controversies especially in relation to ethnic background. In one case, a young man from Somalia was sentenced to prison for rape, and afterwards his sisters were sentenced for menacing witnesses. When reporting on the second case, a newspaper mentioned that the girls were of Somali origin, which the Press Council (in a divided decision) criticized. The newspaper loyally published the decision, but in the editorial the newspaper claimed to persist in its practice. Even the Prime Minister, who is also the Minister of the Press, declared his support for the newspaper against the Press Council. The case was somewhat ridiculous in the sense that the origin of the sentenced brother was already known, and keeping the sisters' origin secret did not make much sense.[208] In a later case the same newspaper reported that a dancing instructor 'with dark complexion and long, black hair' was charged for sexual assault. The Press Council found the information acceptable arguing that it was merely information, not taking into consideration that the rule pertaining to ethnic origin etc. is exactly about factual information.[209]

§5. Hidden Camera

375. One area in which the Press Council has made a lot of decisions is regarding the use of hidden camera. Often it is not possible to obtain information by asking directly, and questions such as 'do you deal illegally with drugs' are not likely to bring forward any information. The use of hidden camera is therefore often a useful tool especially for television journalists. Until 2013 the Guiding Rules contained no specific rule regarding hidden camera, which resulted in the Press Council developing the legal position based on an interpretation of the rules regarding privacy. With the revision in 2013, a specific rule on hidden camera was included in the Guiding Rules. The rule codifies two of four conditions regarding use of hidden camera developed by the Press Council. The other two, however, still apply. The Press Council's practice is rather clear.

376. The use of hidden camera is as a point of departure to be avoided. This implies that the journalist must consider whether the relevant information may be obtained in an open way, which may often be the case. It may be more entertaining

208. 23/2002.
209. 2006-6-429.

for the involved journalists as well as the television viewers to watch programmes featuring the use of hidden camera, but this is not accepted by the Press Council. The Council is sensitive to the fact that the mere use of hidden camera implicitly alleges that something fishy is going on, cf. Case 14-70-00609, where it was criticized that a television programme included recordings made by hidden camera although the recordings did not document that anything critical was taken place. It should be noted that it is irrelevant for the Council whether the filming has taken place on a freely accessible location or not (*see* Chapter 3, §4 and the relevance of this distinction as regards the criminal nature of the act):

(1) *If* the information cannot be obtained by other means and *if* the information is of public relevance, then the use of hidden camera is acceptable according to the new rule in the Guiding Rules and the Council's practice. In 2006-6-360, recordings were made at a home for elderly people with a critical approach as regards the standards of care. The station had asked the manager of the institution to accept the making of a programme, which was rejected. However, the Press Council found that the information could not be gathered sufficiently in other ways, and that the subject, the treatment of elderly people, was of public interest.
(2) The ones unwittingly participating in the recording should have the option of commenting the recorded incidents before the actual broadcasting.
(3) The ones unwittingly participating in the recording should be made anonymous eventually by blurring voices as well as visual appearance. The requirements may vary according to the role of the ones participating. In the case dealing with the home for elderly people, the recording of the residents required extensive blurring, and, obviously, the broadcasting of washing a resident's behind was heavily criticized by the Press Council.[210] As for persons involved in critical activities, the Council still requires anonymity, but here black bars hiding the eyes may suffice.

377. The Supreme Court has rejected to issue an injunction in a case involving hidden camera.[211] A television station wanted to make a programme on an institution treating alcoholics. A journalist who had consumed sufficient alcohol to appear drunk called the institution, and the reception and hospitalization were filmed in secret. The television put the programme on the list and invited the unwitting participants for commenting an hour or so before the broadcasting of the programme. The filmed, rather than wanting to participate in the programme, made a request for an injunction, which was granted by the District Court. The Court argues that the recordings were done at a not freely accessible place, *see* the Penal Code section 264a (*see* Chapter 3, §4), and the Court finds that the issue in question is of public interest, but that (at least some of) the information could be obtained in other ways, and that the main participants had indicated their willingness freely to participate.

210. Later the journalists received a suspended sentence of fourteen days' imprisonment for this unnecessary breach of privacy (judgment by the Copenhagen City Court, 3 Jun. 2010).
211. *UfR* 2010.1853H. *See also* UfR 2012.1788H and UfR 2012.2328H.

The criteria for accepting hidden camera, set up by the Press Council, are not fulfilled. Thus, the Court actually employs ethics of journalism in a case dealing with injunction according to the law. However, the injunction is overruled by the Supreme Court which explicitly rejects that violation of ethics of journalism may constitute sufficient ground for issuing an injunction. Besides, the Supreme Court states that even if some of the recordings showed persons located at a not freely accessible place, the violation is of relatively minor importance seen in conjunction with media's right to report issues of public interest.

§6. The Significance of Agreements, Wishes and Consent

378. Journalists make all sorts of agreements when working: agreements to protect the sources, agreements as to which questions the interviewee will answer, etc. On the one hand, agreements may themselves be violating ethics of journalism, if, say, an advertiser is guaranteed favourable comments in the media. On the other hand, acceptable agreements must be adhered to, and the Press Council has criticized the publishing of pictures on the front page when the parties had agreed that no picture would be published.[212] Likewise, the Press Council has criticized when media have violated agreements regarding use of citations in a programme or article.[213] Also violating conditions for an interview has been criticized.

379. The indication of not wanting to be the object of public commenting is hardly relevant. If a case is of public interest, it is not for the involved to decide whether he/she wants to appear in the media.[214] On the contrary, it is for the media to inform the public, and withholding information of public interest is against a fundamental principle of ethics of journalism, as mentioned in the Guiding Rules. In other situations, the wishes of the involved should be respected. In a case the author of a letter to the editor had indicated that he did not want his letter to be edited. This was done anyway, which was against ethics of journalism.[215] Normally, newspapers announce that letters are subject to editing, and to do so is not a problem as long as it does not distort the content,[216] but in that particular case, the wishes of the author ought to be respected.

380. Consent is relevant especially in cases dealing with privacy. If a person has consented to appear in one media, he/she cannot prevent coverage in other media relating to the same story.[217] Whether consent to appear with one private story entails a right for the media also to cover other private stories may not be quite clear according to the Press Council.[218]

---

212. 2004-6-84. It was not a secret source, but the informant, a doctor, did not want her name published. The newspaper admitted the error (which is rather unusual).
213. 2009-6-0920 and 2017-70-01107.
214. *PÅ* 2001, 16.
215. 2004-6-94.
216. 2004-6-112.
217. 4/1999, 2006-6-334, 2007-6-478.
218. 2005-6-240. The courts are more strict, interpreting consent to the particular story, *see* Ch. 3, §4.

§7. Concluding Remarks

381. The Press Council makes decisions as to whether the content of the media is in accordance with ethics of journalism, not as to whether the content is unlawful, a point which is often stressed by the Council. Sometimes the decisions are very similar to the judgments of the courts, and in fact sometimes complainants use a critical decision from the Council as an argument in subsequent court proceedings.[219] But sometimes the two sets of rules and case law give different results. In cases involving hidden camera, the Press Council is critical unless the use of this means was necessary for the content of the feature, whereas the court obviously must consider whether an act is unlawful, and normally shooting photos and films of persons in public places is not unlawful. The Press Council is critical towards journalists violating agreements, but the agreements are usually not binding agreements in a legal sense, and there would be no sanction of such violations by the courts. Conversely, the Press Council is not likely to criticize behaviour even if it is criminal or if the purpose is to inform on public interest issues, and if considerations for privacy do not play a part. Thus, the courts have in quite a few cases (lightly) sanctioned journalists' criminal behaviour even if the purpose obviously was to obtain and disseminate information (*see* above Chapter 2, §4), but the behaviour is not violating ethics of journalism, on the contrary.

382. Sometimes views and points are drifting from one set of rules to another. The Press Council has in some privacy cases argued in relation to freely or non-freely accessible location,[220] a criterion set out in section 264a, but not necessarily relevant for ethics of journalism. And the courts have applied the consideration whether an act was necessary to obtain important information of public interest, a criterion first employed by the Press Council in relation to the use of hidden camera.[221]

383. It may not always be easy for journalists and media to act in a situation with several sets of rules operating: European human rights law (which constitutes a part of Danish law, but may not always fit well with statutory law), Danish law, especially criminal law, ethics of journalism according to the standards of the Press Council and local ethics and custom, whether explicit or not.

219. As an example: *UfR* 1987.859Ø.
220. 2004-6-62.
221. *UfR* 2008.671H: A journalist carrying a knife on a public location. *See* Ch. 2, §4.

Chapter 7. Copyright Protection in the Media Sector

§1. Introduction

384. Copyright provides the person who created a literary or artistic work (the author) with the exclusive right to control the work. Hence, the author of a literary text, a musical work, a film, a stage piece, art, etc. must consent to others' exploitation of the work. The existence of copyright must be viewed in light of the fact that creative works can be relatively easily copied and disseminated by others. The value of the work lies not in the physical appearance, but in the aesthetic and intellectual effort that underlies the work. Without a legal monopoly, the – often significant – intellectual effort does not stand in reasonable proportion to the risk that others steal the work and exploit it commercially.

385. The exclusive right ensures continued incentive for authors, musicians, artists and others to create literature, music, art, etc. to the benefit of themselves and society at large. A number of statutory limitations to the exclusive right ensure that society as a whole, regardless of the exclusivity, has access to the artistic creations against a reasonable remuneration to the author.

386. Copyright is of vital importance for the media industry, including the many new digital media services and platforms.[222] A very large part of the content on the media consists of literary or artistic works protected by copyright. A movie that appears on television, for instance, contains various copyrights, including the copyright of the author of the manuscript, the producer, the participating actors, the musical composer and the broadcaster who subsequently makes the movie available to the public.

387. The advent of the many new digital media services and platforms only means that the close relationship between media and copyright-protected works is likely to grow.

§2. Legal Sources

I. International Treaties

388. As literary and artistic works have always crossed national borders, and even more so in the digital age, there is a long tradition of international cooperation with regard to copyright. Denmark is a party to the most important international

222. *See* Trzaskowski (ed.) et al: *Internetretten* [*Internet Law*] (Ex Tuto Publishing, 2017), p 23. *See also* the EU Commission's communication on Copyright in the Knowledge Economy (COM 2009/532 final of 19 Oct. 2009).

treaties within the area of copyright, including the Berne Convention for the Protection of Literary and Artistic Works, the World Convention, the Rome Convention and the Agreement of Trade-Related Aspects of Intellectual Property Rights.[223]

II. EU Regulation

389. In recent years, the international harmonization, however, primarily occurred under the auspices of the EU, which has adopted a series of directives in the field of copyright. At the time of finalization of this update (November 2018), the most important EU Directives regarding copyright of relevance to the media sector are:

- Directive 2014/26/EU on collective management of copyrights and related rights.
- Directive 2004/48/EC on the enforcement of intellectual property right.
- Directive 2001/29/EC on the harmonization of certain aspects of copyright and related rights in the information society (in the following called the Infosoc Directive).
- Directive 96/9/EC on the legal protection of databases.
- Directive 93/83/EC of 27 September 1993 on the coordination of certain rules concerning copyright and rights related to copyright applicable to satellite broadcasting and cable retransmission.
- Directive 92/100/EC on renting rights and lending rights.

III. The Copyright Act

390. The present copyright Act is Consolidated Act No. 1144 of 23 October 2014 (the Copyright Act).[224,225] For many years there has been close cooperation between the Nordic countries (Denmark, Finland, Iceland, Norway and Sweden) with regard to copyright law. In recent years the Copyright Act has been increasingly influenced by EU law.

391. The geographical scope of the Act is laid down in the Copyright Act sections 85–88. In accordance with the general principle of territoriality, copyright protection under the Copyright Act requires a geographical connection to Denmark. The requirement is usually satisfied if the author is a Danish citizen, resident or

223. *See* Thomas Riis, *Intellectual Property Law in Denmark* (DJØF Publishing, 2012), 24.

224. Regarding the Danish Copyright Act in general, *see*, *inter alia*, Jens Schovsbo, Morten Rosenmeier & Clement Salung Petersen, *Intellectual Property Right* [*Immaterialret*] (DJØF Publishing, 2018), Ch. 2; Peter Schønning, *Ophavsretsloven med kommentarer* [*The Copyright Act with Commentaries*], 6th edn (KarnovGroup, 2016), and Thomas Riis, *Intellectual Property Law in Denmark* (DJØF Publishing, 2012), Ch. 1.

225. An unofficial English version is available at the Ministry of Culture's homepage www.kulturministeriet.dk.

headquartered in Denmark, or if the work is published first in Denmark or published in Denmark simultaneously with another country. EU/EEA residents are treated as Danish residents.

392. As a result of the commitments, Denmark has assumed under the international treaties and conventions, the geographical scope of the Act is extended so that foreign works are in general protected in Denmark similar to Danish works. In certain areas, however, it is a prerequisite that there is reciprocity, i.e., the country from which the work stems has also ratified the international conventions and thus is also bound by the rules on national treatment.[226]

393. The scope of the Act with regard to satellite broadcasting follows from Directive 93/83/EC, as implemented in section 87 of the Act. Pursuant hereto satellite broadcasting shall be deemed to occur in Denmark if the programme-carrying signals intended for reception by the public under the control and responsibility of a broadcaster in Denmark are introduced into an uninterrupted chain of communication leading to the satellite and down towards the earth. Satellite broadcasting shall also be deemed to occur in Denmark if the introduction in the chain of communication occurs in a State that is not a member of the European Economic Area and which does not provide the level of protection provided for under Directive 93/83/EEC in the following cases:

- if the programme-carrying signals are transmitted to the satellite from an uplink station situated in Denmark;
- if there is no use of an uplink station situated in an EEA Member State and a broadcaster with its headquarters in Denmark has commissioned the introduction into the chain of communication.

§3. What Is Protected by Copyright?

394. According to the Copyright Act section 1(1), copyright is attached to literary or artistic works, including all kinds of literature (novels, articles, poems, interviews, etc.), musical works, stage works, cinematographic works, programmes made for TV, photographic works, fine arts, applied art and architecture. The enumeration in paragraph 1 is not exhaustive.

395. Even if it is not explicitly stated in the Copyright Act, the central requirement in determining if a literary or artistic work enjoys copyright protection is whether the work is *original*, i.e., the result of the author's own intellectual creative contribution.[227] The originality requirement, which is interpreted in accordance with EU copyright law and practice, is not an aesthetic or artistic assessment of the quality of work, but the author must have made his/her unique mark on the work.

---

226. *See* Jens Schovsbo & Morten Rosenmeier, *Immaterialret* [*Intellectual Property Right Law*] (Jurist- og Økonomforbundets Forlag, 2015), 58.
227. *See* Thomas Riis, *Intellectual Property Law in Denmark* (DJØF Publishing, 2012), 29.

396. In practice, most literary and artistic creations are considered as original. A title of a work can in itself be protected if it is sufficiently original. Photographic pictures are protected by copyright if the originality requirement is satisfied; otherwise, pictures are protected by the neighbouring right in section 70.

397. There are no conditions other than the originality requirement and a work that fulfils this requirement automatically enjoys copyright protection. Hence, a copyright neither can nor must be registered under Danish law. The often applied copyright notice © is not required in order to obtain protection, but may serve the interest of the author by indicating that the right owner regards the work as copyright protected and intends to enforce the right.

398. Copyright exists regardless of whether a work is created in analogue or digital form, including on the Internet, or in physical form, e.g., on paper or canvas. Copyright law is, in other words, technology-neutral.[228] What matters is only whether the basic requirement of originality is met, in which case, for example, a journalistic article, a novel, a musical work or a movie is protected, also when it is created or transmitted to the Internet or other digital media.

399. As the creation of a literary or artistic work is linked to a human effort, only individuals can claim copyright. Copyright can only be claimed by the author of the work. Chapter 5 of the Copyright Act, however, also provides independent rights to persons other than the author of the work, so-called *neighbouring rights*, including performers who take part in the creation or projection of works (such as musicians, singers, actors, etc.), producers of audio and video recordings (record and film companies and the like), broadcasting companies and photographers.

400. Copyright can be assigned by contract as any other property right pursuant to section 53(1). The assignment follows the general principles of contract law. Section 53(2) states that the transfer of a copy of a work does not, unless otherwise agreed, include the transfer of the copyright itself.

401. In case of assignment, section 53(3) establishes an interpretative rule according to which agreements regarding assignment of copyright are generally subject to a restrictive interpretation. Thus, if the author has consented to third-party use of the works in certain contexts, such as radio broadcasting of a musical work, the agreement would be interpreted as not conferring the right to other forms of exploitation not explicitly described in the agreement, e.g., webcasting.

228. This principle was expressly stated with the implementation of the Infosoc Directive, but was held to exist even before.

402. If no agreement on assignment exists, the main rule is that copyright to a work produced as part of an employment relationship can only be transferred to the extent it is necessary considering the employer's ordinary activities.[229]

§4. Scope of Copyright

I. Exploitation Rights

403. Pursuant to section 2, copyright implies the exclusive right to control the work by reproducing it or making it available to the public. Hence, if someone other than the author wants to exploit the work, it requires permission from the author. The reproduction right also implies that the author has exclusive right to produce digital copies of analogue work (and vice versa). This is important with regard to the media sector where analogue works, e.g., books, articles, radio and television programmes increasingly are being digitized.

404. Pursuant to section 4(1), adaptations of existing works are protected as independent works. The author of the adaptation has a right to control his/her work, but is without prejudice to the copyright to the original work. The same applies to compilations of existing works or parts thereof, *see* section 5.

405. Preparation of a new and independent work which is inspired by a protected work's underlying ideas and thoughts is not an infringement of the original work, *see* section 4(2). In other words, only the specific expression of a work is protected.[230]

406. The author's exclusive right to make the work available to the public covers three different forms of exploitation of the work, *see* section 2(3) and (4): (1) the public distribution of copies (distribution rights), e.g., by sale, lending or rental; (2) public exhibition of copies (such as viewing a work of art at an exhibition or presentation of a book in a public library); and (3) public performance of the work, including broadcasting of radio and television programmes and making works available to the public on demand via the Internet or other digital networks.

II. Moral Rights

407. The Copyright Act section 3 provides the author with the so-called moral rights. These consist of the right of paternity and the right of integrity. The right of paternity implies that when a work is exploited the author's name shall be stated to

229. *UfR* 1978.901H, where the publishing of a newspaper article in a book, in the absence of an agreement, required the journalist's consent. *See also UfR* 1994.349H, where the rerun of a TV programme was held to be part of the broadcaster's ordinary activities.
230. Hence, the mere idea of painting a picture of a certain motif, or making a movie about a certain event, is not protectable under copyright.

the extent and in the manner required by proper use. Proper use means that if it is impossible, unreasonably burdensome or unreasonably disturbing in the context to state the name, it will not constitute an infringement of copyright not to do so.

408. The right of integrity implies that the work must not be altered or made available to the public in a manner or in a context which is prejudicial to the author's literary or artistic reputation, or to his/her individuality.[231] Use of works in commercials will normally be an infringement. The rights of paternity and integrity cannot be waived except in respect of a use of the work which is limited in nature and extent, *see* section 3(3).

§5. Limitations on Copyright

409. In order to balance the author's interest in obtaining an economic return of the work with society's interest in a reasonable exploitation of the work, Chapter 2 of the Copyright Act contains a number of limitations or exemptions to copyright. The most important of these in relation to the media sector are outlined below. The limitations regarding temporary reproductions (section 11a) and radio and TV programmes (sections 30–35) are described in Parts 6 and 7.

410. Under Article 5(5) of the Infosoc Directive exceptions to copyright: (1) can only be applied in certain special cases; (2) must not conflict with the normal exploitation of the work; and (3) must not unreasonably prejudice the legitimate interests of the right holder. Article 5(5) has not explicitly been implemented into Danish law, but it follows from the Member States' general obligation to interpret national law in conformity with EU law that the provision also applies in Danish law. The following limitations to the Danish Copyright Act should be read with that in mind.

I. Reproduction for Private Use

411. According to section 12(1), anyone is entitled to make or have made, for private purposes, single copies of works which have been made public if this is not done for commercial purposes. This, in practice very important, exception means that natural persons (as distinct from legal persons) without the author's consent can make individual copies for himself/herself and his/her family, friends and acquaintances. Copies taken for private use must not be used for any other purpose; i.e., for distribution or for public performance.

231. In *UfR* 1979.685Ø the soundtrack of a television programme (but not the programme itself) was performed at a political meeting. The right of integrity was found to be violated.

412. It should be noted that the right to make reproductions for private use does not provide the right to, e.g., make copies of computer programs and databases in digital form. Here, the specific rules on computer programs in sections 36–37 apply.[232]

413. For types of work other than computer programmes and databases the reproduction in digital form (whether it be from an analogue or digital original) is only permitted if it is done exclusively for the personal use of the copying person himself/herself or his/her household, *see* section 12(2)(5). This provision implies that it is permissible to take copies of a CD or DVD to the person or household's PC, media player, car, summer residence, etc., but not to friends and acquaintances outside the household.

414. The reproduction right according to section 12(2)(5) is further limited by section 12(3), which states that the right does not include digital copies on the basis of a copy that has been borrowed or hired. This means that it is not allowed to make a digital copy of copies which are borrowed from the library or from friends or acquaintances.

415. As it appears, the right to make copies of digital works is stricter than the general right to make copies for private use under section 12(1). This is due to the significant risk of uncontrollable distribution connected to digital copying, and the fact that the proliferation of CD burners, MP3 players, etc. has made digital copying for private purposes both easy and cheap. However, the clear tendency now towards using streaming media (Spotify, Netflix, YouTube etc.) means that copying for private use is decreasing.

II. Quotations

416. Under section 22 of the Copyright Act it is permitted to quote from a work, which has been made public, in accordance with proper usage and to the extent required for the purpose. The right to quote applies for all works but has inherently greater importance for literary works. Appliance of the quotation right requires that the source shall be indicated in accordance with proper usage, *see* section 11(2).

417. The conditions laid down in section 22 mean that the provision has a rather narrow scope. Generally, the quotation must be fair in relation to the work which is quoted from. This implies that the quotation must comprise of a small part of that which is quoted from. Apart from this, there are no firm rules on the precise scope of the quotation right, which then must depend on a case-by-case assessment.

418. Considerations to the freedom of expression and information imply that the press has rather wide access to the usage of quotations from other news media. The same is assumed to be the case for product reviews and debate in news media. The

232. Implementing Art. 5 of Directive 91/250/EC on the legal protection of computer programs.

right to quote from music and films is relatively limited.[233] The fairness requirement is normally a barrier to apply quotes in advertising. Works of art and 'still' pictures from movies are not covered by section 22, as it is not possible to quote from these types of works.

419. The quotation rule also applies to works in digital media. However, the right to quote is probably even stricter when it comes to digital content due to the significant possibility to copy, manipulate and exploit digital content. This, too, depends on case-by-case assessment.[234] Sampling, i.e., the use of small parts of musical works in a new work, is in general not a lawful quotation under section 22.

III. Report of Current Events

420. In order to secure the media's right to freedom of information, section 25 stipulates that if performance or exhibition of a work is part of a current event and is used in film, radio or television, the work may be included to the extent the work forms a natural part of the reporting of the current event. It is, e.g., permitted in a television news programme to broadcast a live performance from a musical festival, however, only to the extent that it is a natural step in the news reporting of current events.[235]

421. The wording of the provision only covers film, radio and television. New media like the Internet is not covered. However, a radio or television programme in which a performance or exhibition is included in compliance with section 25 may subsequently be made available on the Internet or other digital media.

IV. Access to Public Proceedings and Documents

422. In order to safeguard the freedom of information and a free debate, section 26 determines that proceedings in Parliament, municipal councils and other elected public authorities, in judicial proceedings and in public meetings held to discuss general matters may be used without the author's consent. However, the author shall have the exclusive right to publish compilations of his/her own statements.

423. In addition, where copies of copyright-protected works have come in to an administrative authority or court in connection with its activities, the copyright does

233. *See UfR* 1999.547Ø where a video rental store's use of short film trailers was found to fall outside the scope of s. 22.
234. In *UfR* 1998.525Ø 1,500 samples of thirty to forty seconds of musical works were made available on a website. The Court held this to fall outside the scope of s. 22.
235. It is a requirement that there is a timely connection between the current event where the work is performed, and the news reporting. This precludes videotaping for subsequent distribution of a current event broadcasted in a news programme on TV, *see UfR* 1990.579Ø.

not prevent others from demanding access to copies, including demanding a transcript or a copy, in accordance with the provisions of the legislation on access to public documents, *see* section 27.[236] The same shall apply to works produced within the administrative authority or court.

424. According to section 28, copyright-protected works can also – to the extent justified by the purpose – be used in connection with: (a) judicial proceedings and proceedings before administrative tribunals; and (b) proceedings within public authorities and institutions under Parliament.

V. Distribution of Copies

425. Section 19(1) establishes that where a copy of a work has been sold or otherwise assigned to others within the European Economic Area with the consent of the author, the copy may be further distributed. In such case, the exclusive right to that particular copy (but not the copyright as such) is said to be exhausted.

426. It is important to emphasize that section 19 only covers the transfer of *physical* copies of the work, not digital. Hence, services that are disseminated via the Internet in digital form, such as music or movie files, are not covered. Case law from the Court of Justice from the EU indicates, however, a tendency to equate physical and digital copies.[237] Moreover, the rule of exhaustion does not apply to distribution to the general public through rental, *see* subsection 2. Further, copies of cinematographic works and copies of computer programs in digitized form may not be distributed to the public through lending without the consent of the author, *see* subsection 3. However, this does not apply if a copy of a computer program in digitized form constitutes a part of a literary work and is lent together with it.

427. Denmark has adopted the principle of regional exhaustion, *see* the wording of section 19(1), according to which the exhaustion only occurs within the EEA. Accordingly, parallel imports throughout the Community are permitted, but the right holder retains protection against parallel imports from third countries.[238]

VI. Extended Collective Licence Agreements and Compulsory Licences

428. Exploitation of a copyright-protected work requires as a main rule an individual agreement with the author. However, conclusion of individual agreements is

---

236. The rules on access to public documents are described in Ch. 5.
237. Cf. Case C128/11, *UsedSoft*, and Case C-174-15, *Openbare Bibliotheken*.
238. In Case C-479/04, *Laserdisken ApS v. Kulturministeriet*, the Danish company Laserdisken ApS claimed that Art. 4(2) of the Infosoc Directive was invalid and did not preclude a Member State from retaining international exhaustion. The CJEU, however, rejected both claims.

not feasible when there is mass use of works, as for example, is the case of broadcasting entities' use of musical works in radio and television programmes or cable or satellite retransmission of works in radio and television programmes.

429. Therefore, section 50 of the Copyright Act establishes a system of so-called extended collective licence agreements where collective organizations – representing the right holders on behalf of their members – enter into agreements with users of copyright-protected works, specifying the permitted use of the works and the conditions in this respect.

430. Due to the statutory provisions on the extended collective licence agreements, the effects of the collective agreements are extended to right holders who are not represented by the collective organizations, *see* section 50(1). For these, the licensing agreement takes character of a compulsory licensing agreement (*see* below). This way exploitation of works can be done without the authors' individual consent and include all right holders of works of that specific nature, also those who are not members of the particular collective organization.

431. The collective organizations must be approved by the Ministry of Culture and represent a substantial part of the right holders, *see* section 50(3).[239] More detailed provisions regarding the collective organizations are laid down in a special act[240] implementing Directive 2014/26/EU on Collective Rights Management.

§6. Duration of Copyright

432. Copyright lasts for seventy years after the year of the author's death, *see* section 63. Where there is more than one author, the right lasts for seventy years after the last survivor. Neighbouring rights typically last for fifty years after the first performance, publication or disclosure took place. Upon expiration, copyright-protected work can freely be used without the consent of the author.

§7. Enforcement

433. Chapter 7 of the Copyright Act contains rules on sanctions in case of violations of copyright. Gross or negligent violations of copyright may be punishable by fines pursuant to section 76. In case of copyright piracy involving particularly aggravating circumstances, punishment may increase to imprisonment in one year and six months.

239. Whether the organization represents a 'substantial' part in conditioned on, *inter alia*, the number of members and represented works. It is not a condition that more than half of the authors are represented.
240. Act No. 321/2016.

434. It is relatively rare that penalties are imposed for copyright violations. The most common sanction is the provision of an adequate remuneration (compensation) for the exploitation of the work and compensation for any additional damage caused by the violation, *see* section 83. When setting the additional damages consideration shall be given to such matters as the infringed party's loss of profits and the offender's unfair profits. Compensation can also be set to the infringed party for non-financial damage.

435. Pursuant to section 84, the court can by sentence decide that copies infringing copyright-protected works shall be recalled or removed from the channels of commerce, be destroyed or be handed over to the infringed party.

436. In order to stop the infringing activities as soon as possible, without having to wait for a judgment in a normal trial, cases of copyright infringement frequently start with the infringed party applying for a preliminary injunction against the violation.

§8. Special Provisions Regarding Radio and Television

I. Radio and Television Broadcasts

437. Pursuant to section 69(1), a radio or television broadcast may not be rebroadcast by others or in any other manner be performed in public without the consent of the broadcaster; nor may the broadcast, without consent, be photographed or recorded on tape, film or any other device by means of which it can be reproduced.

438. Section 69 provides broadcasting organizations with the exclusive right of their broadcasts. The exclusive right only covers the broadcast as a technical signal. The content of the broadcast is not covered by the exclusive right. If the content is created by a third party or includes works created by a third party, the third party therefore acquires copyright to this content subject to the general rules of the Copyright Act, in particular section 1, and the radio or television enterprise must through conclusion of individual agreements or extended collective licence agreements acquire the necessary rights to the exploitation of the works. If the broadcasting enterprise itself has created the content, the copyright of course belongs to the broadcasting enterprise itself.

439. The exclusive right to broadcasts has a duration of fifty years after the end of the year in which the broadcast took place, *see* section 69(2). Section 69(3) states that a number of the limitations to copyright, including the right to reproduction for private use shall apply *mutatis mutandis* to the right to broadcasts.

II. Web- and Simulcasting

440. It is becoming increasingly common for broadcasters to make programmes available on their websites on the Internet (webcasting), either simultaneously with the primary broadcast (in which case it is often called simulcasting), or, what is more common, at a subsequent time as on-demand services. Section 2(4)(1)[241] expressly states that copyright-protected works which are made available on demand (point to point) on the Internet, mobile phones or other interactive media are considered public performances, and thus are covered by copyright. Because broadcasters as described according to section 69 have the exclusive right to make public performances of the broadcasts, the right also includes making the broadcasts available on the Internet.

III. Public Service Broadcasters' Right to Use Protected Works in Broadcasts

441. In order to fulfil their public service obligations, public service broadcasters need to use a substantial amount of copyright-protected works, including music, in their broadcasts. It is therefore necessary to have flexible rules that ensure that the public service broadcasters can easily get access to the relevant works while at the same time ensuring that authors' interests, including the right to equitable remuneration for exploitation, are protected.

442. To that end, section 30(1) stipulates that the public service broadcasters (DR, TV2 and the regional TV2 companies) are entitled to broadcast published works provided the requirements regarding extended collective licence according to section 50 (*see* above) have been met.[242] Hence, the public service broadcasters can, via agreements with the relevant collective right holder organizations, acquire the right to use all the relevant works at an agreed fee, also with regard to authors who are not represented by the various organizations.

443. The right does not apply to dramatic or cinematographic works. Although the Copyright Act does not explicitly state so, the right does also not apply to programmes made available on demand on the Internet and other interactive platforms.[243] Further, the right under section 30(1) does not apply where an unrepresented right holder has prohibited the broadcaster to deploy the work, *see* section 30(2).

241. Corresponding with the Infosoc Directive Art. 3(1).
242. Pursuant to s. 30(3) the extended collective licence agreement can be expanded to include other broadcasters than public service broadcasters. However, this option has not been utilized.
243. *See* Søren Sandfeld Jakobsen, *Lærebog i elektronisk medieret* [*Textbook of Electronic Media Law*] (Jurist- og Økonomforbundets Forlag, 2006), 280 ff.

444. The right under paragraph 1 neither applies to broadcasts transmitted via satellite, unless the broadcaster makes a simultaneous broadcast via a terrestrial network, *see* section 30(3).[244] The purpose with this rule is to safeguard right holders who may have concluded agreements on the exploitation of the rights to different parties in different countries. If the statutorily extended collected licence agreement covered primary transmission by satellite only, these right holders would not be able to avoid the works from being transmitted via satellite to other countries in violation of the concluded agreements. For satellite transmission the public service broadcasters therefore have to obtain individual licences from authors who are not represented by a collective organization.

IV. Public Service Broadcasters' Use of Their Archives on Demand

445. Section 30a stipulates that works which have been made public and are a part of the public service broadcasters' own productions can be repeated and made available on demand, provided that the requirements regarding extended collective licence according to section 50 have been met. The right also applies to the making of copies which are necessary for the reproduction. The author may issue a prohibition to the broadcaster against the reproduction of the work.

446. The right according to section 30a does, however, only apply to works which are part of productions broadcast before 1 January 2007. The making available of works after this date is not covered by a statutory-based extended collective licence and is hence conditioned on conclusion of individual licence agreements with all involved right holders.

V. Ephemeral Recordings

447. Under section 31, broadcasters may for the purpose of their broadcasts record works on tape, film or any other device that can reproduce them provided they have the right to broadcast the works in question.[245] As most broadcasts are not made 'live', but are recorded and transmitted at a later time, a statutory right to make such ephemeral recordings is necessary in order not to violate the right holders' right of reproduction according to section 2. Digital recordings are also covered.[246] The provision applies to all broadcasters, not just public service broadcasters.

244. The provision corresponds with Art. 3(2) of Directive 93/83/EC of 27 Sep. 1993 on the coordination of certain rules concerning copyright and rights related to copyright applicable to satellite broadcasting and cable retransmission.
245. The provision corresponds with Art. 11*bis*(3) of the Berne Convention.
246. *See UfR* 2003.284H where ephemeral recordings of thousands of music works and other sound recordings on a digital hard disk were found not to be a violation of s. 31.

VI. Broadcast of Debate Programmes

448. Section 32 states that broadcasts of debate programmes in which general questions are discussed may be used without the consent of the author. However, the author shall have the exclusive right to publish compilations of his/her own statements.

VII. Cable Retransmissions

449. Cable retransmission of terrestrial radio and television broadcasts is regarded as a renewed public performance of the works and thus requires consent of the authors, *see* section 2.[247] This constitutes a problem for the cable companies who, unlike broadcasters, have no influence on the programmes which are retransmitted and therefore have no real opportunity to clear the relevant rights by individual contracts.

450. Accordingly, section 35(1) establishes an extended collective licence agreement for cable retransmission, *see* section 50 (described above). It is a condition of the licence agreement that the cable retransmission takes place simultaneously with the terrestrial broadcast and without alteration. The retransmission right under section 35(1) applies to all types of protected works, but does not apply to rights held by broadcasters (in particular the right pursuant to section 69). In 2014, the provision in section 35 was amended in order to cover certain forms of digital retransmission of radio and television broadcasts.[248]

VIII. Use of Sound Recordings in Broadcasts

451. Section 68 establishes a compulsory licence for broadcasters to use published sound recordings in broadcasts on radio and television. The compulsory licence is a restriction on the exclusive rights of performing artists and producers of sound recordings according to sections 65 and 66. Their rights are hence reduced to a right to remuneration. In case of disagreement, the remuneration is determined by the Copyright Licensing Board pursuant to section 47.

247. In accordance with Art. 11*bis* of the Berne Convention. *See also* Arts 8 and 9 of Directive 93/83/EC.
248. Cf. Amendment Act No. 741 of 25 Jun. 2014.

Part III. Regulation of AVMS

Chapter 1. The Broadcasting Act

§1. Historical Background: From State Monopoly to a (Partly) Free Market

452. The first radio broadcasting act was implemented in 1926.[249] In 1959, television was incorporated in the Act on the same basic principles that applied to radio, i.e., with the exclusive right of the State – via the state-owned broadcasting institution DR (formerly called DR) – to provide programme services which were funded through a public levy called radio and television licence.

453. The state exclusivity was primarily motivated by the fact that radio and television broadcasting via the then only existing broadcasting network, the analogue terrestrial broadcasting network, was based on a scarce resource, namely the number of radio frequencies assigned to Denmark, which was regarded as a public good that the state was best suited to manage.

454. In exchange for the exclusive right DR was imposed an obligation to provide public service for all the people, i.e., provide programmes that were versatile, cultural and informative. A designated board, which was partly politically appointed, was established in order to control that the programme planning fulfilled the public service remit. Hence, legislation on radio and television was in the first many years in fact a law on one institution: the public monopoly, DR.

455. The developments in the 1960s and 1970s of cable and satellite networks created new ways of transmission compared to traditional terrestrial broadcasting, which allowed a multiplication of the number of radio and television channels available to households. Until then only a handful of Swedish, Norwegian and German television channels could be received through the surplus of signals pouring into the Danish territory from our neighbouring countries' terrestrial transmitters. Some foreign radio stations were also available to Danish listeners through medium and long wave frequencies.

---

249. *See* in detail Lars M. Banke et al., *Radio- og tv-lovgivning* [*Radio and Television Regulation*] (Thomson Publishing, 2004) and Søren Sandfeld Jakobsen & Sten Schaumburg Müller, *Medieretten* [*Media Law*] (Jurist- og Økonomforbundets Forlag, 2013), Ch. 12.

456. Now, using cable networks and satellites, an increasing number of broadcasting channels could be transported from abroad to the Danish households. This changed significantly the technological prerequisites for the state monopoly, which, although somewhat slower, affected the political considerations behind the legislation, as it became increasingly difficult to defend the state monopoly on broadcasting.

457. In the 1980s and onwards, this led to gradual but constant liberalizations of the broadcasting legislation. First, the Danish broadcasting market was opened up in relation to cable and satellite channels transmitted from abroad.

458. Second, DR's monopoly on national broadcasting was abolished through the introduction of local radio and television in the mid-1980s, and, in particular, the establishment of the nationwide TV2 in 1988. In 1992, the Danish market in general opened since it was permitted for others than DR and TV2 to provide programme services from the Danish territory via satellite or cable.

459. In 2000, and again in 2011, the fourth, fifth and sixth nationwide radio channel (the first three are allotted by statute to DR) were awarded to the market subject to a public tender. As certain public service obligations are attached to these channels, this relatively small amendment represented a significant innovation in relation to the traditional notion of public service because it means that public service is no longer closely linked to specific institutions (DR/TV2).

460. Further, in 2006, a special 'public service pool' in the amount of DKK 75 million was established to support the production of Danish television drama and documentaries. Only commercial broadcasters can receive funding from the special pool. The pool, which has since been increased, was a first step in linking public service funds to specific types of content rather than specific institutions.

461. Along with the liberalization of the regulation due to technological developments and increased competition on the broadcasting market, the political influence on the DR's management and programme planning was also relaxed. Today, DR's Board, which is still politically appointed, must not interfere in editorial decisions regarding the programme service and the daily financial and administrative management.

462. The establishment in 1988 of the state-owned public service broadcaster TV2 introduced not only competition on nationwide, public service television in Denmark, but also the use of advertising in the Danish broadcasting regulation – something that had hitherto been forbidden (and still is with respect to DR). However, the Danish rules on advertising were – and to some extent still are – more strict than the minimum rules set forth in the Directive on AVMS Directive EU regulation.

463. The implementation of the the AVMS Directive resulted in the Danish television advertising rules being adjusted more to the EU rules. However, differences still exist, as explained below. It should be noted that a revision to the AVMS Directive was adopted in November 2018.[250] As the update of this publication ended shortly before, and as no draft implementation act has been presented yet, the revised AVMS Directive will only be briefly mentioned.

464. In recent years the increasing media convergence and the development of video on demand and streaming media has led to changes to the Broadcasting Act. For example, DR and TV2 are authorized to diversifying into digital media platforms and to pursue new services such as video on demand, webcasting and podcast. Moreover, by 1 November 2009 Denmark switched completely from analogue to digital signal on the terrestrial television network.

465. In addition, the implementation of the AVMS Directive represented a huge step into the online world, as it means that the former sharp distinction between broadcasting (linear transmission of content) and programme services made available online (on demand) is abolished.

§2. The Broadcasting Act

I. Scope

A. Material Scope

466. The Broadcasting Act[251] (the Act) applies to the provision of programme services. After the implementation of the AVMS Directive,[252] the notion of programme services covers not only traditional broadcasting, i.e., the provision of radio and television programmes to the general public (point-to-multipoint)[253] regardless of the transmission platform (terrestrial, cable, satellite, Internet or other IP-based networks), but also provision of on-demand (point-to-point)[254] AVMS, *see* section 2.

467. In order to be an on-demand audiovisual media service comprised by section 2[255] of the Act, several conditions must be fulfilled. Most of these conditions do not appear expressly in the Act, but can be derived from the preparatory work and the AVMS Directive. First, the service must have a *commercial purpose.* Audiovisual content which is purely private in nature, e.g., a private website with video clips, is thus not covered. Next, the service must have the same basic character as

250. Directive 2018/1808/EC.
251. Consolidated Act No. 444 of 8 May 2018 with subsequent amendments.
252. Directive 2007/65/EC, implemented by Act No. 1269 of 16 Dec. 2009.
253. That is, one-way communication from the radio broadcaster to an unspecified group of recipients who cannot communicate back to the sender and thus have no influence on either the content or timing of the transmission.
254. That is, communication directly to a specific recipient on the basis of the recipient's individual request thereof.
255. Transposing the AVMS Directive Art. 1.

a traditional *mass medium,* i.e., include information, entertainment or education targeted at the general public. Services that are directed against a limited number of recipients (including e-mail-based services, newsgroups, chat services, etc.) thus fall outside.

468. The requirement that the service must be treated as a mass medium also means that the service must be subject to *editorial control,* i.e., the service provider must exercise effective control over the selection and composition of the displayed content. This implies that 'social' or 'user generated' services (e.g., weblogs, services like Facebook, YouTube etc.), which allow the users of the service to make content available to other users of the service without the service provider's prior control, were previously not covered. However, this has changed with the 2018 revision of the Directive, where so-called 'video sharing platforms' are now covered by parts of the Directive.[256]

469. Last but not least, the service must include 'programmes', which according to the directive means a quantity of moving images with or without sound constituting an individual unit in a single programme plan or a catalogue which in form and content can be compared with a conventional television programme. This condition does not seem quite clear, especially when the directive also insists that the programme concept is to be interpreted dynamically and take account of the television media's continued development.

470. The extension of scope from traditional broadcasting to AVMS represents an essential change of paradigm in European and Danish broadcasting regulation, as the Directive breaks with the idea that AVMS, by definition, consist of traditional broadcast media, i.e., point-to-multipoint services. Now, on-demand-based AVMS and video sharing platforms are included under the regulation. Hence, the regulation now takes a technology neutral approach where the character of the content is determining for the application of the regulation – not the technological platform over which the content is transmitted.

471. However, the step into the on-demand world is in practice probably relatively modest. The many conditions attached to the notion of AVMS imply that – at least in the contemporary media environment – in fact only a handful of on-demand services will be covered by the new framework (i.e., only those who have significant similarities with traditional broadcasting services, e.g., VOD services like Netflix).[257]

472. Moreover, not all the rules in the Directive/the Act apply to on-demand-based AVMS.[258] Only a few, relatively soft 'ground rules' apply to on-demand services, including requirements regarding identification of the service provider (name, contact address, etc.), a prohibition regarding programmes which encourage hatred

256. Cf Directive 2018/1808/EU Art. 1, subs 1, litra b) aa).
257. *See* more detailed Søren Sandfeld Jakobsen in *UfR* 2008B.68ff.
258. *See* Ch. IIB of the Directive.

based on race, sex, religion or nationality and some basic requirements for the content of advertisements, including a requirement that on-demand advertisements must be clearly identifiable as such, must not discriminate and must not be harmful to minors. The rules on product placement, *see* below Chapter 4, §4, also apply to on-demand-based media services. The rest of the rules applicable to programme content still only apply to traditional broadcasting, i.e., point-to-multipoint services.

473. The Act distinguishes between provision of programme services (content) and the mere distribution of programmes (e.g., by cable TV operators), *see* Chapter 2 of the Act and further below. The Act only contains a few provisions regarding distribution, as distribution of programme services – like other electronic communication services – is primarily regulated in the telecommunications regulation.

B. Territorial Scope: The Country of Origin Principle

474. When radio and television programmes can be transmitted and received across national borders, the question arises which country's law regulates the broadcast – is it the law in the country from where the transmission takes place or the country where it is received?[259] The issue is governed by the so-called country of origin principle, originally set forth in the 1989 TV without Frontiers Directive and continued in the AVMS Directive with the extension that the principle now also applies to on-demand-based media services covered by the Directive.[260] The country of origin principle in the AVMS Directive is transposed into the Broadcasting Act.[261]

475. The country of origin principle implies first that a broadcaster is subject to the regulation – and the powers of the controlling authorities – in the country where it is legally established (the principle of home country control). Second, other Member States must not hinder retransmission of broadcasts from broadcasters legally established under the jurisdiction of other Member States, but must mutually recognize broadcasts from other countries (mutual recognition).

476. The country of origin principle means that a broadcaster is exclusively governed by the laws of the country where it is established, regardless of which countries receive the transmissions. It is, however, important to note that this only applies to broadcasters (as opposed to, e.g., an advertiser) and to issues covered by the AVMS Directive (i.e., in particular advertising and sponsorship and protection of minors and the public order).[262]

---

259. *See* Lars M. Banke et al., *Radio- og tv-lovgivning* [*Radio and Television Regulation*] (Thomson Publishing, 2004), 293 et seq., and Jakobsen & Schaumburg-Müller, *Medieretten [Media Law]* (Jurist- og Økonomforbundets Forlag, 2013), 616 et seq.
260. *See* Art. 2 and 2a.
261. Cf. Executive Order No. 697/2016 s. 2.
262. *See* the CJEU in united Cases C34-C36/95 (*De Agostini*).

477. With regard to disputes concerning matters that are not regulated by the Directive, and do not involve the broadcaster, the question of jurisdiction and applicable law must be determined on basis of the general principles of jurisdiction in private international law.

478. The country where a broadcaster is considered to be established in accordance with the country of origin principle is the country where the headquarters are located and where the editorial decisions regarding the programme planning are made. This again is determined based on several criteria, including particularly the country where a significant proportion of the staff works.[263]

479. The consequence of the country of origin principle is that a television channel which in all relevant matters – language, content, commercials – is targeted at viewers in one Member State can be subject to the exclusive jurisdiction of another Member State, namely the country where it is established (if different from the recipient country). Most of the commercial broadcasters who are present in Denmark with channels especially targeted at Danish viewers, are established in other EU countries, notably the UK, and thus fall outside of Danish jurisdiction according to the Broadcasting Act. The same goes for many providers of on-demand audiovisual services present in Denmark.

480. Obviously, this creates a risk of 'forum shopping' where a broadcaster establishes itself in one Member State specifically to circumvent the more strict rules of another Member State to which the broadcaster wants to direct its transmissions.[264]

481. In case of abuse of the country of origin principle, Member States can derogate from the country of origin principle and claim jurisdiction over a foreign broadcaster transmitting to its territory. Pursuant to the AVMS Directive the derogation presupposes a prior dialogue between the two involved Member States (the country of establishment and the recipient country) and the EU Commission, *see* Article 3, paragraphs 2–6.[265]

263. *See* Art. 2 of the Directive.
264. It is frequently debated in Denmark whether the commercial broadcaster Visat/TV3, which is formally established in the UK, effectively shall be regarded as established in Denmark (and thus subject to Danish jurisdiction) because it broadcasts programmes in Danish and with Danish content and advertisements directly to Denmark. However, the Danish Radio and Television Board has in two occasions, the latest on 4 Nov. 2010, decided – after consulting the UK regulator Ofcom – that TV3 fulfils the conditions under the AVMS Directive for being regarded as established under UK law.
265. With Recitals 31–34.

Chapter 2. Public Service Broadcasting

§1. The Concept and Mission of Public Service Broadcasting

I. Background

482. Already with the first Broadcasting Act of 1926, which laid the framework for the State monopoly on television broadcasting, constraints were put on the content of broadcasting. Hence, programmes should be of 'versatile, cultural and informational nature'.[266] These general obligations were over time and under the general influence of the English language and the regulation of the 'model', the British BBC, named public service obligations.

483. In the first decades the public service obligations were interpreted as a commitment to 'educate' the population culturally, partly because of the State's (at the time) significant influence on the overall programme planning (via the representation of the Radio Council), and partly because of the prevailing education concept, which was used as an indicator of what type of content the general public ought to be presented to.

484. Today, the broad public service obligations are summarized in the concepts of 'quality, versatility and diversity' in section 10 of the Broadcasting Act. Meanwhile, the interpretation of the public service concept has evolved in the direction of greater responsiveness to the public's needs and interests. This is partly due to a changed position on the State's role as 'educator' of the population, but also, and especially that the State's monopoly on broadcasting has been repealed and replaced by a large and varied picture of both state-owned and private, commercial and non-commercial, nationwide and local programme service providers.

485. This implies that the public service institutions today are not only undertaking overall societal obligations, but also very much have to compete on market conditions to maintain and consolidate their position as media undertakings who serve the entire population.

486. The standards from which public service obligations are presently assessed therefore comprise the total broadcasting market, including the commercial channels, and not only similar licence-funded public service enterprises' programme schedule. When this scale is used, the public service enterprises' programme schedule must constantly guarantee them a relatively high market assessed in relation to

266. *See* in detail Lars M. Banke et al., *Radio- og tv-lovgivning* [*Radio and Television Regulation*] (Thomson Publishing, 2004), Ch. 3, and Jakobsen & Schaumburg-Müller, *Medieretten* [*Media Law*] (Jurist- og Økonomforbundets Forlag, 2013), 642 et seq.

the total market offerings. Otherwise, the collection of the licence fees, which hitherto has formed the bedrock of the public service enterprises' financing, cannot be legitimized.[267]

487. It is also important to note that the question of whether the public service obligations are met must be evaluated in light of the public service undertaking's overall programme offerings – not isolated individual programmes.

488. There is no clear and unambiguous definition of the public service concept. This is intentional, since the public service obligations must be very broadly defined in order to ensure the public service institutions an extensive freedom – within the overall limits – to fill in and interpret the public service requirements so that they always reflect the continuous developments of society.[268]

489. The public service concept can be said to have two dimensions. The first is aimed at the relationship between the public service institutions and the population, and is expressed in a broad range of requirements to ensure that the programmes offered are of high quality, are varied and encompass the demands of the whole population.

490. The second dimension, which is less visible in the Broadcasting Act, concerns the public service institutions' independence, primarily of the State, but also by commercial interests. The independence is vital in order to serve the freedom of information and expression in a democratic society like the Danish. The way the broadcasting regulation has reflected these two dimensions has, as will be seen, evolved through the years.

II. The Content of the Public Service Obligations

A. *Versatility*

491. As mentioned above, section 10 of the Broadcasting Act stipulates that the public service institutions in their programme planning shall aim at 'quality, versatility and diversity'. Section 10 contains a number of additional requirements which, however, primarily serve as clarifications of the overall requirements.

492. The most important of the overall requirements is the requirement regarding versatility. This concept must be understood very broadly as including: (1) versatility in relation to various programme genres (news, information, entertainment, culture, etc.); (2) versatility with respect to the different layers of society (i.e., the

267. Lars M. Banke et al., *Radio- og tv-lovgivning* [*Radio and Television Regulation*] (Thomson Publishing, 2004), 50.
268. This lack of clear definition is held not to violate the EU rules on state aid, *see* the EU Commission's recent update on its communication on the application of state aid rules to public service broadcasting (OJ C/257 of 27 Oct. 2009) and Søren Sandfeld Jakobsen, *Juristen* 10 (2009): 287.

different attitudes and cultures that exist in society, including minority groups' right to be heard in the debate; and (3) diversity in relation to the programme arrangement, i.e., that all relevant stakeholders and opinions are heard in the arrangement of a programme.

493. The versatility requirement in relation to the different opinions in society has been tried in case law in relation to political broadcasts in connection with elections and EU Referenda. In the Supreme Court's decision referred in *UfR* 1960.33H, it was found that DR had a duty to treat all legitimate political parties equally in connection with television programmes prior to elections to Parliament – in this case by including them all in a final televised party leader round (where DR had otherwise decided that only parties that were already represented in Parliament could participate).

494. In *UfR* 1989.148H, the Supreme Court modified the principle of equality in relation to EU Referendums, since the court found that DR had acted lawfully when inviting only those parties that were represented in parliament to the closing televised debate. The Court attached particular importance to the debate programme was arranged essentially as an informative programme and that both supporters and opponents of the specific proposal that was voted on (and which could only be voted yes or no to) were fairly equally represented in all programmes up to the referendum, including the final debate.[269]

B. Diversity

495. The diversity requirement is largely covered by the broad versatility concept, but serves to highlight that there should be a balanced schedule of programmes aimed at the entire population. The programme offering must include all programme categories, and there is no programme category which in itself meets the public service requirement better than others. Public service enterprises are in other words not limited to broadcast only the programme categories that are not or very rarely offered by the commercial entities.

496. The diversity requirement also serves to underline the obligation for public service enterprises to provide individuals, institutions, etc. who are subject to attacks or accusations in a programme, a reasonable opportunity to be heard in the debate. A similar requirement follows from the general standard regarding 'good press ethics' pursuant to the press code of ethics applicable to all mass media.[270]

269. The two Supreme Court decisions are commented by Torben Jensen in *UfR* 1989B: 129.
270. *See* Ch. 6 above.

C. Quality

497. Unlike the requirements regarding versatility and diversity, which have been part of the public service concept from the beginning, the quality requirement is relatively new. That does not mean that it has not always been assumed that public institutions should provide quality programmes. It rather reflects the emphasis on quality as a public service parameter in the modern media world with many competing broadcasters.

498. The quality standard is directed first against the programme development to express a technical, professional and journalistic quality. Second, the requirement is directed externally, to the public's perception and expectations that the programmes reflect a programmatic and aesthetic quality. This dimension of quality requirements is inherently difficult to measure and assess, since the perception of when a programme is an expression of quality is not objective, but subjective, as it varies from person to person. For similar reasons, the use of quality requirements in the definition of public service certainly is not unproblematic.

D. Other Requirements

499. In addition to the core concepts of quality, versatility and diversity, the Broadcasting Act section 10 adds a number of additional requirements for public service, including that a variety of programmes must be offered, that decisive emphasis must be placed on the freedom of information and expression, that emphasis also must be placed on objectivity and impartiality and that the public must be ensured access to essential information regarding society as well as debate. These requirements can all be seen as clarifications of the overall public service obligations, especially the versatility requirement.

500. The objectivity requirement emphasizes the obligation that actual facts produced for a programme are correct and reflect sound source criticism. The requirement of impartiality means that the public service entities *as institutions* may not take a position in controversial matters, and that their employees may not use their position to promote personal interests. The requirement does not prevent the public service enterprises from taking a critical angle or position in relation to a certain programme, e.g., a documentary programme regarding a controversial topic, as part of their freedom of information and expression.

III. The Public Service Institutions' Independence

501. The purpose of the requirement in section 10 that the public service enterprises shall put decisive emphasis on the freedom of information and expression is, in addition to securing a diverse and varied range of programmes where the opinions of minorities are also heard, to avoid political and commercial interference in the programme planning. Hence, the requirement also protects the public service enterprise's own right to information and expression. Attempts by outsiders, be they political or commercial interests to exert pressure on broadcasting enterprises, must in other words be rejected.

IV. Public Service on the Internet and Other New Media

502. Subject to an amendment in 2000,[271] section 10 of the Act also stipulates that the public service obligations must not only be carried out through traditional radio and television, but also via 'the Internet or similar'. This inclusion of the Internet and other new media platforms in the public service obligation shall ensure the public access to public service content also on the new media, and ensure the public service undertakings the best possible position to compete with other media companies. Furthermore, the platform-neutral provision of public service content expresses that public service is no longer linked to specific platforms and ways of transmission (broadcasting), but adapts to the technological developments and the trend of new technological media platforms and media convergence.

V. Public Service Activities

503. It follows from section 11(1) of the Act that public service activities are performed by the state-owned broadcasters DR, TV2 Danmark A/S and the regional TV2 stations.

504. In addition to the public service activities attached to specific state-owned institutions, public service obligations are also attached to two specific radio channels which cannot be the state-owned public service institutions. Just recently, it has been politically decided to launch a new television channel and a new radio channel which equally cannot be allotted to the state-owned public service institutions. Consequently, section 11(2) has been amended authorizing in general the Minister of Culture to include under the public service obligations television and radio channels (and corresponding on-demand audiovisual services) from other providers than the state-owned public service broadcasters.[272]

505. This continues an essential change of principle in the Danish broadcasting legislation the last decade where public service as a concept is no longer exclusively tied to certain state-owned institutions, but follows the right – by statute or subject to a public tender – to provide programme services on a given frequency.[273]

506. The change of principle was also cemented by the inclusion in 2006 of a new section 11a, according to which – initially on a trial basis – a 'Public Service

271. Act No. 1272/2000.
272. Cf. draft bill No. L 37, adopted by Parliament on 29 Nov. 2018.
273. *See also* report from the Ministry of Culture and the Ministry of Science: Convergence in the network society (2001), 113 ff.

Pool' was established. The pool, which is administered by the Danish Film Institute and amounts to DKK 47 million (approximately EUR 6 million) annually, financed by the public service licence funds, will be used to subsidize the production of Danish television drama and documentaries and is reserved to commercial broadcasting enterprises, i.e., others than DR and the regional TV2 stations.[274]

VI. Financing Public Service

507. It has always been a cornerstone of the public service concept that the public service obligation is counterbalanced by a right to have the public service activities wholly or partly financed through licence fees. However, due to a political agreement in 2018 it has been decided to phase out the licence fee system and to let the public service obligations be financed over the annual state budget in the future.[275]

508. As part of the planned privatization of TV2/Danmark A/S, the enterprise's share of licence fees ceased as of 1 January 2005, thus leaving it to the station itself to finance the public service activities solely by its commercial activities.

§2. The Organization and Financing of Public Service Broadcasting

I. Introduction

509. The public service institutions include DR, the regional TV2 stations (who since 2002 have been legally separated from TV2/Danmark and are now independent, state-owned institutions) and TV2/Danmark (the nationwide TV2's main channel), provided TV2/Danmark has received authorization from the Minister for Culture subject to section 38a.[276]

510. DR has existed since the implementation of the first radio broadcasting act from 1926, when the institution was called Statsradiofonien and had a monopoly on broadcasting – and later on television. DR's public service activities today comprise of six TV channels and eight radio channels, which are distributed via (digital) terrestrial networks, DAB and the Internet. Further, DR provides public service activities on its website (www.dr.dk).

511. DR is an independent public institution and thus not covered by the Minister for Culture's instruction power.[277] Hence, DR's decisions, notably regarding the programme services, can and must not be influenced by the minister or the

274. Detailed rules are laid down in Executive Order No. 1127/2008.
275. Cf. draft bill No. L 36, adopted on 29 Nov. 2018.
276. As mentioned, the authorization was issued on 17 Dec. 2003.
277. The Broadcasting Act s. 15.

political system as such. This is of course essential for the undertaking's performance – along with the rest of the press – as the public's 'watchdog' in a democratic society.

512. DR is almost exclusively (more than 90%) financed by licence fees. The rest of the revenue comes from commercial activities not connected with the public service activities. According to section 15(2), DR is not eligible to receive advertising revenue – either from the traditional broadcasting activities or the online activities on the Internet, mobile media, etc. This prohibition applies to the institution as a whole, i.e., also the institution's activities outside of the public service obligations. Likewise, DR may as a main rule not make use of sponsorship agreements, *see* section 13. DR may not require user fees for the provision of its public service activities (besides the general licence fee collection).

513. The regional TV2 stations were established in connection with the establishment of the nationwide TV2 in 1986. In 2002, the regional stations were organizationally and financially separated from the parent. The regional TV2 stations therefore today consist of 8 independent, state-owned companies. They each dispose of a twenty-four hour channel on the digital terrestrial network, send regional programmes in the 'windows' on the nationwide TV2's programme schedule and conduct public service activities on their website. The regional stations have as their primary purpose to provide a public service to the entire population in their respective geographical areas. They are funded through a direct share of the licence fees and income deriving from the sale of programmes and other benefits.

514. The nationwide TV2 (TV2/Danmark) was established by statute in 1986 and launched in 1988. The main purpose of TV2 was to create competition on the Danish television market by providing an alternative to DR's monopoly on nationwide television. That way the total Danish television supply was strengthened in relation to the increasing competition from abroad. In addition to the public service channel, TV2 Danmark, which is distributed via the terrestrial television network, the TV2 group also transmits – via cable and satellite – the channels TV2 Zulu, TV2 Charlie, TV2 News, TV2 Fri, TV2 Sport, the subscription-based VOD service 'TV2 Play' and activities on their website.

515. Until the transformation from a public foundation to a state-owned private limited company in 2003, TV2 derived its total revenues from advertising revenue (about 70%), revenues other than advertising and a part of the public licence fees. After the transformation the revenues from licensing fees with effect from 2005 have lapsed. Hence, TV2 is currently funded on purely commercial terms.[278]

278. The Station is still entitled to receive state funding for specific projects.

II. Public Service Contracts

516. All the public service enterprises (DR, TV2/Danmark and the regional TV2 stations) must comply with the public service obligations set forth in section 10 as described above. DR and the regional TV2 stations are annually concluding a public service contract with the Minister for Culture, *see* sections 12(2) and 31(4).[279] The purpose of the contract is to specify the framework for the public service activities and the operational tasks which are considered to fall within these frameworks. The present public service contracts are entered into for the period 2019 to 2023. DR and each of the regional TV2 stations shall prepare an annual statement on its fulfilment of the public service contract.[280] The Radio and Television Board shall issue an opinion on the statement.[281]

517. Notwithstanding the use of the word 'contract', it is not a contract in traditional private law terminology, which, if necessary, can be enforced by the courts.[282] The contract must be seen more as a political instrument to complete the very vague public service definition in section 10 and to control that the public service institutions fulfil their public service obligations. When the law does not operate with a public service contract with respect to TV2/Danmark's public service obligations, it is because a specification of these follow from the issued permit for TV2 to provide programme services, including public service activities, *see* section 38a.

III. Value Tests

518. Pursuant to section 44b, the Radio and Television Board, on application or on its own initiative, decides whether DR's and the regional TV2 companies' launch of significant new services and significant changes to existing services can be approved. A 'new service' means a larger coherent concrete initiative on a platform that is not imposed on DR or the regional TV2 companies under the public service contracts or is approved by the Radio and Television Board. In assessing whether a new service is 'significant', emphasis is placed, *inter alia*, on the distribution of the service (how many are expected to use it), how many financial resources the service will require, the news value of the service in relation to existing public service activities and its duration.

519. In the decision itself, the Radio and Television Board must conduct a 'value test', i.e., balance the service's public service value for society against the impact of the service on other services on the market. The assessment must include whether there are similar or alternative offers on the market, the market structure, the market

279. The contracts can be found on the Minister for Culture's webpage, www.kum.dk.
280. *See* ss 12(3) and 31(5).
281. *See* s. 40(2).
282. *See* the preparatory works.

position of the DR, or the regional TV2 companies, the extent of competition, and potential impacts on private initiatives, including editorial competition.

520. The background of the requirement of the value test is a political desire for an increased control that DR is not using its public licence means to launch new services which can make undue harm to the commercial market players. However, until now there have only been a couple of cases before the Radio and Television Board, and in none of those cases the Board carried out a value test (because the Board did not find that the service in question was a significant new service).

521. The value test also serves the purpose of complying with the conditions pursuant to the 2009 EU Commission recommendation for aid to public service enterprises (e.g., in the form of licence fees) not to be considered illegal state aid.[283]

IV. Other Activities than Public Service

522. Pursuant to section 14, DR is entitled, possibly by establishing independent subsidiaries or in cooperation with other companies, to carry out so-called 'other activities', i.e., broadcasting and other media-related activities that are not associated with the public service obligations. Until 2003, TV2/Danmark had a similar statutory right, but after the transformation to a limited company such express authorization is no longer needed. The regional TV2 stations are banned from engaging in other programme service activities, but are allowed to engage in other forms of media-related activities, *see* section 33(2).

523. It is generally a precondition for the exercise of other activities that it takes place on competitive terms, *see* sections 14(4) (DR) and 33(5) (the regional TV2 stations) and Executive Order No. 62/2016, which, e.g., prohibits cross-subsidization from the licence-funded part of the activities to the commercial part. It is not as such prohibited to lend capital from the public service part to the commercial part, but the capital must not stem from the licence means and the loan must be subject to normal market terms, i.e., lending rates and other terms must correspond to what a private investor would require in the same situation. Furthermore, there must be a separation between the public service activities and other activities in terms of accounting.

V. Organization

A. *Danmarks Radio*

524. Section 15(1) stipulates that DR is organized as an independent public institution. The independence of the Minister for Culture and the State as a whole ensures the institution a free and independent position in relation to the state power,

283. OJ C/257 of 27 Oct. 2009.

both in relation to the programme planning and other administrative matters.[284] The Minister for Culture may therefore in principle not interfere in DR's editorial decisions and related matters in general.

525. Certain modifications apply to this main rule. The Minister for Culture can issue detailed rules on, for example, DR's other activities, *see* section 14(4) and (5), and the statute for DR, *see* section 15(4). Furthermore, the Minister is entitled to appoint three members of the DR's Board (section 16(1)), to approve DR's annual account (section 19(2)), to approve borrowings in excess of 4% of DR's income (section 15(3)), and to assist in a possible decision regarding a transfer of funds from the Treasury to finance specific parts of DR's activities (section 20(1)).

526. The management of DR is regulated in the Broadcasting Act, sections 16–18. DR is headed by a board of eleven members appointed by the Minister for Culture for four years at a time. The Minister appoints three members (including the Chairman), the Minister and Parliament jointly appoints six of the other members and the permanent staff of DR appoints the remaining two members (and an alternate for this).

527. The composition of the Board shall reflect media, cultural, managerial and professional insight, *see* section 16(2). Members of Parliament cannot be members of the board. Pursuant to section 17, the Board has the overall programme responsibility and is liable for the compliance with the rules on DR. The Board also determines the general guidelines for DR's activities and hires the Director General and the rest of the general management.

528. The Director General is subject to section 18 responsible for the day-today programme service. As is the case with the Minister for Culture, the politically appointed board members may not interfere with the daily programme planning or the content of individual programmes. The Director General is also responsible for the daily administrative and financial management of DR.

B. The Regional TV2 Stations

529. As with DR a Board of Directors constitutes the overall management of the eight regional TV2 stations, *see* section 36. The Board consists of five to seven members elected for four years.[285] The Board has the overall programme responsibility and is accountable for the observance of the rules of the Act. The Board establishes the general guidelines for the regional stations and hires the managing director (who is responsible for the day-to-day management, including the day-today programme service).

---

284. *See* Lars M. Banke et al., *Radio- og tv-lovgivning* [*Radio and Television Regulation*] (Thomson Publishing, 2004), 84 et seq.

285. In order to avoid political interference s. 36(2) stipulates that Members of Parliament and local politicians cannot be Board Members.

530. Section 34 provides that each of the eight regional stations shall have a Board of Representatives which shall reflect a wide variety of aspects of the regional culture and community. The Board of Representatives elects the Board of Directors (except for one employee-elected member).

C. TV2/Danmark

531. Subject to a political agreement in 2002 on the media policy for 2002–2006, it was decided to convert TV2's nationwide activities – TV2/Danmark – to a state-owned limited company with a view to a subsequent privatization, i.e., a full or partial sale of the shares to private investors.[286] The transformation of TV2/ Danmark was legally/technically carried out by a transfer of TV2/Danmark's assets and liabilities to a specially incorporated public company, TV2/Danmark A/S, after which the independent public institution ceased to exist.[287]

532. The Minister for Culture is given authority to sell the shares in TV2/ Danmark A/S and thus privatize the company. As mentioned, the privatization has not yet taken place.[288] The programme service permission from the Minister for Culture to TV2 ensures that in case of privatization the new owners shall, subject to the Government's sovereign assessment, be capable of complying with TV2's public service obligations. Through a requirement that any change of control of the privatized company (e.g., through sale of shares or shareholders' agreements) must be approved by the Ministry of Culture, the State will be able to control future changes in the ownership of a privatized TV2.

533. As a consequence of the conversion to a public limited company, the rules on management of TV2 now entirely follow the general rules of the Public Companies Act.[289] The company's senior management consists of a Board of Directors with six members (including four staff-elected). The daily management is handled by the general management, appointed by the Board.

286. The conversion was implemented by Act 438/2003 on TV2/Danmark A/S. The Act was accompanied by an amendment of the Broadcasting Act which in general adapted the Act to TV2's future status as a private company.
287. The transfer was done with full succession vis-à-vis creditors.
288. Primarily because of several pending state aid cases with the EU Commission and before the EU courts.
289. Act No. 470/2009 with amendments.

Chapter 3. Private Broadcasting

§1. Provision of Programme Services

534. The Broadcasting Act section 1(1) contains an exhaustive enumeration of the entities entitled to provide programme services. The state-owned public service broadcasters DR, the regional TV2 stations and TV2 Denmark A/S have a statutory-based programme permission. Private enterprises need to obtain a programme licence or be registered. Providers of on-demand AVMS are entitled to provide programme services without a licence or even a registration.

I. The Statutory Right to Provide Programme Services

535. As mentioned, section 1 of the Broadcasting Act provides the public service undertakings DR, the regional TV2 stations and the nationwide TV2 with a statutory right to provide programme services. An administrative licence is thus unnecessary. The statutory right applies only to the public service activities, *see* section 45(1). Programme services which fall outside of the public service activities require – like the services of other enterprises – a permission or registration. The nationwide TV2's right to provide programme services is – following the privatization of the station in 2003[290] – conditioned on the Minister for Culture's permission to engage in public service activities subject to the rules in Chapter 6a of the Act, *see* below. The Minister issued the permission to TV2 on 17 December 2003.

II. Permission or Registration

536. From sections 1(1) and 45 it follows that provision of programme services for other enterprises than the state-owned public service broadcasters requires *either* a permission from *or* registration with the Radio and Television Board. A permission is only required if the programme services require access to scarce spectrum resources. In other cases only a registration is required. Permissions are issued subject to a public tender.

537. The difference between a permission and registration is that while a permission is issued based on an assessment of various criteria laid down in the regulation, this is not the case for registration. Here, some basic information about the enterprise, its activities and financing scheme are registered without any legal assessment. The difference is, *inter alia*, reflected by the fact that the Radio and Television Board can make the issuance of a permission subject to the fulfilment of certain conditions regarding the programme activities. The permission may be

290. *See* Act No. 438/2003.

revoked temporarily or permanently if the conditions are not complied with, *see* section 50. The permission may also be subject to payment of a licence fee in accordance with section 45(3).

538. Terrestrial broadcasting is based on scarce spectrum resources. In accordance with the foregoing, access to provide programme services on this platform is subject (for other than public service enterprises) to a permission from the Radio and Television Board based on a public tender. For example, the fourth, fifth and sixth FM radio channels are allocated by tender. The exact procedure for each tender is laid down in executive order form, *see* section 45(5).

539. With regard to programme services provided via satellite or cable network where no frequency scarcity exists, no permission is required. Accordingly, enterprises falling under Danish jurisdiction that provide programme services via these platforms only have to register with the Radio and Television Board in accordance with section 47.

540. As of 1 November 2009, the analogue terrestrial television network was switched off and replaced by the digital terrestrial network.[291] Although the digital technology implies that the number of channels on the new platform is increased, the digital terrestrial network – as the analogue – rests on scarce spectrum resources. The starting point is therefore in accordance with the foregoing that the provision of programme services on the digital platform requires permission from the Radio and Television Board.

541. However, pursuant to sections 3–4 the licence to administer the broadcasting possibilities on the digital platform has – subject to a tender – been awarded to a single enterprise, who acts as a distributor ('gatekeeper'), i.e., an intermediary between the providers of programme services and the end users. Consequently, the individual programme service providers do not apply for frequency resources, but enter – on commercial terms – into agreements with the gatekeeper who administers the frequencies. The providers of programme services should therefore only be registered pursuant to section 47(1).

542. In cases where a permission is required, i.e., where the programme services rely on scarce frequency resources, a permission must also be obtained from the Danish Energy Agency under the Frequency Act.[292] However, with regard to frequencies specially reserved for broadcasting purposes, the Agency can issue a frequency authorization on the mere fact that an authorization to provide programme services has been issued under the Broadcasting Act.[293]

291. *See* Executive Order No. 1287/2007.
292. Act No. 1100 of 10 Aug. 2016 on Radio Frequencies s. 6.
293. *See* ss 35–36 of the Radio Frequency Act.

543. If the permission according to the Frequency Act is cancelled, the Minister for Culture may decide that the permission for providing programme services under the Broadcasting Act also lapses.

544. It should be noted that a permission from the Radio and Television Board is also required for providers of programme services established outside the EU if the programme activities are based on technical facilities which Denmark has at its disposal, e.g., radio frequencies or uplink to a satellite from the Danish territory.

III. Information Regarding Audiovisual Media Service Providers

545. In order to ensure that users have knowledge of exactly who is responsible for the content of AVMS (whether it be broadcast or on-demand AVMS[294]), Executive Order No. 697/2016 section 13 stipulates that audiovisual media service providers shall give the users at least the following information:

(a) the name of the media service provider;
(b) the geographical address at which the media service provider is established;
(c) the details of the media services provider, including his/her electronic mail address or website, which allow him/her to be contacted rapidly in a direct and effective manner;
(d) information on the Radio and Television Board as the competent supervisory body.

§2. Programme Distribution

546. The Broadcasting Act distinguishes between the provision of programme services (as described above), i.e., the dissemination of the content itself, and the mere *distribution* of the content. Distribution differs from programme service activities in that the distributor does not undertake the primary broadcast of the radio or television signal to end users, but only receives such a signal and transports it to end users.

547. Programme distribution is regulated by a few provisions in the Broadcasting Act Chapter 2, but otherwise the Act does not apply to distribution since the Act is primarily targeted at the content side. A service which exclusively or mainly consists of the conveyance (transportation) of radio or television is also a telecommunications service subject to the telecommunications regulation.

548. If follows from Chapter 2 of the Broadcasting Act that the Act deals with two forms of distribution to end users: distribution on the digital terrestrial network and distribution of communal aerial installations. Other forms of distribution (e.g.,

294. For providers of on-demand services similar requirements already follow from the E-Commerce Directive s. 7.

satellite) are thus not governed by the Broadcasting Act. In contrast to the provision of programme services, distribution of programmes does as a rule not require a permission or registration under the Broadcasting Act. There are also no longer restrictions on who can establish communal aerial installations.

I. Distribution of Terrestrial Digital TV Network

549. The media convergence has made it possible to convert the analogue terrestrial network to a digital broadcasting network, which implies access to an increased number of channels of better quality as well as new digital services such as video on demand, data services, etc. The transition from analogue to digital network was completed by 1 November 2009; as of this date the analogue signal was shut off.

550. The regulatory framework underlying the digital switch is set forth in the Broadcasting Act sections 3–4, containing some general guidelines on the establishment and operation of the digital terrestrial television network, while the more specific rules are established in executive orders.[295]

551. In accordance with these rules and the overall principles of the Broadcasting Act, distribution of television programmes on the new digital terrestrial television network requires permission from the Radio and Television Board subject to a tender, *see* section 3. The right to administer and distribute the broadcasting possibilities on the digital platform is made subject to payment of a concession fee, *see* section 4.

552. Accordingly, the right to administer the frequencies on the digital network was in 2008 – subject to a public tender[296] – awarded to the Swedish company Boxer, which then acts as a gatekeeper that operates the network on normal commercial terms and – given the network's capacity constraints – concludes agreements with various content providers, including 'ordinary' TV channels, pay channels, video on-demand providers and providers of interactive data services. The permission has a duration of twelve years. In 2016, Boxer's Danish operations were purchased by the Danish energy company SE.

553. Section 3(4) contains an exception to the general rule that the frequency options (exclusively) are managed by the gatekeeper, in that it authorizes the Minister for Culture the power to grant the public service enterprises DR and the nationwide TV (but not the regional TV2 stations) a licence to provide programme services on the new platform directly, i.e., without the gatekeepers intervention. Pursuant to the authorization, the Minister for Culture has awarded the public service enterprises several of the available so-called 'MUX', i.e., frequency possibilities on the new network.

---

295. Notably Executive Order No. 1287/2007.
296. *See* for details, www.bibliotekogmedier.dk/medieomraadet/medieprojekter/arkiv/dtt-udbud/.

II. Distribution Through Communal Aerial Installations

A. *The Concept of Communal Aerial Installations*

554. The Broadcasting Act section 2(2) defines 'communal aerial installations' as cable-based systems for distributing audio and video applications for premises used for private households. The origin of the concept stems from the way such facilities were created in the beginning, namely as a result of a relatively small group of residents, e.g., a housing association or group of parcel owners in a residential neighbourhood, who jointly established a 'communal aerial antenna', which each member of the association were connected to.

555. This enabled them to receive radio and television signals from foreign cable networks or satellites and redistribute the signals to the members of the association, thereby making it possible to receive a much larger number of channels than each household with a common ground antenna were able to.

556. With the development in the early 1990s of the nationwide cable networks, the so-called 'hybrid network', many communal aerial installations connected to the hybrid network and receive programmes directly from here. Many residents, particularly in major urban areas, are not connected to a communal aerial installation in the above-mentioned traditional sense but are directly connected to one of the two nationwide cable networks operated by two competing undertakings, YouSee and Stofa.

557. The growing media convergence has created new types of cable-based networks which, as the traditional communal aerial networks and nationwide cable networks, are designed for distribution to private households. For example, in these years many electricity supply companies establish local or regional fibre networks connected to individual households. Networks based on fibre technology have so much capacity that they can be used for distribution of telephony, data services (Internet, etc.) and radio/television programmes over a single line. Hence, fibre networks have become direct competitors to cable-based and satellite distribution.

558. The question is whether such networks fall within the definition of communal aerial installations in section 2(2). To the extent that these fibre networks have the same characteristics as communal aerial installations, this is probably the case.

B. *Requirements for Distribution*

559. According to the Broadcasting Act section 5(1), distribution through communal aerial installations can only take place 'without changes and while the broadcast or transmission occurs'. This ensures that the end users can receive the programmes in 'real time' and without changes, i.e., at the same time and manner as others.

560. This also means that texting and the like, or deferred distribution, may only be carried out with the broadcaster's consent, just as an editing of the programmes by the distributor would require consent from the right holders[297] – and would also mean that the activity no longer could qualify as distribution but provision of programme services comprised by section 2 of the Broadcasting Act, *see* above.

C. Use of Decoders

561. Communal aerial installations and other cable systems are not only used for 'free to air' programmes, but also distribution of programmes subject to payment. These are, in order to ensure the payment, coded (encrypted) by the programme providers. The handling of encrypted programmes requires that the aerial network is equipped with a decoder system that can decode the coded programmes. To ensure that the development of various decoding schemes does not lead to a bottleneck situation where certain broadcasters are barred from offering their encrypted programmes because they are not compatible with the applied encrypted system, section 7 of the Broadcasting Act authorizes the Minister of Science to establish detailed rules to ensure competition.[298]

D. Must-Carry Rules

562. The Broadcasting Act section 6(1) contains the 'must-carry' rules. The purpose of the must-carry obligations is to ensure that the part of the population that receives radio and television programmes via cable-based networks has access to certain TV channels which are available to the rest of the public. Previously, the owners of communal aerial installations were required to ensure that the main public service channels from DR and the regional TV2 stations were distributed in the network. DR and TV2's niche-oriented channels as well as DR's public service radio stations were not covered by the must-carry rules.

563. However, the public service channels are now accessible to everyone via the Internet. Accordingly, the must-carry obligations were in 2013 eased and now cover only the sign language interpreted news programmes from DR and TV2/Danmark, programmes from DR1 and DR1 with vision interpretation and the TV channel 'Folketinget' (The Parliament).

297. *See* Part II, Ch. 7 on copyright.
298. *See* Executive Order No. 515/2001.

§3. Local Radio and Television

I. Background

564. A permanent access to provide local radio and television was introduced in 1985 (for radio) and 1987 (television).[299] The purpose of introducing local radio and television was to strengthen the public's ability to transmit and receive opinions and views within the local area – in practice the individual municipality. Thus, the overall aim was to strengthen freedom of expression and information on the local level – not to build a commercial market for local radio and television. This also implied that the regulatory regime at first in particular supported non-profit institutions' opportunities to establish radio and television stations.

565. In 1988, the use of advertisements was permitted on local radio and in 1989 on local television. But even with the possibility of funding through advertising, at that time the Broadcasting Act contained so many requirements and restrictions that the possibility of running a profitable commercial local radio or television station was limited.

566. In particular the requirement that the local station had a very strong attachment to the municipality in question – with no possibility of establishing cooperation with other local broadcasting companies in other areas (so-called networking) made profitability difficult when considering the relatively small number of residents and businesses in most Danish municipalities. In 1996 partial access to networking was allowed, and by 2002 the last restrictions regarding networking were repealed. Now, the local broadcasters are even obligated to form networks with the other broadcasters holding a licence within the geographic area covered by the frequency.

567. In 2005, the local radio and television boards were closed down and the power transferred to the Radio and Television Board. In addition, the public aid scheme was simplified and the special must-carry rules for local broadcasting were lifted. To simplify the regulation, the special rules on local radio and television were either incorporated in other chapters of the Act or transferred to executive orders. Today the rules are laid down in two executive orders on commercial and non-commercial local radio services, respectively, and an executive order on non-commercial local television services.[300] Provision of commercial local television services follow the same rules as nationwide commercial television, hence no special rules apply.

---

299. *Ibid.*, 42 f.
300. Now Executive Order No. 1459/2016, Executive Order No. 1460/2016 and Executive Order No. 1098/2017.

II. Permission to Provide Local Broadcasting Services

568. Access to provide local broadcasting basically rests on the same – today quite liberal – rules on access to provide nationwide programme services.[301] Thus, permission from the Radio and Television Board is only required in cases where the use of scarce radio spectrum is required. In other cases the activity only requires registration.

569. Permissions are issued subject to a public tender in the form of a 'beauty contest'. Permits may be renewed. A permission may be withdrawn temporarily or permanently if it is not used or if the holder does not meet its obligations or otherwise violates the law.

III. Requirements for the Provision of Programme Services

570. Previously, a wide range of requirements applied to local programme entities to ensure that the local broadcasting actually was local and was independent of local interests, including the requirement that the operator may have only local programme activities as assigned, that a majority of the Board members would live in the local area and a ban on commercial enterprises – apart from newspapers and local magazines – having a dominant influence in the broadcaster. These requirements are now lifted and all there is left is a requirement for non-commercial local broadcasters (especially local television broadcasters) that a certain share of the programmes has local content.

571. Advertising and sponsorship in local broadcasting follow the same rules that apply to nationwide broadcasting, i.e., the rules in the Broadcasting Act Chapter 11. Similarly, the restrictions regarding programme content aimed at children and youth, and the prohibition of discrimination because of race, sex, religion, etc. correspond with the content rules that apply to nationwide broadcasting.

IV. Public Subsidies to Non-commercial Local Radio and Television Broadcasters

572. Pursuant to section 43 of the Broadcasting Act, the State provides, through the licence fees, subsidies to non-commercial local radio and television broadcasters. The subsidies are granted by the Radio and Television Board. Conditions can be attached to the subsidy, and a broadcaster can be met with a repayment claim if the subsidy is not used as intended. The subsidy is an operational subsidy and is calculated on basis of the local broadcaster's own, independent programme activities.

301. *See* s. 47 and the Executive Order on local broadcasting Ch. 2.

Chapter 4. Advertising, Sponsorship and Other Content Rules

§1. Various Forms of Commercial Communication

573. The Broadcasting Act has always contained restrictions in relation to programme content, including in particular advertisements. During DR's monopoly the public service rules delimited the permissible content, and advertising and sponsorship were not allowed.

574. With the launching of TV2 in 1988 and local commercial broadcasting advertising was allowed – albeit with significant restrictions in relation to the extent, placement and content. Since then the advertising rules – in line with the Act as a whole – have been liberalized considerably, and today the Danish rules in many respects correspond to the minimum standards imposed by the EU's 1989 'television without frontiers' Directive, now the AVMS Directive.

575. However, as will be seen, the Danish Broadcasting Act still contains a number of restrictions on advertising placement and extent, just as there are still important restrictions regarding, e.g., advertising to minors, advertising of special products, political advertising and – subject to the implementation of the AVMS Directive – product placement.[302]

576. Programme sponsorship, i.e., third party's contribution to the financing of a programme with a view to promoting its name, logo, etc., was permitted in 1990. The rules apply to all broadcasters, including DR. Besides content rules on public service, advertising and sponsorship, the Broadcasting Act also contains some very general content rules regarding programmes aimed at protecting children and young people from inappropriate content, and content which is discriminatory in relation to race, sex, religious beliefs, etc.

§2. Restrictions on Advertising

577. Rules on advertising on radio and television follow from the Broadcasting Act Chapter 11 and Executive Order No. 801/2013, which, following the AVMS amendment act to the Broadcasting Act,[303] now implement the AVMS Directive. The 2018 amendments to the AVMS Directive, cf. Directive 2018/1808/EU, has not yet been implemented in Danish law.

578. The rules on advertising in the Broadcasting Act are supplemented by the general rules in the MPA[304] as well as special sector rules on, e.g., advertising in television of healthcare products.

302. *See* Art. 3g of the AVMS Directive.
303. Amendment Act No. 1269/2009.
304. Act No. 426/2017.

579. The advertising rules can from an overall perspective be divided into rules regarding:

- placement
- extent
- identification
- special products
- religious and political movements etc.
- advertising which can harm children and adolescents.

I. Regarding Placement

580. Pursuant to the Broadcasting Act section 73(1), advertisements on traditional television may as a main rule only be transmitted in blocks to be inserted between programmes. Radio advertisements may be scheduled at any time during the programme service, *see* section 74. The rules do not apply to on-demand audiovisual services which can be placed in or in conjunction with a programme.

581. Two exceptions apply to the prohibition in section 73(1) on placing advertisements outside blocks. According to 73(2), advertisement blocks may interrupt sports television programmes where breaks occur or programmes that are transmissions of performances or events where there are intervals for the audience (e.g., theatre or concerts). It is a condition that the interruption takes into account the programme's natural breaks, duration and nature in such a way that the integrity and value of the programme shall not be compromised nor the owner's rights infringed.

582. Second, section 76(2) stipulates that it is allowed to advertise pharmaceutical products and healthcare services subject to provisions of the Pharmaceuticals Act and the Act on Advertisement of Healthcare Services. This means in practice that it is permissible to advertise alcoholic beverages, non-prescription drugs and dietary supplements. This also applies to on-demand audiovisual services.

583. Despite those exceptions to the prohibition regarding advertisement 'breaks' in television programmes, the Danish rules on this matter remain stricter than the (minimum) rules set forth in the AVMS Directive. Whether that will still be the case following the 2018 amendments to the AVMS Directive is uncertain, as no implementation regulation has yet been presented.

II. Regarding Extent

584. Section 75 of the Broadcasting Act provides that advertising on radio and television (but not on-demand AVMS or Teletext) can never exceed a maximum of twelve minutes per hour.

III. Regarding Identification

585. The Broadcasting Act section 72 stipulates that advertisements must be clearly identifiable as such, so that the content and presentation distinguish them from regular programmes. This rule also applies to on-demand audiovisual services.[305]

586. Although the requirement regarding identification sounds simple, a vast amount of decisions from the Radio and Television Board concern this particular issue. The cases most often concern the question of whether a product displayed in a television programme is exposed so extensively that it is in effect an advertisement that should have been clearly identified and placed in an advertising block. With regard to DR, who is not permitted to make use of advertisements at all, any kind of advertisement, identifiable or not, constitutes a breach.

587. In order to constitute hidden advertising, and in accordance with practice under the AVMS Directive, the highlighting of the product must fulfil 3 cumulative conditions: (1) it must be intended by the media service provider; (2) it should be intended as an advertisement; and (3) it may mislead the public as to its nature (i.e., it must be unclear to the recipient that is an advertisement). Whether the media service provider has received payment for the advertising is obviously an important factor in the assessment, but is not a requirement in itself. Thus, certain communication can qualify as hidden advertising though no payment was made in return.

588. Practice shows that the Radio and Television Board, in its assessment, reviews the three aforementioned conditions. Particularly difficult is to assess whether a given use of a product or service in a programme can be said to be a natural and editorial well-founded highlight as part of the programme's content and purpose, or appears as – and is meant as – an advertisement. In the latter case the highlighting is not justified.[306]

589. A specific case concerned a news host who in a feature of approx. 70 seconds in a news programme spent 16 seconds raising a football with a specific label in front of him, while he repeatedly took time to make sure that the ball turned so that the label was clearly visible to the viewer. No payment was received in connection with the display of the football, and there was no oral mentioning of the label in the news feature. The Radio and Television Board found that it was an unnecessary and unjustified highlight of the specific football label which could not be justified by the editorial context and purpose of the news feature (a record attempt in football).[307]

---

305. As a supplement to the similar rule in the E-Commerce Directive Art. 9.
306. Sandfeld Jakobsen & Schaumburg-Müller, *Medieretten* [*Media Law*] (Jurist- og Økonomforbundets Forlag, 2013), 670 et seq.
307. Decision of 24 Nov. 2011.

590. Another case concerned a talk show host who was wearing a polo shirt with an advertisement for a specific product. There was no agreement between DR and the product vendor. The Radio and Television Board did not find that the case constituted covert advertising since the advertisement on the shirt did not appear significantly in the picture and there was no oral mentioning of the product during the programme.[308]

IV. Regarding Advertisements on Special Products

591. In accordance with the general ban on tobacco advertisements, section 76 prohibits the broadcasting of advertisements for tobacco products or products primarily used in connection with smoking. This also applies to on-demand AVMS.

V. Regarding Advertisements for Religious and Political Movements

592. According to the Broadcasting Act section 76(3), advertisements for employers' organizations, trade unions, religious movements, political parties, political movements and elected members or candidates for political assemblies are not allowed on television (but, conversely, are allowed in radio and on-demand AVMS). Regarding political messages in general, it follows from section 76(4) that advertisements for political messages are not allowed on television during the period from the date on which an election for a political assembly or a referendum is called until the election or the referendum has been held. If the date of the election or the referendum is announced more than three months before it is held, the advertisement-free period comes into force three months before the election or referendum is held.

VI. Regarding Advertisements Which Can Harm Children and Adolescents

593. Pursuant to the Executive Order on Advertisements, it is prohibited to include advertisements which can harm minors mentally or morally, exploit or mislead them, undermine social values or parents, teachers or others' authority and responsibility, display minors in dangerous situations or give a misleading impression of the products. In addition, there are special rules restricting children's and persons associated with children's programmes' involvement in advertisements. Most of these rules also apply to on-demand AVMS.

308. *Ibid.*

VII. Other Restrictions

594. Besides the above-mentioned rules, which target specific types of advertisements, the Executive Order on Advertisements contains a number of more general content requirements for television advertisements, including that they must comply with the general provisions set forth in the MPA and other relevant laws and generally accepted standards, be decent, honest and truthful, may not encourage violence or be discriminatory and must not depict or refer to people without their prior consent. These rules also apply to on-demand audiovisual services.

VIII. Supervision of the Advertising Rules

595. The advertisement and sponsoring rules are supervised by the Radio and Television Board, *see* sections 44 and 78 of the Broadcasting Act and the Executive Order on advertising Chapter 5. In cases involving advertising of pharmaceutical products, the Radio and Television shall obtain an opinion from the relevant authorities (the Medicines Agency and the Health Protection Agency) before the decision is made.

596. The Radio and Television Board's sanctions in case of violation of the advertisement rules include the issuance of orders, publication of the decision, right to reply and fines.

§3. Sponsorship

597. Sponsorships are in general permitted under Danish law.[309] DR, however, may as a main rule not apply sponsorships in connection with their own programme productions, cf. the Executive Order on Advertising section 25.

598. Section 79 of the Broadcasting Act defines sponsorship as any contribution, direct or indirect, to the financing of programmes in radio, television and on-demand AVMS, including Teletext pages, from a natural or legal person not engaged in the transmission or production of programmes in radio, television, on-demand AVMS, films, sound recordings, etc. with a view to promoting its own name, brand (logo), image, activities or products.

599. Hence, the decisive question is whether there is a contribution to the financing of a programme with the purpose of promoting the sponsor itself, including its products or services.

600. As with advertisements the use of sponsorships must be clearly identifiable, *see* section 80. Identification shall be made by appropriate credits appearing at

309. Cf. Sandfeld Jakobsen & Schaumburg-Müller, *Medieretten* [*Media Law*] (Jurist- og Økonomforbundets Forlag, 2013), 681 et seq.

the beginning or end, or both, of the programme, showing the sponsor's name, trademark (logo), product or service. Such credits may not, however, occur in the programme itself. On Teletext the sponsor's name, trademark, product or service shall appear on the individual pages sponsored.

601. Sponsorship of a programme may give rise to uncertainty among viewers and listeners about whether the sponsor – through the financial contribution – also exercise influence over the programme content or the programme enterprise as such. Section 81 therefore stresses that the content and scheduling of a sponsored programme must not be influenced by the sponsor in such a way as to affect the responsibility and editorial integrity of the programme enterprise. Section 82 specifies that the sponsored programme must not encourage the sale of the sponsor's (or a third party's) products or services or promote the products or services thereof.

602. Also relating to the uncertainty which sponsorship can create regarding sponsor's possible influence over the programme content, section 84 expressly prohibits sponsorships in news and current affairs programmes in television and audiovisual media services. News and current affairs radio programmes that do not form part of the overall public services may be sponsored.

603. Further, programmes may not be sponsored by enterprises whose principal activity is to produce or sell tobacco products or other goods primarily used in connection with smoking.[310] No radio programmes forming part of the overall public services and no television programmes may be sponsored by employers' organization or trade unions or by political parties or religious movements.[311] This may change when the newly revised AVMS Directive of 2018 is implemented.

§4. Product Placement

604. The legal position with regard to product placement has always been somewhat unclear and has varied from Member State to Member State.[312] In order to clear this uncertainty the Audiovisual Media Service Directive established new and specific rules on product placement. Following the adoption of the AVMS Directive product placement, which was previously not legal in Denmark, was gradually legalized.[313] For political reasons, however, in 2013 the previous ban on product placement was reintroduced, although with significant exceptions.[314]

310. *See* s. 83.
311. *Ibid.*
312. *See* Recital 61 to the AVMS Directive.
313. Act No. 1269 of 16 Dec. 2009.
314. Act No. 513 of 27 May 2013.

605. The Danish rules on product placement are found in the Broadcasting Act section 85a and the Executive Order on Advertisement sections 31–35. In accordance with the AVMS Directive product placement is defined as 'any form of audiovisual commercial communication consisting of the inclusion of or reference to a product, a service or the trade mark thereof so that it is featured within a programme, in return for payment or for similar consideration'.

606. According to section 85a, product placement in television and on-demand AVMS produced in Denmark is prohibited. As mentioned, the definition of product placement corresponds with the definition set forth in the Directive.

607. By way of derogation, however, television and on-demand AVMS may display purchased programmes containing product placement produced abroad within the genres of short and documentary films, feature films, films and series produced for television or on-demand AVMS, sports programmes and light entertainment programmes, cf. section 32(3) of the Advertising Order. Hence, product placement in purchased programmes from abroad – except for news programmes and programmes on current affairs – is allowed.

608. However, this implies that a number of conditions have to be met, cf. section 32(2), e.g., that the editorial independence of the media service provider must not be affected by the product placement, and that the viewers must be clearly informed that product placement appears in the program. The identification must take place in an appropriate way at the beginning and end of the program, and when a television program continues after an advertisement interruption.

609. There is very little case law regarding product placement. In a case[315] of a Danish-produced television program (where product placement as mentioned above is prohibited), the Radio and Television Board did not find that the inclusion of cars of a particular brand in the program constituted illegal product placement, as the panel held that the broadcaster had not received any financial support from the car dealer. Moreover, since the cars were found to be an editorially natural part of the program, there was also no violation of the general prohibition of hidden advertising, cf. above.

610. In accordance with the AVMS Directive, a narrow exception to the rules on product placement is made with respect to so-called 'product sponsoring', where companies lend out or simply give away products in order for these products to be used in programmes. Product sponsoring is permitted if (1) the deliverance of the product, service or trademark has no significant value; and (2) no relevant media service provider or attached person has received payment or other remuneration in relation to the inclusion of or reference to the product, service or trademark in the programme.[316]

315. Decision of 29 Aug. 2014.
316. *See* the Broadcasting Act s. 85(3).

611. The term 'significant value' is defined as a residual value which is not of minor importance. Minor importance is to be understood as a monetary or other economic value for the relevant media service provider besides the value of the expense which is saved by including or referring to the product, service or trademark in the programme.[317]There is no case law regarding product sponsoring.

§5. Other Content Rules

612. In addition to the rules on advertising, sponsorship, product placement and the previously mentioned public service rules, the broadcasting regulation also contains some more general content rules, which apply to audiovisual programmes as well as advertisements and other audiovisual commercial communication.

613. Pursuant to the Broadcasting Act section 48, the Minister for Culture may lay down rules on the programme services, including rules regarding content, promotion of programmes of European origin and the provision of the programme services, including protection of minors. Detailed rules are set forth in Executive Order No. 697/2016. The rules correspond with the programme content requirements stipulated in the AVMS Directive, including the requirement that programmes may not in any way create incitement to hatred on grounds of race, sex, religion, nationality or sexual orientation. The rules also apply to on-demand audiovisual services.

317. *See* the Advertising Order s. 33(2).

Chapter 5. From Media Licence to State Budget Financing

614. Historically, DR's and the regional TV2 stations' public service activities have always been financed through licence fees which are imposed on television sets and other devices (nowadays also computers, tablets ad mobile phones) that are capable of receiving audiovisual programmes and services. The nationwide TV2 was previously also financed partly by the licence fees. However, subject to the conversion to a publicly owned limited company, as of 2005 TV2 has no longer received licence fees. Rules on licence fees follow from the Broadcasting Act Chapter 10 as detailed in Executive Order No. 1580/2014. However, pursuant to a political agreement and a recent amendment of the Broadcasting Act (November 2018),[318] the media licence will be phased out over the next four years. Instead, the public service activities will be financed through direct subsidies via the annual state budget.

318. Draft bill No. L 36, adopted by Parliament on 29 Nov. 2018.

Chapter 6. Right to Information

615. The Broadcasting Act also reflects the EC rules regarding access to events of significant interest to society and short extracts for the purposes of general news programmes, which rules aim at promoting media pluralism, safeguard the freedom to receive information and protect the interests of the viewers.

§1. Access to Events of Significant Interest to Society

616. The 1997 amendment to the TV Without Frontiers Directive of 1989[319] introduced a new Article 3A (now Article 14 in the AVMS Directive) authorizing Member States to take appropriate measures ensuring that broadcasters under their jurisdiction do not broadcast on an exclusive basis events which are regarded by that Member State as being of major importance for society in such a way as to deprive a substantial proportion of the public in that Member State of the possibility of following such events via live coverage, or deferred coverage on free television.

617. Member States who make use of the authority shall draw up a list of designated events, national or non-national, which it considers to be of major importance for society. Consequently, Denmark in 1997 issued an executive order with a list of events of major importance for the Danish society, including the Olympic Games and a number of football and handball matches in connection with the European and World football and handball Cup.

618. The conditions and procedures under which an exclusive right owner pursuant to the executive order was obliged to offer the rights to free TV broadcasters did, however, give rise to considerable critics and practical problems, and the executive order was repealed again in 2001.[320] The list was, however, reintroduced in 2015 by way of an executive order.[321]

619. Pursuant to section 2 of the executive order, an event of material mutual interest is a sporting event which satisfies at least two of the following conditions: (1) it is of interest to persons other than those normally following the sport or sport in question on television; (2) It belongs to a sport that is traditionally central to Danish sports culture, and (3) It is generally followed by many viewers. Based on this definition section 3 identifies the events which are of major social interest, including the Olympic Games and the largest international football and handball events (and the qualifying matches leading up to these events).

319. Directive 97/36/EC amending Directive 89/552/EC (the 'TV Without Frontiers' Directive).
320. Despite the fact that Denmark has no longer special legislative measures regarding broadcast of major sports events and other events of significant interests to society, Denmark is still under an obligation to comply with Art. 3A para. 3 of the 1997 amendment directive, according to which Member States shall mutually respect one another's list (if any) of events of major importance.
321. Executive Order No. 546/2015.

620. According to section 3 of the Order, 'a significant proportion of the population is prevented from following an event on free television' unless (1) the event is broadcast on a television channel which at least 90% of all households has access to; and (2) receiving the event does not have any costs for the households except for the media licence and any subscription payment to a cable TV provider or the like (provided the channel is located in the cheapest package or offered as single channel).

621. The more specific terms for providing access for the public to an exclusive right follow from section 5 of the Order. In short, the holder of the exclusive right is bound to agree to share the exclusive right with other broadcasters, and shall offer the right to other broadcasters (who comply with the terms of the Order, i.e., reaches a significant proportion of the population via free broadcast) in due time before the event in order to determine whether some of these other entities wish to enter into an agreement on fair market conditions.

§2. Access to Short Extracts for News Programmes

622. Pursuant to Article 15 of the Audiovisual Media Service Directive Member States shall ensure that those exercising exclusive rights concerning an event of high interest to the public should grant other broadcasters the right to use short extracts of the events for the purposes of general news programmes on fair, reasonable and non-discriminatory terms.

623. In order to ensure that the right of access to short extracts applies on a trans-frontier basis only where it is necessary, Article 15(2) stipulates that if another broadcaster established in the same Member State as the broadcaster seeking access has acquired exclusive rights to the event of high interest to the public, access shall be sought from that broadcaster.

624. The extracts shall be used solely for general news programmes and may be used in on-demand services only if the same programme is offered on a deferred basis by the same media service provider.

625. The AVMS Directive does not define the term 'general news programmes', but it appears from the recitals that short extracts can be used also by dedicated sports channels.[322] Compilation of short extracts into programmes serving entertainment purposes, however, is not covered.

626. Article 14(5) leaves it to the Member States to more precisely determine the modalities and conditions regarding the provision of short news extracts, in particular any compensation arrangements, the maximum length of short extracts and time limits regarding their transmission. However, where compensation is provided for, it shall not exceed the additional costs directly incurred in providing access.

322. *See* Recital 39.

627. With regard to the maximum length of the short extracts, it appears from the recitals that these should as a general rule not exceed ninety seconds.[323]

628. Article 15 AVMS has been implemented in the Broadcasting Act section 93, subparagraph 3–5 and the Copyright Act section 25a. The new provisions in the Broadcasting Act section 93 reflect the overall principles of the Directive and provide the Minister of Culture with an authorization to set forth more detailed provisions with regard to the access to and application of the short extracts. This has been done by Executive Order No. 106/2010. There is no case law yet in Denmark regarding the right to short extracts.

629. With regard to the notion of 'events of high interest to the public', which is not defined in the Directive, the preparatory works to the new provisions in section 93 of the Broadcasting Act states that an event is only of high interest to the public if it appeals to a significant group of persons which is broader than those who normally follow events of that kind. Accordingly, the concept of events of great interest to the public in Danish law is defined as events that have a news value that appeal to a larger circle of persons and at the same time is of interest to people other than those usually accompanying events of a similar nature, cf. section 2 of the Executive Order.

630. This implies that, e.g., the premier national football league is not considered an event of high interest to the public, as it does not interest a broader group than those who are normally interested in that event, even though this group in itself is considerable. Conversely, an event like the Football World Championship is followed by a much broader group of persons than those who are normally interested in football, and thus qualify as an event of high interest to the public.

631. The Directive does not define what should be understood as a 'short' excerpt. This question is left to the Member States, cf. Article 14(6). However, it is clear from the recitals to the Directive that a short extract should, as a rule, not be longer than 90 seconds. According to section 3 of the Order, the short extract may not be longer than the purpose of the information, but only in special situations longer than 90 seconds.

632. The right to access short extracts shall be completely free of charge, cf. section 6(3) of the Executive Order, according to which the television undertaking, which is obliged to give access to short excerpts, cannot claim compensation for the costs involved.

633. The new right to access to short extracts not only affects the broadcasters holding the exclusive broadcasting rights to the event of high public interest, but

323. *Ibid.*

also, potentially, a variety of holders of 'neighbouring rights' to the event pursuant to the Copyright Act, e.g., performing artists and producers of musical or cinematographic works.[324]

634. In order to ensure that these right holders cannot obstruct the broadcasters' right to access to short extracts a new provision is inserted in the Copyright Act section 25a, according to which right holders who are affected by the right to short extract pursuant to section 93 of the Broadcasting Act cannot prevent broadcasters' reproduction and making available to the public of the short extracts.

324. *See* the chapter on Copyright in the Media Sector, Part II, Ch. 7.

Chapter 7. Access to Networks

§1. Introduction

635. Obviously, it is not enough for a media undertaking to produce media content. The content must also reach the audience.[325] Previously, media content was dominantly distributed via print media (newspapers, magazines, etc.) and broadcasting networks. Today, the content is increasingly being disseminated via electronic communication networks such as the Internet and other IP-based networks, mobile networks, etc. Hence, in order to reach the end users, providers of media content services are more and more dependent on being able to dispose of or via agreements have access to an electronic communication network.

636. As access to electronic communication networks is regulated in the telecommunications regulation, the chapter will focus on these rules, notably the Radio Frequency Act and the so-called interconnection rules in the Telecoms Act.

637. Under Danish law, the main rule is that anyone is entitled, without permission from a public authority, to establish an electronic communication network, save where the network is based on scarce radio frequencies, in which case a permission is required.

638. Instead of establishing own infrastructure, telecom providers can also rent-free space on other providers' networks. Pursuant to the interconnection rules, providers who hold a strong position on the market are obligated to give new providers access to their network on fair and equal terms

§2. Access to Networks and Access to Provide Content Services, Respectively

I. Broadcasters

639. Under Danish law, access to a telecommunication infrastructure and access to provide media content services are regulated in two different set of rules, the Broadcasting Act and the telecoms regulation, respectively.[326]

640. As described in the chapter on the Broadcasting Act, the provision of broadcasting services in general requires permission in accordance with section 1

325. *See* more detailed Sandfeld Jakobsen & Schaumburg-Müller, *Medieretten* [Media Law] (Jurist- og Økonomforbundets Forlag, 2013), Ch. 16.
326. *See* in general Sandfeld Jakobsen & Schaumburg-Müller, *Medieretten* [*Media Law*] (Jurist- og Økonomforbundets Forlag, 2013), Ch. 16, and Tom Latrup-Pedersen, *Telekommunikationsret* [*Telecommunications Law*] (Thomson Reuters Publishing, 2008), Ch. 1, 16 ff. and Ch. 5.

of the Broadcasting Act. The public service broadcasters have a statutory permission directly in the act, while other providers must obtain permission from the Radio and Television Board.[327]

641. However, permission is not required if no scarce radio frequency is necessary for the programme service, as is the case if the programme service is distributed via cable or satellite. In such case the provider is only obliged to be registered with the Radio and Television Board. Providers of on-demand AVMS under the Broadcasting Act who do not make use of scarce frequency resources are not obligated to be registered with the Radio and Television Board.[328]

642. In addition to an authorization under the Broadcasting Act, in cases where the media content service makes use of a scarce radio frequency, an authorization to use the radio frequency itself (in order to build up a network based on the frequency) is also required pursuant to the Radio Frequency Act (*see* below). However, with regard to frequencies specially reserved for broadcasting purposes the Danish Energy Agency can issue a frequency authorization on the mere fact that an authorization to provide programme services has been issued under the Broadcasting Act.[329]

II. Other Media Content Providers

643. It should be noted that the requirement for certain broadcasters to obtain permission from the Radio and Television Board to provide programme services only applies to undertakings covered by the Broadcasting Act. Accordingly, providers of media content services which are not AVMS as defined in section 2 of the Act and the underlying EU Directive[330] can in general provide their services without any prior authorization, permission or registration.

644. However, media content providers falling outside the scope of the Broadcasting Act, e.g., providers of on-demand services on the Internet or mobile platforms (which services are not AVMS), still need to get access to a distribution network in order to reach the end users. They will normally do so by concluding an

327. For example, the public service broadcasters have a statutory right under the Broadcasting Act to provide programme services on the digital terrestrial broadcasting network, which by 1 Nov. 2009 replaced the analogue terrestrial network. The Swedish enterprise 'Boxer' has, subject to a public tender held by the Radio and Television Board, been assigned the right to administer the remaining frequencies. Accordingly, media content providers (other than the public service undertakings) who want to provide services on the new digital network will have to conclude an agreement with Boxer on ordinary, commercial terms. The content providers are not required to have permission from the Radio and Television Board; they only have to be registered. *See* above Ch. 1 on the Broadcasting Act.
328. *See* s. 47(1) of the Broadcasting Act.
329. *See* ss 35–36 of the Radio Frequency Act (Consolidated Act No. 1100/2016).
330. The Audiovisual Media Service Directive, 2007/65/EC, Art. 1.

agreement with a network operator on normal commercial terms. If they wish to establish their own network, the rules in the telecoms regulation must be observed, *see* below.

§3. The Must-Carry Rules

645. As described in the foregoing chapter section 6(1) of the Broadcasting Act contains the 'must-carry' rules, according to which the owners of communal aerial installations are required to ensure that certain public service channels are distributed in the network.

§4. Access to Networks under the Telecoms Regulation

646. As described, providers of programme services who have obtained permission under the Broadcasting Act will normally automatically also obtain permission from the Danish Energy Agency to establish or make use of an electronic communication network according to the Radio Frequency Act.

647. Other media enterprises, however, e.g., programme providers who do not need permission according to the Broadcasting Act, cable companies who do not provide programme services themselves, but only distribute programmes from third party, or providers of content falling outside the scope of the Broadcasting Act have no automatic access to a radio frequency or a network.

648. Thus, these media undertakings must either enter into an agreement with a network operator (such as a cable or satellite operator, an Internet provider, a mobile operator, etc.) or – which is more unusual – establish their own network infrastructure.

649. Agreements between content providers (providers of broadcasting or on-demand media services) and network operators are as a starting point not subject to special regulation, but are entered into on ordinary, commercial terms. If the media undertaking is also a provider of electronic communication services under the Telecoms Act, the special rules on access and interconnection may apply. These rules are described below.

650. If a media undertaking chooses to establish own infrastructure, the general rules under the telecommunications regulation, primarily the Telecoms Act and the Act on Radio Frequencies, must be observed. These rules are also described further below.

651. The main rule under this regulation is, as under the Broadcasting Act, that access to establish electronic communications networks or provide electronic communications services do not require authorization from a public authority, save where the access is depending on the use of scarce radio frequencies.

652. This means that media undertakings that do not provide AVMS or other content services themselves, but only distribute media services provided by third party, such as operators of cable or satellite television networks under Danish jurisdiction, are neither required to obtain a programme licence pursuant to the Broadcasting Act, nor required to obtain an authorization under the telecoms regulation. Hence, they are free to establish an electronic communication network of any kind and offer to content providers (broadcasters and others) to distribute their content services to the end users. Only if radio frequencies are needed, a licence is required under the Radio Frequency Act, *see* immediately below.

I. The Radio Frequency Act

653. Issues regarding allocation of radio frequencies are regulated by the Radio Frequencies Act.[331] Besides reflecting the principles regarding allocation of radio frequencies set forth in the underlying EU Telecoms Regulation,[332] the Act also reflects the agreements concluded by the International Telecommunication Union (ITU),[333] in which Denmark participates.

654. As mentioned, the use of radio frequencies – being a scarce public resource – is subject to a licence provided by the Danish Energy Agency, *see* section 6(1) of the act. The granting of individual frequency licences is allowed under the 2002 EU Telecoms Package. The EU Regulation specifies, though, that the individual rights shall be granted through open, transparent and non-discriminatory procedures.[334] A frequency licence is required regardless of what kind of communications service is being transmitted via the frequency.[335] Thus, the use of radio frequencies for broadcasting purposes also requires a licence pursuant to the Frequency Act.

655. According to the Frequency Act sections 3–4, the Minister of Energy issues the overall guidelines for the Energy Agency's administration of the Danish radio frequencies. The Agency then prepares a more detailed 'frequency plan' regarding the use of the available frequencies.

656. The allocation of available frequencies is based on a 'first come, first served' principle, *see* section 7. However, if the number of applicants exceeds the number of spare frequencies, the licences are awarded subject to an auction (based solely on the price offers) or a public tender (based on a number of criteria).

657. Licences are awarded for a limited period of time, however, long enough to enable the licence holder to make a reasonable return of the investment (often fifteen or twenty years), in some cases with the possibility of prolongation.

---

331. Consolidated Act No. 1100/ 2016 on Radio Frequencies.
332. *See* EU Parliament and Council decision 676/2002 and the Framework Directive (2002/21/EC), Art. 9.
333. *See*, www.itu.int.
334. The Authorization Directive (2002/20/EC), Art. 5.
335. *See* the preparatory works to the act.

658. In conformity with the developments in the underlying EU regulation, the present Frequency Act represents certain liberalizations in comparison with the former act. Previously, a specific frequency was reserved for specific services (e.g., mobile communication, data broadband services, etc.). Under the present Act, the IT and Telecoms Agency can decide that a certain frequency is not subject to any restrictions with regard to choice of service.

659. Likewise, allocated radio frequencies could previously only be assigned with consent of the regulator. Now, in accordance with the underlying EU legislation, frequencies can be transferred without consent, however, provided that the transfer does not unduly restrict competition on the relevant market, *see* section 21. The Energy Agency and the Competition Council oversee the effect on competition resulting from a licence transfer.

II. The Interconnection Rules in the Telecoms Act

660. Undertakings that wish to distribute media content services to end users but do not own or have a network of their own at their disposal can get access to another operator's network by entering a commercial agreement with a network operator with spare capacity on its network, e.g., a cable or satellite network operator, an Internet service provider or a mobile network operator.[336]

661. If, however, the operator holds a dominant position on the market and is reluctant to offer the new provider access on reasonable terms, the new entrant, if it is a provider of public electronic communications services covered by the Telecoms Act, can, subject to certain conditions, get access to the dominant providers' network in accordance with the so-called interconnection rules laid down in Part IV of the Telecoms Act (with appurtenant executive orders),[337] corresponding with the underlying EC directive on access and interconnection.[338]

662. The Danish telecoms regulation (as the underlying EU Regulation) applies to *infrastructure services* (provision of networks or transport of communication, whereas *content services* (e.g., radio and television services, on-demand audiovisual services, web services, etc.) are not covered.[339]

663. This means that media content providers (broadcasters, providers of on-demand AVMS, etc.) are normally not providers of electronic communications services encompassed by the Telecoms Act, and therefore cannot make use of the interconnection rules to get access to a telecom operator's network. Instead, content providers, if a voluntarily agreement with a network provider cannot be reached,

336. *See* Sandfeld Jakobsen & Schaumburg-Müller, *Medieretten* [*Media Law*] (Jurist- og Økonomforbundets Forlag, 2013), Ch. 16, and Tom Latrup-Pedersen, *Telekommunikationsret* [*Telecommunications Law*] (Thomson Reuters Publishing, 2008), Ch. 9.
337. Consolidated Act No. 128 of 7 Feb. 2014 on Electronic Communications Network and Services.
338. Notably Directive 2002/19/EC (the Access Directive).
339. *See* Recital 5 of the Framework Directive.

must apply the general competition law as set forth in the Competition Act and Articles 101 and 102 of the Treaty, which supplement the interconnection rules set forth in the telecoms regulation.[340]

340. *See* the Chapter on competition law.

Chapter 8. Standards and Interoperability

664. Technical standards, protocols, logical interfaces, etc. can be regarded as languages which enable different elements in a communication infrastructure, e.g., networks, terminals and software, to 'speak together' and function as a unit. If different elements do not apply same standards, they can still be able to work together if they are interoperable, i.e., are based on open standards which make it possible for others to develop elements that can work together, even though they might be based on other standards.[341]

665. Lack of common standards and interoperability increases the risk of markets characterized by many proprietary standards unable to work together, which again will lead to limited competition and lack of innovation and growth. Thus, harmonized standards or at least a high degree of interoperability is needed, especially considering the vast technological developments and convergence which characterizes the media sector these years.

666. As technology is not depending on national borders, it is most appropriate that common or harmonized standards are developed and adopted on an international level. This is also the case in the media and communications field where standards and requirements regarding interoperability are primarily established in international organizations such as the ITU, CEN (the European Committee for Standardization) and ETSI (the European Standardization Institute for Telecommunication). Denmark is a member of these organizations.

667. The agreements made in the international standardization bodies are often not implemented as formal legislation, but more as 'soft law' instruments (self- or co-regulation), which are easier to amend concurrently with the technological developments.

668. Having said this, there are some formal rules in the EU Regulation regarding standardization and interoperability, most of which have been implemented in Danish law.

§1. The Framework Directive Article 17

669. In the Framework Directive[342] Article 17 EU addresses standardization and interoperability in general. In the recitals to the directive it is stated, as a basis for

341. *See* for further reading Sandfeld Jakobsen & Schaumburg-Müller, *Medieretten* [*Media Law*] (Jurist- og Økonomforbundets Forlag, 2013), Ch. 16, and Tom Latrup Pedersen, *Telekommunikationsret* [*Telecommunications Law*] (Thomson Reuter Publishing, 2008), Ch. 6.
342. Directive 2002/21/EC.

the provisions, that standardization should remain primarily a market-driven process, but that there may be situations where it is appropriate to require compliance with specified standards at Community level to ensure interoperability in the single market.[343]

670. Accordingly, Article 17(1) stipulates that the Commission shall draw up and publish in the Official Journal of the European Communities a list of standards and/or specifications to serve as a basis for encouraging the harmonized provision of electronic communications networks, electronic communications services and associated facilities and services. The Commission may request that standards be drawn up by the relevant European standards organizations.

671. Pursuant to Article 17(2), Member States shall encourage the use of the standards and/or specifications referred to in paragraph 1, for the provision of services, technical interfaces and/or network functions, to the extent strictly necessary to ensure interoperability of services and to improve freedom of choice for users.

672. As long as standards and/or specifications have not been published in accordance with paragraph 1, Member States shall encourage the implementation of standards and/or specifications adopted by the European standards organizations.

673. In the absence of such standards and/or specifications, Member States shall encourage the implementation of international standards or recommendations adopted by the ITU, the International Organization for Standardization (ISO) or the International Electrotechnical Commission (IEC).

674. If the standards and/or specifications referred to in paragraph 1 have not been adequately implemented so that interoperability of services in one or more Member States cannot be ensured, the Commission, pursuant to paragraph 3, can make the implementation of such standards and/or specifications compulsory to the extent strictly necessary to ensure such interoperability and to improve freedom of choice for users.

675. Where the Commission intends to make the implementation of certain standards and/or specifications compulsory, it shall publish a notice in the Official Journal of the European Communities and invite public comment by all parties concerned, *see* paragraph 4.

§2. Interoperability of Digital Interactive Television Services

676. In the market for digital radio and television services, there is a particular risk of bottleneck if platform operators through whose network the services are to be distributed, use closed standards, protocols, etc. that require special access. Although the platform operator may not have a dominant position on the market and

343. Recital 30.

the general competition law is not applicable, lack of openness regarding standards and interoperability may not only impede competition and innovation significantly but also media pluralism and cultural diversity.[344]

677. Article 5 of the Access Directive,[345] cf. also Article 18 of the Framework Directive, seek to counter this by encouraging Member States, in accordance with Article 17(2), to impose on providers of digital television services and digital television equipment to use an open Application programming interface (API) and Electronic Program Guide (EPG) interface that allows other providers to produce services that may be delivered via the platform. The provisions have been implemented in section 48 of the Telecoms Act, which authorizes the Danish Business Authority to lay down rules for multiplex operators (i.e., digital broadcasting operators) to provide access to API and EPG on reasonable and non-discriminatory terms, to the extent necessary to ensure end-users' access to digital broadcasting transmission. The authorization has so far not been used.

678. Digital TV enables access control systems, i.e., digital systems such as encryption (coding) that can be used to control end users' access to the television signal, so that only end users who have the necessary equipment to decrypt (decode) the signal can access this. Access management systems formed the basis of the many pay-TV channels that emerged in the 1990s, but at the same time worried legislator as a closed access control system that other providers cannot easily access may seem like a bottleneck restricting supply and competition.

679. Article 6 of the Access Directive shall counteract this. The rules are implemented in section 49 of the Telecoms Act and Executive Order 393/2011. Under these rules, providers of access control systems, including operators, must ensure that their system allows for cost-effective shift in access control and that broadcasters have the technical capability to broadcast radio and television programs to end users using the appropriate access control system.

344. *See* Recital 31 of the Framework Directive.
345. Directive 2002/19/EC.

Part IV. Cross-Ownership, Competition and State Aid Regulation

§1. Introduction

680. Media pluralism is a vital element of any modern democracy and is an essential pillar of the right to information and freedom of expression as protected by Article 11 of the EU Charter of Fundamental Rights and Article 10 of the Human Rights Convention. However, there is no legal or commonly applied definition of media pluralism. The concept can be defined broadly, as embracing a number of aspects such as diversity of ownership of media undertakings, a variety in the sources of information and in the range of contents available. In other words, the concept can be understood as implying all measures that ensure the public's access to a variety of information sources, opinion, voices, etc. in order to form their opinion without the undue influence of a dominant opinion forming power.[346]

681. Very often the concept of media pluralism is understood in a more narrow sense as only covering the plurality of ownership of media undertakings. This is due to the risk that a concentration of ownership may result in a skewed public discourse where certain viewpoints are excluded or underrepresented and where certain interests, be they political or commercial, can exercise an undue influence on the public opinion and debate.

682. The very tangible risk posed by media concentration has resulted in a number of countries adopting regulation that to a certain extent restricts media undertakings' access to ownership of other media undertakings. Denmark, however, has no general regulation of media ownership. Concentrations that effect competition are subject to the merger control regulation contained in the Competition Act. *See* Part IV, §3 below.

683. In addition, when licences for radio frequencies for media purposes are offered, Danish law contains rules to prevent an undue media concentration and thus – indirectly – ensures effective competition and media pluralism.

346. *See* Commission Staff Working Document on Media Pluralism in the Member States of the EU (SEC(2007) 32), 5.

684. Another area of media law which has gained considerable importance in recent years is state aid to public service broadcasters. The liberalization of the broadcasting market and the advent of the Internet and other new digital media platforms and services have increased the risk that state funding schemes which benefit public service activities can distort or threaten to distort competition in the common market, in violation of Article 107 of the EU Treaty. The application of the state aid rules and the case law from the European Courts of Justice regarding Denmark is described in Part 4.

§2. Media Ownership Rules

I. No General Rules Ownership Rules

685. There is no general regulation on media ownership under Danish law. Hence, no general ownership restrictions exist with respect to changes in ownership, neither *within* a specific media sector (television, radio, print, Internet, etc.) nor *between* different media sectors (cross-ownership). There are no restrictions in *foreign* undertakings ownership in Danish media undertakings either.

686. This means that changes in the ownership of media undertakings are in general only subject to the general merger control rules in the Danish Competition Act, *see* below. The merger control rules, however, are primarily concerned with a transaction's effect on competition in the relevant market, not concerns regarding media pluralism or other media political or societal considerations.

687. The absence of general media ownership rules – and the reliance on general competition law – does not mean that considerations regarding media pluralism do not exist under Danish law. Several provisions scattered around in various acts and other regulatory measures intend to safeguard media pluralism.

II. Provisions Safeguarding Media Pluralism

688. Today, after the liberalization of both the broadcasting and telecommunications regulation, it is a general principle under Danish law that except for radio-based networks and services, anyone – including foreign undertakings – is entitled to establish themselves as a provider of telecoms and media services in Denmark without any licence or authorization. However, where the provision of services is based on the use of radio frequencies, as this is a scarce public resource, a licence from the Danisk Energy Agency is required in accordance with the Radio Frequency Act.[347] If the frequency is used for radio or television purposes, an authorization from the Radio and Television Board is also required pursuant to the Broadcasting Act.

347. Act No. 1100 of 10 Aug. 2016 on Radio Frequencies s. 6.

689. Considerations regarding media pluralism follow from the Act on Radio Frequencies section 14(2), according to which the Energy Agency, when issuing a frequency licence, can impose conditions which restrict the supply of certain services if such restrictions are found to be necessary in fulfilling a common aim, including the promotion of, *inter alia*, media pluralism.

690. Formerly, any transfer of a frequency licence was subject to an authorization. This requirement is eased under the present Act on Radio Frequencies, which in section 22 stipulates that in case of transfer of a frequency licence, the licence holder must not establish a market position which is so significant that the effective use of frequency resources is impeded, and thus detrimental to competition. However, this provision, as its predecessor, only serves competition purposes (and as such supplements the general provisions set forth in the Competition Act), not considerations regarding media pluralism.

691. Considerations regarding media pluralism are also indirectly contained in the Broadcasting Act. As mentioned, the general rule under Danish law is that a licence for carrying out media activities is not required, save where the activities are based on a radio frequency. If the frequency is to be used for radio or television purposes, an authorization from the Radio and Television Board is required. Pursuant to Chapter 8 of the Broadcasting Act, the issuance of programme licences in general shall be subject to a public tender. When deciding between the applicants in a specific tender, the Minister for Culture or Radio and Television Board can normally put emphasis on whether the programme catalogue is of a versatile nature.

692. As Danish law does not contain general rules on media ownership, no restrictions for political parties and organizations exist either. In relation to advertisements in television, however, section 76 of the Broadcasting Act stipulates that advertisements for, *inter alia*, political parties, political movements and elected members or candidates for political assemblies are not allowed on television.

693. Further, advertisements for political views and messages are not allowed on television during the period from the date on which an election for a political assembly or a referendum is called until the election or the referendum has been held. If the date of the election or the referendum is announced more than three months before it is held, the advertisement-free period comes into force three months before the election or referendum is held.

§3. The Competition Act

I. An Overview

694. In the absence of special media ownership rules, changes in the ownership structure of Danish media undertakings are only regulated by the general competition rules set forth in the Danish Competition Act,[348,349] including the rules on merger control.

695. The Danish Competition Act is aligned with the EU Competition Rules set forth in the EU Treaty. Hence, the Danish Competition Act is fundamentally based on two prohibitions: a prohibition against anti-competitive agreements, concerted practices, etc. (section 6 of the Act, *see* Article 101 of the Treaty) and a prohibition against abuse of a dominant position (section 11, *see* Article 102).

696. Pursuant to section 2, the Competition Act applies to any economic activity which takes place in a market for goods or services, no matter whether the business activity is profitable or not or how the business is organized (limited liability company, cooperative undertaking, trade union, etc.). The Act also applies to aid from public funds granted for commercial activities.

697. The Act also applies to public business activities, i.e., a business activity performed by a central or local government administration, which consists in supply of or demand for goods or services, provided the activity is of importance for the competitive conditions. The Act does not apply to activities under the executive powers of a public authority, i.e., activities which consist of stipulating citizens' rights and obligations in pursuance of statutory rules.

698. If an anti-competitive practice is a direct or necessary consequence of public regulation, the prohibitions do not apply, *see* section 2(2). The decision whether an anti-competitive practice is a direct or necessary consequence of public regulation rests with the relevant minister. The Act applies to anti-competitive practices which affect the Danish market. Thus, undertakings located abroad are also covered if their anti-competitive agreements etc. affect the Danish market.

699. The two main prohibitions regarding anti-competitive agreements and abuse of dominance both rely on a determination of the 'relevant market'. The relevant market is, as under EU law,[350] defined on the basis of an examination of

348. *See*, *inter alia*, Kirsten Levinsen et al., *Konkurrenceloven med kommentarer* [*The Competition Act with Commentaries*] (Jurist- og Økonomforbundets Forlag, 2009); Caroline Heide-Jørgensen, *Lærebog i konkurrence- og markedsføringsret* [*Textbook of Competition and Marketing Law*] (Jurist- og Økonomforbundets Forlag, 2017). *See also* information on The Competition Agency's website, www.ks.dk.

349. Consolidated Act No. 869 of 8 Jul. 2015.

350. *See* Council Regulation 139/2004/EC on the control of concentrations between undertakings (the EC Merger Regulation), and Commission Notice on the definition of relevant market for the purposes of Community competition law (OJ 1997 C 372/05).

demand substitutability, supply substitutability and potential competition, *see* section 5a. As is the case under EU Competition Law, market definitions on the Information and Communication Technology and media markets sometimes give rise to uncertainties due to the growing convergence between the Internet, media and communications sectors.[351]

700. The prohibition in section 6 against anti-competitive agreements etc. covers, e.g., agreements regarding prices, market division, limitations to production, etc. Certain statutory exceptions exist to the prohibition.[352] In addition, the Competition Council (the politically independent body that enforces the Competition Act) can decide to issue individual exemptions if an agreement, although it separately viewed must be regarded anti-competitive, has such general favourable effects that it should be allowed.

701. Similarly, a number of block exemptions, i.e., exemptions for certain categories of agreements with general favourable effects, e.g., agreements on research and development and technology transfer agreements, have been issued.[353]

702. Finally, the undertakings involved in an anti-competitive agreement etc. can apply for a so-called non-intervention statement, i.e., a statement from the Council that the agreement in question – based on the facts at hand – is not covered by the prohibition, *see* section 9.

703. The prohibition in section 11 against abuse of a dominant position covers, e.g., the setting of unreasonable prices, supply limitations or discriminatory conduct towards certain customers. The Competition Council can, subject to notification, issue a non-intervention statement to the effect that a certain conduct does not fall under the prohibition.

704. Besides the prohibitions regarding anti-competitive agreements etc. and abuse of a dominant position, the Competition Act also applies to aid granted from the public funds to business activities. The Competition Council can order the termination or repayment of such aid if the aid granted directly or indirectly has as its object or its effect the distortion of competition and may not be legitimate according to public regulation, *see* section 11a.

---

351. *See*, *inter alia*, the Eastern High Court's decision of 22 Jun. 2009 in Case B-3926-06 regarding the Danish public service broadcaster TV2's rebates in connection with annual agreements on TV advertisements.
352. *See* s. 7 (the *de minimis* rule) and 8 (regarding agreements which, although anti-competitive, are permissible because they in different ways contribute positively to society).
353. *See* s. 10. The block exemptions basically correspond with the block exemptions issued under EU Competition Law.

II. The Merger Control Regulation

705. As of 2000, the Competition Act also comprises a merger control regime, which to a large extent is based on the same substantive rules as the EU Merger Control Rules.

706. According to section 12, the merger control rules apply to mergers where the aggregate annual turnover in Denmark of all undertakings involved is at least DKK 900 million and the aggregate annual turnover in Denmark of each of at least two of the undertakings concerned is at least DKK 100 million, *or* the aggregate turnover in Denmark of at least one of the undertakings concerned is at least DKK 3.8 billion and the aggregate worldwide turnover of at least one of the other undertakings concerned is at least DKK 3.8 billion.

707. According to section 12a(1) and (2), mergers arise where:

- two or more previously independent undertakings merge;
- one or more persons already controlling at least one undertaking, or one or more undertakings acquire, whether by purchase of securities or assets, by contract or by any other means, direct or indirect control of the whole or parts of one or more other undertakings;
- a joint venture performing on a lasting basis all the functions of an autonomous economic entity is created.

708. Mergers covered by the threshold rules must be notified to the Competition Council before the merger can be carried out. If the merger is assessed to create or strengthen a dominant position as a result of which effective competition would be significantly impeded, the Council can prohibit the merger. If the Council approves a merger, the Council may attach conditions and obligations to the approval. The merger control regime has been applied in several cases concerning the media market, of which two recent cases shall be mentioned here. In 2016, the largest privately owned media, JP/Politiken, who *inter alia* holds some of the largest newspapers and online news media, wished to purchase the business news media Børsen. However, in early 2017, the notification of the merger to the Competition Council was ultimately withdrawn.[354] In its review of the merger, the Competition and Consumer Agency had found that the merger would have significantly hampered competition in a number of markets including the market for news in print and online, the market for rights to news articles and the market for media surveillance. The merger would have strengthened the position of JP/Politiken in these markets and this position could potentially be used to raise prices or reduce supply to the detriment of subscribers and advertisers. Different commitments offered by the merger parties in order to ensure effective competition were deemed insufficient

709. During the examination of the case, the competition authorities carried out some of the most extensive investigations and calculations in a Danish merger case,

354. Cf. press release of 24 Jan. 2017 from the Danish Competition and Consumer Agency.

among other things in order to make a precise definition of the relevant markets. The merger parties had strongly argued that the market definitions and delimitations should not just focus on Danish market players but also consider new global media players such as Google and Facebook. The Agency, however, noted that the market delimitation, among other things, was based on the fact that Facebook and Google did not produce news content themselves, but only exhibited other people's edited news. Hence, the services of Google and Facebook were not substitutable with traditional news services.

710. In September 2017,[355] the Competition Council, subject to a very thorough market investigation, approved that SE, a provider of e.g. broadband and TV distribution services, took over the TV distribution company Boxer subject to binding commitments from SE. The commitments imply that SE until 2020 has a duty to maintain the so-called 'free choice' products offered by Boxer today (the free choice products being the possibility for the customers to put together their own selection of TV channels instead of being forced to choose between various programme packages put together by the distributor). SE also undertakes not to raise the prices of Boxer's free choice products with more than the rise in the consumer price index until 2020. Finally, the commitments mean that SE must not demand that consumers also buy SE's broadband products in order to purchase Boxer's television products.

711. The Competition Council has estimated that the merger without commitment would increase the risk that SE after the acquisition would abolish Boxer's free choice products or raise their prices. This would significantly reduce competition for the distribution of television channels to the detriment of consumers.

§4. State Aid

I. Introduction

712. If Member States grant financial aid to certain undertakings, sectors or the production of certain goods, rather than to undertakings in general, the aid can distort competition on the relevant market.[356] In order to ensure an internal market in which competition is not distorted by state aid granted by Member States, the EC Treaty Articles 107–109 contain provisions regarding state aid. As technological changes have dramatically altered the media markets over the past generation, notably the broadcasting and audiovisual market, creating multiple distribution platforms and replacing former state monopolies with competitive markets consisting of both state-owned and private market players, the regulation on state aid has gained considerable importance as an instrument to ensure effective competition.

355. The Competition Council's decision of 27 Sep. 2017.
356. *See*, in general, e.g., Bent Iversen et al., *Regulating Competition in the EU* (DJØF Publishing, 2008), Ch. IX, and K. Bacon (ed.), *European Community Law of State Aid* (Oxford University Press, 2009).

713. This is particularly the case with respect to public service broadcasters who through various means are depending on state funding. Consequently, the Commission in 2001 issued a communication on the application of state aid rules to public service broadcasting, setting out the framework governing state funding of public service broadcasting.[357] The communication was updated in 2009 in light of the rapid technological and market changes.[358]

714. The state aid rules and the Commission's communication are of vital importance to the audiovisual media sector and form the legal basis in the ongoing cases against the Danish public service broadcaster TV2. Hence, this part will outline the state aid rules, the new communication and the most important case law, including notably the TV2 cases.

II. The State Aid Rules

A. The Prohibition in Article 107(1)

715. Article 107(1) of the EC Treaty contains a prohibition on state aid: 'Save as otherwise provided in this Treaty, any aid granted by a Member State or through State resources in any form whatsoever which distorts or threatens to distort competition by favouring certain undertakings or the production of certain goods shall, in so far as it affects trade between Member States, be incompatible with the common market.'

1. State Aid

716. According to practice from the Commission, who subject to the ECJ's control has the competence to decide whether state aid measures are in accordance with Article 107(1), the decisive factor in determining whether a state measure constitutes state aid is the financial effect of the benefit on the recipient's competitive position. In other words: whether the aid gives the recipient a financial advantage which it would not be given under normal competitive conditions and which means that the recipient undertaking's financial position is improved so its competitive position is likewise improved in relation to its competitors. The effect of the state aid, not its purpose, is the decisive element in the assessment of state aid.

717. The very broad concept of state aid means that it is not relevant whether the undertaking concerned receives the aid directly or indirectly. Further, the legal basis for granting the aid is irrelevant. The prohibition on state aid covers not only measures set forth by statute or other primary or secondary legislative means, but also aid provided on basis of, e.g., an administrative decision or agreement.

357. OJ C 320 of 15 Nov. 2001.
358. OJ C 257/01 of 27 Oct. 2009.

718. The assessment of whether an undertaking is given a financial advantage which it would not be given under normal competitive conditions is decided on basis of the market economy investor principle, according to which a measure does not constitute state aid as long as the terms on which the state provides resources to an undertaking would be acceptable to a private investor under normal market conditions.

2. Favouring Certain Undertakings or the Production of Certain Goods

719. In order for a state aid measure to be declared incompatible with the common market under Article 107(1), the measure must favour certain undertakings or the production of certain goods. This so-called selectivity requirement means that the measure should contain an element of specificity or discrimination, i.e., the measure must favour certain undertakings, a group of undertakings, a specific sector or region in comparison with others which are in a comparable legal or factual situation. Measures which benefit all the undertakings of a Member State will not be covered by the state aid prohibition. The selectivity criterion, as the other criteria in Article 107(1), is interpreted very broadly.

3. Distorts or Threatens to Distort Competition

720. The prohibition in Article 107(1) only applies to aid measures which distort or threaten to distort competition within the common market. This criterion is very broad and is closely linked to the criteria regarding selectivity (*see* above), as aid which gives a selective advantage will improve the financial position of those who receive it in relation to their competitors, thus normally leading to a distortion of competition in the relevant market. Hence, if an aid measure selectively benefits an undertaking, competition will as a main rule be distorted. Not only state aid which actually distorts competition, but also potential competition is covered.

4. Affects Trade Between Member States

721. Finally, it is a condition under Article 107(1) that the state aid measure affects trade between Member States. This condition is also interpreted very broadly. The ECJ has held that when state aid strengthens the position of an undertaking compared with other undertakings competing in intra-Community trade, that trade must be regarded as affected by that aid.[359] Hence, the presumption that state aid distorts competition, *see* above, leads to the presumption that such distortion also affects trade between Member States if it can be shown that the undertakings receiving the aid participate in intra-Community trade.

359. Case 730/79, *Philip Morris*.

B. Exceptions to the Prohibition

722. The prohibition in Article 107(1) is not absolute but is modified both by other provisions on state aid in Articles 107–108 and by other provisions of the Treaty. Article 107(2) lists certain forms of support which are compatible to the common market, and Article 107(3) lists certain forms of aid may be considered to be compatible with the common market. Article 108(2), paragraph 3 empowers the Council to decide that a specific aid measure is to be considered as compatible with the common market. To the extent that these modifications are relevant to the media market they will be described immediately below, along with Article 106(2) of the Treaty, which is extremely important to state aid in relation to public service broadcasting.

723. The fact that the state aid prohibition is interpreted relatively broadly means that the Member States must notify numerous small aid measures. In order to reduce the administrative burden of this mass of notifications, and recognizing that the Commission does not consider that aid measures without appreciable effect are covered by the state aid prohibition, the Commission in the early 1990's in its administration of the state aid rules introduced a *de minimis* rule. The rule is now codified in the Commission Regulation on state aid.[360] The *de minimis* rule is based on the assumption that state aid to an individual undertaking below EUR 200,000 over a three-year period does not affect trade between Member States and/or distort or threaten to distort competition.

III. The Communication on the Applicability of State Aid Rules to Public Service Broadcasting

724. The communication underlines the important role played by public service broadcasting in general in relation to the social, democratic and cultural life in EU, as recognized by the Treaty, in particular Articles 16 and 106(2) and the Amsterdam Protocol. The latter expressly states that the provisions of the Treaty establishing the European Community shall be without prejudice to the competence of Member States to provide for the funding of public service broadcasting insofar as such finding is granted to broadcasting organizations for the fulfilment of the public service remit as conferred, defined and organized by each Member State, and insofar as such funding does not affect trading conditions and competitions in the Community to an extent which would be contrary to the common interest, while the realization of the remit of that public service shall be taken into account.[361]

725. The communication also stresses, by reference to the Council Resolution concerning public service broadcasting,[362] that the concept of public service broadcasting is not limited to traditional point-to-multipoint broadcasting, but also needs

360. Commission Regulation 1998/2006 on the application of Arts 107 and 108 to *de minimis* aid.
361. *See* para. 11.
362. OJ C 30, 5 Feb. 1999, 1.

to benefit from technological progress and to bring the public the benefits of the new audiovisual and information services and the new technologies and to undertake the development and diversification of activities in the digital age.[363]

726. In relation to the applicability of the prohibition laid down in Article 107(1), the communication states that state financing of public service broadcasters in general can be considered to affect trade between Member States.

727. Regarding the existence of a financial advantage the communication refers to the ECJ's decision in the *Altmark* case,[364] according to which public service compensation does not constitute state aid provided that four cumulative conditions are met. First, the recipient undertaking must actually have public service obligations to discharge, and the obligations must be clearly defined. Second, the parameters on the basis of which the compensation is calculated must be established in advance in an objective and transparent manner. Third, the compensation cannot exceed what is necessary to cover all or part of the costs incurred in the discharge of the public service obligations, taking into account the relevant receipts and a reasonable profit.

728. Finally, where the undertaking which is to discharge public service obligations, in a specific case, is not chosen pursuant to a public procurement procedure which would allow for the selection of the bidder capable of providing those services at the least cost to the community, the level of compensation must be determined on the basis of an analysis of the costs which a typical undertaking, well-run and adequately equipped so as to be able to meet the necessary public service requirements, would have incurred in discharging those obligations.[365]

729. If the conditions laid down in the *Altmark* case are not fulfilled, and the state funding of the public service undertaking thus constitutes state aid within the meaning of Article 107(1), it is possible for public service broadcasters to be exempted from the prohibition on state aid by virtue of Article 106(2) of the Treaty.

730. According to this provision 'undertakings entrusted with the operation of services of general economic interest or having the character of revenue-producing monopoly shall be subject to the rules contained in this Treaty, in particular to the rules on competition, in so far as the application of such rules does not obstruct the performance, in law or in fact, of the particular tasks assigned to them. The development of trade must not be affected to such an extent as would be contrary to the interests of the Community'.

731. As stated in the Commission's communication, the ECJ has clarified that in order for a state funding measure to be exempted under Article 106(2) three conditions must be met.

---

363. *See* para. 12.
364. Case C-280/00.
365. *See* para. 23.

732. First, the service must be a service of general economic interest and clearly defined as such by the Member State (*definition*). The communication notes that the definition should be as precise as possible, and it should leave no doubt as to whether a certain activity is to be included in the public service remit or not. On the other hand, the communication acknowledges that given the specific nature of the broadcasting sector, and the need to safeguard the editorial independence of the public service broadcasters, a qualitative definition entrusting a given broadcaster with the obligation to provide a wide range of programming and a balanced and varied broadcasting offer is generally considered legitimate under Article 106(2).[366] The definition of the public service remit may also reflect the development and diversification of activities in the digital age and include audiovisual services on all distribution platforms.

733. The definition of the public service mandate falls within the competence of the Member States, and the role of the Commission is only to check for manifest errors. A manifest error would occur if the included activities could not reasonably be considered to meet the democratic, social and cultural needs of each society.[367]

734. The second condition that must be complied with in order to benefit from the exemption under Article 106(2) is that the public service remit should be *entrusted to the public service undertaking* by means of an official act, e.g., by legislation, contract or binding terms of reference.[368] According to the communication, it is 'desirable' that an appropriate authority or appointed body monitors its application in a transparent and effective manner. The competence to choose the mechanism to ensure effective supervision of the fulfilment of the public service obligations rests with the Member States.

735. With respect to the third condition, *the proportionality test*, the Commission according to the communication considers whether or not any distortion of competition arising from the public service compensation can be justified in terms of the need to perform the public service and to provide for its funding.[369] The amount of public compensation must as a general rule not exceed the net costs of the public service mission, taking also into account other direct or indirect revenues derived from the public service mission.

736. In relation to public service activities on the new digital distribution platforms such services, in order to meet the proportionality test, must address the democratic, social and cultural needs of the society and must not entail disproportionate effects on competition and cross-border trade, which are not necessary for the fulfilment of the public service remit. To this end, Member States shall consider, by means of a prior evaluation procedure based on an open public consultation, whether significant new audiovisual services serve democratic, social and cultural

366. *See* paras 44–47.
367. *See* para. 48.
368. *See* paras 50–55.
369. Paragraphs 40 and 81.

needs while duly taking into account its potential effects on trading conditions and competition. This implies an assessment of the overall impact of a new service on the market by comparing the situation in the presence and in the absence of the planned new service.[370]

IV. The TV2 Cases

737. Subject to a complaint from commercial Danish broadcasting operators, the Commission in 2003 decided to launch a State aid probe into possible overcompensation of the Danish Public Service Broadcaster TV2 by the Danish State.[371][372] This resulted in a complex of court cases which ultimately was decided by the Court of Justice of the European Union (CJEU) nearly fifteen years later.

738. In 2004, the Commission decided that part of the aid granted by Denmark to TV2 between 1995 and 2002 in the form of licence fee resources and other measures, namely DKK 628.2 million (approximately EUR 84 million), constituted overcompensation of TV2's net costs of its public service activities.[373]

739. The Danish State argued that the funding scheme only compensated TV2 for the net costs related to the public service remit and thus that in accordance with the conditions established in the *Altmark* case the aid did not constitute state aid under Article 107(1). The Commission rejected this, as it found that the criteria for calculation of the aid were not objective and transparent. The Danish State further argued that the conditions for exempting the aid under Article 106(2) were fulfilled. The Commission rejected this, as it found that the condition regarding proportionality was not met.

740. Consequently, the Commission ordered Denmark to recover that sum from TV2, together with interest. The Commission found the rest of the state aid granted to TV2 in the aforementioned period to be compatible with the common market.

741. TV2 and Denmark brought actions before the General Court for annulment of the Commission's decision. Also, the two commercial broadcasters SBS and Viasat brought actions before the Court of First Instance for annulment of the part of the decision that found the aid granted to be compatible with the common market.

742. In its judgment of 22 October 2008, the General Court ruled in favour of TV2 and Denmark, thus annulling the Commission's decision of 2004.

---

370. Paragraph 88.
371. Judgment of the Court of First Instance in Joined Cases T-309/04, T-317/04, T-329/04 and T-336/04.
372. *See* IRIS No. 2, 2003, 3–4.
373. Decision 2006/217/EC of 19 May 2004 on measures implemented by Denmark for TV2/Denmark.

743. The Court found that the Commission's decision of 2004 was based on an inadequate statement of reasons, amounting to an infringement of essential procedural requirements. According to the Court, the failure to provide an adequate statement of reasons was attributable to the Commission's complete failure to examine seriously, during the formal investigation procedure, the actual conditions which governed the setting of the amount of licence fee income payable to TV2. Moreover, the Court found that the Commission's assertion that the Danish authorities did not regularly check the level of the accumulated reserves was an unsubstantiated claim which was expressly disputed by Denmark during the formal investigation procedure.

744. As it appears, the judgment was based on formal grounds. However, the judgment also contains points regarding some of the material aspects of the case, which have now found their way to the Commission communication, *see* above. First, the Court noted that Member States enjoy a broad discretion for defining what they regard as services of general economic interest, and they can legitimately define such services as to cover broadcasting of full-spectrum programming. Second, the Court noted that licence fees, though paid by the users, shall be regarded as state funds, as the obligation to pay the licence fee does not arise from a contractual relationship between TV2 and the person liable to pay, but simply from the ownership of a television or radio receiver in accordance with statutory law.

The judgment from the General Court did not end the case. Since the decision was annulled for formal reasons, the Commission could start the case again and make a new decision. Hence, in April 2011 the Commission adopted a new decision, which, contrary to its first decision, approved the state aid granted for 1995–2002 pursuant to Article 106(2), considering that the compensation was necessary and proportionate to the costs of fulfilling public service obligations and therefore did not lead to unfair distortion of competition.

745. Again, the case (which consists of several linked cases) was brought before the General Court and subsequently the CJEU. In 2017, the CJEU essentially upheld the Commission's decision from 2011 except for TV2's advertising revenues for 1995 and 1996, which the Court, contrary to the Commission, found constituted state aid.[374]

746. The case now continues in the Danish court system since TV2's competitors – the plaintiff in the EU cases – have claimed compensation due to the fact that most of the financing of TV2 in the period 1995–2002 actually constituted state aid, and although that state aid might be approvable it was not notified to the EU and thus was illegal for this reason alone.

374. Cf. Case C-657/15 P and C-660/15 P.

Part V. Supervision: Media Regulator – The Radio and Television Board

747. Provisions on the Radio and Television Board are set out in the Broadcasting Act Chapter 7.[375] The Board was established in 2001 and took over the functions hitherto performed by three boards, the Satellite and Cable Board, the Radio and Television Advertising Standards and the Committee on Local Radio and TV.

748. Besides the tasks acquired from the three boards were a series of other tasks, *see* below. In 2005, the competence hitherto carried out by the local radio and television boards (in relation to local radio and television) were also transferred to the Radio and Television Board. Hence, the Board now decides and oversees all broadcasting development entities covered by the Broadcasting Act.

749. Pursuant to section 39(1) of the Act, the Radio and Television Board is appointed by the Minister for Culture. However, the Board is independent of the Minister for Culture and the Board's decisions cannot be submitted to the Ministry of Culture or other administrative authority, *see* section 40(1). The Board's decisions can, of course, be brought before the courts.

750. The Board is established for four years at a time and consists of ten members who – in light of the diverse tasks assigned to the Board – shall represent legal, economic, administrative, media and cultural expertise. The chairman shall be a lawyer.

751. The Board is partly funded through fees charged for issuing a permit or registration of programme activities. The secretarial functions (preparing cases and draft decisions etc.) are carried out by the Agency for Culture and Palaces.

752. According to section 40, the Board performs a number of official tasks with regard to broadcasting, *see* below. The Board must also give an opinion about DR's and the regional TV2 stations' corporate statements for fulfilling their public service contracts. Finally, the Board advises the Minister for Culture on broadcasting policy issues.

375. More detailed rules on the board's activities are laid down in a set of rules of procedure, *see* Executive Order No. 1527/2013 issued in accordance with s. 39(3) of the Broadcasting Act.

753. The Board's official tasks are specified in sections 41–42 and include issuing authorizations for conducting programme service in cases where such authorization is necessary (as is the case for distribution on the new digital terrestrial television platform and programme services on platforms using scarce spectrum resources) or registration of providers of AVMS in cases where authorization is not required.[376]

754. In cases where programme service authorizations are issued subject to a public tender, the Board as a rule carries out these tenders.

755. According to section 44, the Board also makes decisions regarding advertising and sponsorship of programmes, including ruling on advertising identification, placement, extent and content. The Board also makes decisions regarding the rules on product placement as well as the right to reply in relation to factual information in advertisements.

756. Besides making decisions on programme authorizations, the Board also regularly monitors the programme entities that have obtained authorizations. The Board can issue orders if an authorization or the rules in the Broadcasting Act are violated, and can cancel the programme authorization in the event of serious or repeated violations.

757. According to the Broadcasting Act section 44a the Board also oversees TV2's public service activities, criticizes any breaches of conditions attached to TV2's public service permit and the law as a whole and can make recommendations to the Minister for Culture on the possible cancellation of TV2's public service authorization. Moreover, the Board makes decisions regarding DR and the regional TV2 stations initiations of significant new services or significant changes to existing services, cf. section 44 b.

---

376. *See* in detail Part III, Chs 1 and 2.

Selected Bibliography

Banke, Lars et al. *Radio- og tv-lovgivning* [*Radio and Television Regulation*]. Thomsons Forlag, 2004.

Baumbach, Trine, 'Medieansvar eller redaktøransvar i forbudssager – har det nogen betydning' [Media liability and editor's liability in injunction cases. Does it have any importance?], *UfR* 2018B.36.

Baumbach, Trine, *Medieret. Frihed og ansvar* [*Media Law. Freedom and Liability*], Karnov 2017.

Baumbach, Trine, 'Bærende hensyn og god presseskik' [Critical considerations and ethics of journalism], in Anita Rønne et al. (eds.), *Fred, forsoning og mægling. Festskrift til Vibeke Vindeløv* [Peace, reconciliation and mediation. *Festschrift* to Vibeke Vindeløv*]*, Jurist- og Økonomforbundets Forlag, 2017, pp. 258 ff.

Baumbach, Trine, 'Anonyme, uredigerede debatindlæg – skal ingen bære ansvaret?' [Anonymous debate – Nobody's liability?], in Nis Jul Clausen et al. (eds.), *Ikke kun retsfilosofi – festskrift til Sten Schaumburg-Müller* [Not only legal philosophy. *Festschrift* to Sten Schaumburg-Müller], Jurist- og Øjkonomforbundets Forlag, 2016, pp. 57–72.

Borberg, Vibeke, 'Mediernes brug af skjult kamera på privat område' [The Media's Use of Hidden camera on private locations], *UfR* 2014B.258.

Frese Jensen, Malene et al. *The Principal Danish Criminal Acts,* 3rd edn. DJØF Publishing, 2006.

Germer, Peter. *Ytringsfrihedens væsen* [*The Essence of Freedom of Speech*]. Juristforbundets Forlag, 1973.

Greve, Vagn, Poul Dahl Jensen & Gorm Toftegaard Nielsen, *Kommenteret Straffelov. Almindelig Del*, [*The Criminal Code. A Commentary. General Part*] Jurist- og Økonomforbundets Forlag, 2013.

Jakobsen, Søren Sandfeld & Sten Schaumburg-Müller, Nyt kapitel om Medier og persondata [*New Chapter on Media and Personal Data*], presently available on the website of Jurist- and Økonomforbundet, 2018.

Jakobsen, Søren Sandfeld & Sten Schaumburg-Müller, Persondatabehandling i journalistisk øjemed [*Processing of Personal Data for Journalistic Purposes*], *Juristen*, 2017, pp. 54–62.

Jakobsen, Søren Sandfeld & Sten Schaumburg-Müller, *Mediejura for journalister og andre mediearbejdere* [*Media Law for Journalists and Other Media Workers*] Jurist- og Økonomforbundets Forlag, 2016. Jakobsen, Søren Sandfeld & Sten

Schaumburg-Müller, Retten til at blive glemt – og forholdet til medierne og informationsfriheden [*The Right to Be Forgotten – and the Relation to Media and Freedom of Information*] *Juristen*, 2015, No. 5, pp. 176–186

Jakobsen, Søren Sandfeld & Sten Schaumburg-Müller, *Medieretten* [*Media Law*] Jurist- og Økonomforbundets Forlag, 2013.

Jakobsen, Søren Sandfeld & Sten Schaumburg-Müller, 'Pressenævnets kompetence' [The Jurisdiction of the Press Council], *Juristen*, 2013, No. 4, pp. 185–193.

Jakobsen, Søren Sandfeld. 'Danish Supreme Court Upholds Injunction to Block the Pirate Bay', *IRIS*. Legal Observations of the European Audiovisual Observatory, 2010-8.

Jakobsen, Søren Sandfeld. 'The Case Regarding the Danish Muhammed Drawings', *IRIS*. Legal Observations of the European Audiovisual Observatory, 2006-8.

Jørgensen, Oluf. *Det drejer sig om ytringsfrihed* [*It's All About Freedom of Speech*], 3rd edn. Ajour, 2014.

Lambert, Peter & Iben Gjessing, *Medieansvarsloven med kommentarer* [*The Media Liability Act-. A Commentary*], Jurist- og Økonomforbundets Forlag 2017.

Lauridsen, Preben Stuer. *Pressefrihed og personlighedsret* [*Press Freedom and Privacy Protection*]. Gyldendal, 1988.

Levinsen, Kirsten et al. *Konkurrenceloven med kommentarer* [*The Competition Act with Commentaries*]. Jurist- og Økonomforbundets Forlag, 2018.

Nielsen, Gorm Toftegaard, Thomas Elholm & Morten Niels Jakobsen, *Kommenteret straffelov. Speciel Del* [*The Criminal Code. A Commentary. The Special Part*] 11. udgave, Jurist- og Økonomforbundets Forlag 2017.

Petersen, Clement Salung, Morten Rosenmeier & Jens Schovsbo, *Immaterialret – ophavsret, patentret, brugsmodelret, designret, varemærkeret* [*Intellectual Property Law – Copyright, Patent Law, Utility Models, Design and Trade Mark Law*], Jurist- og Økonomforbundets Forlag, 2018.

Pressenævnets Årsberetninger [*Annual Reports from the Press Council*].

Riis, Thomas, *Intellectual Property Law in Denmark* (DJØF Publishing, 2012).

Rytter, Jens Elo. 'Når journalister bryder loven' [When Journalists Violate the Law]. *Juristen,* 2008, pp. 269–281.

Schaumburg-Müller, Sten, 'Strafansvar for indholdet af onlinemedier – Om formidleransvar for medier, der ikke er omfattet af medieansvarsloven', [Criminal liability for online content – On liability for intermediaries not covered by the Media Kliability Act], *UfR* 2018B. pp. 113–123

Schaumburg-Müller, Sten, 'Denmark. Freedom of speech and online media', in Mart Susi, Jukka Viljanen, Eiríkur Jónsson & Artūrs Kučs (eds.), *Human Rights Law and Regulating Freedom of Expression in New Media*, Routledge 2018.

Schaumburg-Müller, Sten, 'Hypotetisk samtykke og privatlivets fred' [Hypothetical Consent and Protection of Private Life], in Nis Jul Clausen, Annette Kronborg, Nina Dietz Legind & Bent Ole Gram Mortensen (eds.), *Festskrift til Hans Viggo Godsk Pedersen*, Jurist- og Økonomforbundets Forlag, 2017, pp. 495–510.

Schaumburg-Müller, Sten, 'Om retlig beskyttelse af aktiv journalistik – En kommentar til UfR 2014B.258 om mediernes brug af skjult kamera på privat område' [On Legal Protection of Active Journalism – A Commentary to the Media's Use of Hidden Camera, *UfR* 2015B.9-14

Schaumburg-Müller, Sten: 'Hvilke emner har almen interesse?' [Which Topics are of 'General Interest'?] in Hinrichsen, Rytter & Rønsholdt (ed.), *Ret, informatik og samfund*, Jurist- og Økonomforbundet, 2010.

Schønning, Peter. *Ophavsretsloven med kommentarer* [*The Copyright Act with Commentaries*]. 6th ed. Karnov, 2016.

Trzaskowski, Jan (ed.) *Internetretten* [*Internet Law*]. Ex Tuto Publishing, 3rd ed. 2017.

Udsen, Henrik. *De informationsretlige grundsætninger* [*Basic Principles in Information Law*]. Jurist- og Økonomforbundets Forlag, 2009.

Selected Bibliography

Index

The numbers here refer to paragraph numbers.

Index